Writing Academic Texts D

This edited volume combines cutting-edge research on feminist and intersectional writing methodologies with explorations of links between academic and creative writing practices. Contributors discuss what it means for academic writing processes to explore intersectional in-between spaces between monolithic identity markers and power differentials such as gender, race, ethnicity, class, sexuality and nationality. How does such a frame change academic writing? How does it make it pertinent to explore new synergies between academic and creative writing? In answer to these questions, the book offers theories, methodologies and political and ethical considerations, as well as reflections on writing strategies. Suggestions for exercises, developed against the background of the contributors' individual and joint teaching practices, will inspire readers to engage in alternative writing practices themselves.

Nina Lykke is Professor of Gender and Culture, Unit of Gender Studies, Linköping University, Sweden.

Routledge Advances in Feminist Studies and Intersectionality

Routledge Advances in Feminist Studies and Intersectionality is committed to the development of new feminist and profeminist perspectives on changing gender relations, with special attention to:

- Intersections between gender and power differentials based on age, class, dis/abilities, ethnicity, nationality, racialisation, sexuality, violence, and other social divisions.
- Intersections of societal dimensions and processes of continuity and change: culture, economy, generativity, polity, sexuality, science and technology.
- Embodiment: Intersections of discourse and materiality, and of sex and gender.
- Transdisciplinarity: intersections of humanities, social sciences, medical, technical and natural sciences.
- Intersections of different branches of feminist theorizing, including: historical materialist feminisms, postcolonial and anti-racist feminisms, radical feminisms, sexual difference feminisms, queerfeminisms, cyberfeminisms, posthuman feminisms, critical studies on men and masculinities.
- A critical analysis of the travelling of ideas, theories and concepts.
- A politics of location, reflexivity and transnational contextualising that reflects the basis of the Series framed within European diversity and transnational power relations.

Writing Academic Texts Differently

Intersectional Feminist Methodologies and the Playful Art of Writing

Edited by Nina Lykke

In collaboration with Anne Brewster, Kathy Davis, Redi Koobak, Sissel Lie and Andrea Petö

Routledge
Taylor & Francis Group

NEW YORK AND LONDON

First published 2014
by Routledge
711 Third Avenue, New York, NY 10017, USA

and by Routledge
2 Park Square, Milton Park, Abingdon, Oxfordshire OX14 4RN

First issued in paperback 2016

Routledge is an imprint of the Taylor & Francis Group, an informa business

© 2014 Taylor & Francis

Library of Congress Cataloging-in-Publication Data

Writing academic texts differently : intersectional feminist methodologies
   and the playful art of writing / edited by Nina Lykke.
      pages cm. — (Routledge advances in feminist studies and
intersectionality ; 16)
   Includes bibliographical references and index.
   1. Feminism—Authorship.   2. Women authors.   3. Feminism and
literature.   4. Creative writing.   5. Academic writing.   I. Lykke, Nina,
editor of compilation.
   PN471.W755 2014
   808.02082—dc23
   2014007062

Typeset in Sabon
by Apex CoVantage, LLC

ISBN 13: 978-1-138-28311-4 (pbk)
ISBN 13: 978-0-415-50225-2 (hbk)

Contents

PART TWO
Learning to Write Differently

Exercises

Note on Terminology

Following the practice developed within the framework of the European Women's/Gender/Feminist Studies network Athena (1998–2009), this volume has not harmonized the naming of the field. The different naming practices reflect the diversity of the field.

Acknowledgements

This volume came about as a result of the joint organizing and teaching of several doctoral courses in academic and creative writing in Feminist Studies, organized under the auspices of two international research training networks: NorsGender, the Nordic Research School in Interdisciplinary Gender Studies, funded by the Nordic Council of Ministers' research funding agency NordForsk 2004–2009; and InterGender, the Swedish-International Research School in Interdisciplinary Gender Studies, funded by the Swedish Research Council, 2008–2013.

As director of both the NorsGender and the InterGender research schools, I have given high priority to including courses which introduced writing strategies and writing methodologies in Feminist Studies and intersectional gender research. So in both research school projects, a number of writing courses took place over the years. They were developed together with varying groups of teachers from different countries, and they became very popular among the doctoral students who attended them and contributed with much enthusiasm. I want to thank all teachers and doctoral students who took part in the writing courses of NorsGender and InterGender for inspiring collaborations.

This book emerged out of the joint work on the courses of the two research schools. After several successful courses, a group of teachers decided to take the joint teaching and learning experiences from the courses as a starting point for writing a textbook. A few more participants were invited to join, and the next step was to meet and start working on the synopsis. Thanks to a grant from the Central European University in Budapest, Hungary, it became possible to organize two workshops in the spring of 2010, when the group met to discuss the synopsis and first drafts. Later, in the fall of 2010, one more workshop was held at Linköping University in Sweden, in collaboration with the NorsGender and InterGender research training networks, and combined also with a symposium on feminist epistemologies and writing practices, organized together with the *European Journal of Women's Studies* and the Unit of Gender Studies, Linköping University.

In my capacity of main editor of the volume, I shall warmly thank all the co-editors—Anne Brewster, Kathy Davis, Redi Koobak, Sissel Lie and

Andrea Pető—for great collaborative work. An extra warm thanks to Andrea for taking the initiative to secure funding at Central European University to organize the first two workshops on the book project in 2010. It was a great initiative, and I think we all enjoyed your hospitality a lot.

Warm thanks also to Suruchi Thapar-Björkert and Susanne Gannon, who both learned about the textbook at a late stage and kindly agreed to contribute—Suruchi as co-author of Chapter 3 and Susanne with a poem on Deleuze, a radical example of how to write academic texts differently.

Thank you also to Kathy Davis, the editorial board of the *European Journal of Women's Studies* and the Unit of Gender Studies, Linköping University, for good collaboration around the writing symposium in 2010.

Moreover, I warmly thank Dr Emma Strollo, who assisted in the editing process. You did a great job, Emma, in transforming the contributions into a final manuscript. Thanks a lot also to Dr Liz Sourbut, who took care of the linguistic revisions of the chapters written by non-native English speakers. As always, you managed to transform all odd phrases in excellent ways.

Thank you for permission to reprint the following:

Chapter 4. Lisa Bellear: "Feelings" (Poem). From Lisa Bellear, *Dreaming in Urban Areas*. St. Lucia, Queensland: University of Queensland Press 1996, page 13. Printed with permission from John Stewart (copyright-holder).

Chapter 12. Lisa Bellear: "Artist Unknown" (Poem). From Lisa Bellear, *Dreaming in Urban Areas*. St. Lucia, Queensland: University of Queensland Press 1996, page 41. Printed with permission from John Stewart (copyright-holder).

Finally, thank you to the anonymous Routledge reviewers for their valuable reviews, and a special thanks to Routledge Research editor Max Novick for your support and encouragement.

12 July 2013
Nina Lykke

Editorial Introduction

Nina Lykke, Anne Brewster,
Kathy Davis, Redi Koobak,
Sissel Lie and Andrea Petö

Writing is an inevitable part of academic work. Whether you are a first-year student or an established professor, writing is part of your work. To communicate your research and studies to colleagues, evaluators or the broader public, you will have to commit yourself to writing. Even when academics present their research in lectures, they often do so based on carefully written papers prepared beforehand to ensure the logic of the argument, coherence and inclusion of all the major points. Mastering the different genres of academic writing is crucial for anyone who wants to build an academic career.

As most people within the academic professions will probably admit, the writing process can be very painful at times as well as immensely pleasurable and fun. Sometimes you are stuck; you cannot make the text work even though you may feel that you "know" the points and arguments you want to make and the results you want to communicate. At other times the text may flow freely; your mind and your fingers typing at the computer keyboard seem to be one. You go right ahead making your points and formulating your arguments in precisely the way you think they should be phrased. In short, you are in a state of creative ecstasy. A tricky thing is that these two states—the stuck one and the state of creative ecstasy—may, in fact, be quite close to each other. You may shift from one to the other, and you do not necessarily know beforehand when you are at the turning point where the painful feelings of stuckness will be replaced by the joyful feelings of productivity, empowerment and mastery, or vice versa. Moreover, to be stuck is not necessarily negative; if you admit to yourself that you are stuck, reflections on why this has happened may in fact lead your analysis and writing process in new, productive directions.

This book is an advanced textbook, written with the purpose of helping and inspiring academic and other non-fiction authors to reflect more consciously on the writing processes to which they commit themselves, and in this way perhaps to prolong and enhance the states where they feel productive and experience the pleasure and joy of writing. The contributors to this volume share the belief that you can do things that will help you to consciously push yourself into positions where your writing "flows", and where the writing process works well for you; we claim that even stuck places may be used in a constructive and positive sense. More precisely, we believe that combining modes of more traditional academic writing with methodologies inspired by creative writing can help academic and other non-fiction authors to launch themselves into more joyful and fruitful writing processes. Our shared belief in the empowering dynamics of combining academic and creative writing is based on long-standing teaching practices at all academic levels, from undergraduate to postgraduate education. The contributors to this volume have taught and developed courses on academic and creative writing in various parts of Europe and Australia, and we have also in different ways joined hands and taught writing courses together within the framework of international gender research schools. We have all experimented with style and genre in our own work and have tried out what it means to produce texts in the borderlands between academic and creative writing. Some of us have also published fiction beyond the academy. Besides scholarly work as a professor of Romance languages, Sissel Lie is a Norwegian playwright, poet and fiction writer, and Andrea Pető, in addition to her research and teaching at the Central European University in Budapest, Hungary, has published a successful historical crime novel in Hungarian.

However, encouraging academics and other non-fiction writers to integrate academic and creative modes of writing and if possible to experiment with genres and styles is not the only aim of this book. The discussions on strategies for writing differently are framed by reflections on epistemologies, methodologies, politics and ethics. Following postmodern feminist scholar Laurel Richardson (2000), the contributors to this volume understand "writing as a method of inquiry". We consider writing as something that is not separate from, but totally embedded in, the research process. We share Richardson's claim that the struggle with language—with naming processes, with problems of representing and engaging with "objects" of study, with questions of enunciation (from which position do you tell your text? Is there a visible "I" or "we" in the text or not?), with the narrative and aesthetic structure of the text—is part of the scholarly inquiry. This struggle should not be reduced to a wrapping-up of research results following the "serious" part of the research. Many scholars tend to believe that you first think and then write. But as Richardson (2000) has forcefully emphasized, at least as far as qualitative research is concerned, thinking and writing are two sides of the same coin. As teachers, we have all met students and colleagues who believed they should think through their research first and write it up afterwards but who ended up in troubled situations; they started to write "too late", overestimating the necessity of thinking before writing and underestimating the difficulties involved in the writing process. It is well known to many students and scholars that the real problems often start when you begin to write up your research. However, we have also sometimes met students and colleagues who did not think before they wrote but whose writing was carried forward by both serendipity and a strong scholarly commitment to dig deeper and deeper into a research problem that engaged them passionately, and who produced very good texts using this approach, combining meticulous scholarly methods with a lively and engaging style.

So language should not be considered as a passive medium for transparent communication but instead understood as an active, ambiguous and slippery phenomenon that will inevitably launch the writing subject into unexpected situations—positive as well as negative. This is a tenet of postmodern language philosophy but also a very practical everyday experience of many students and scholars engaged in the process of writing up their research: desiring to be in command of language but also having to admit that language, discourse, genre and style act as tricksters that are not to be controlled "just like that".

Overall, the book is built on the assumption that writing, method, methodology, epistemology, ethics and politics are inextricably linked. For the contributors, questions about writing differently have emerged out of frameworks of feminist reflections on epistemologies, methodologies, ethics and politics. A key concern is the pressing question of intersectionality and the intersections of power differentials and social categorizations, based on gender, race, ethnicity, class, nationality, sexuality, dis/ability, age, etc., that currently hold a central place in many feminist debates. In this volume, we raise questions about *intersectional writing*. What does it mean for academic writing processes if we consciously write intersectionally—that is, in the in-between spaces between monolithic identity categories such as gender, race, ethnicity, class, sexuality, and nationality? How do such frames change scholarly writing?

A central starting point for various kinds of feminist epistemologies is the insistence on a politics of location and the claim that knowledge production should be understood as situated. This epistemological and political stance has methodological and ethical implications as well as repercussions for the writing process. It urges scholars to reflect on the position of enunciation, the embodied location of the textual subject of their scholarly writing (who is the "I"/"we" of the text?) and directs them towards reflections on the politics and ethics of representing and engaging with the "object" of study in their texts.

Moreover, according to a majority of contemporary feminist scholars, the researcher "I" as well as the research "object" must be understood as situated not only in one-dimensional categorizations in terms of gender *or* race *or* ethnicity *or* class *or* nationality *or* sexuality *or* dis/ability *or* age *or* other social categorizations but in a multiplicity of intersecting power relations. As argued forcefully by feminist scholar Jasbir Puar, these multiplicities should not be seen as fixed taxonomies but as "assemblages", i.e. as "interwoven forces that merge and dissipate time, space, and body against linearity, coherence and permanency" (2007, 212).

Against this backdrop, we consider it urgent to explore strategies for *writing intersectionally*, i.e. to develop methods of writing which take into account politics of multiple, mobile and open-ended locations and which aim at unfolding alternative, committed, ethically and politically accountable ways to write the researcher "I" and the so-called "objects" of research into the scholarly text.

The authors in this volume share an ambition to combine the theorizing of intersectional writing processes with suggestions for exercises and writing strategies which may inspire readers to engage in alternative writing practices themselves. All the chapters make suggestions for writing strategies, and a majority of them include exercises that can be tried out either in groups or individually. The exercises and suggestions for writing strategies are consciously constructed in open-ended ways in order to speak to the creative fantasy and intellect of readers and to encourage them to further develop or change the exercises and writing strategies according to their own interests and the particular tasks in which they are engaged.

The book is innovative in its approach. It differs from the majority of general books on academic and creative writing because of its *theoretical and methodological reflections*. A majority of books on academic and/or creative writing are more "technical" and miss the theoretical, epistemological, methodological, ethical and political perspectives that are reflected throughout this volume. Accordingly, the exercises and suggestions for writing strategies are mixed in with the theoretical and methodological considerations throughout, not placed in separate appendices. The volume differs also from most feminist books that include considerations on academic and creative writing because of its focus on *intersectional* writing, but it also differs from feminist books on intersectionality because it not only systematically takes into account theoretical and political aspects but also focuses on the important question of how to *write* intersectionally and includes "hands-on" dimensions in the shape of exercises.

Since publishing, reporting on or popularizing research will always involve writing processes, the book addresses a broad readership. It is written for scholars, teachers and students (from undergraduate to postdoctoral levels) in all disciplines. The volume will be of particular interest to scholars, teachers and students from humanities and social science disciplines (such as anthropology, history, sociology, Film Studies, Media Studies, literature, art history, Textual Studies and various kinds of area studies) and interdisciplinary fields such as Gender Studies, Cultural Studies, Environmental Studies, Science and Technology Studies, etc., where it is possible to experiment with writing processes. However, the theoretical, methodological, political and ethical reflections of the book as well as the writing exercises may also be useful to scholars and students within, for example, the natural, technical and medical sciences, who may use the suggested writing strategies and exercises as inspirations to experiment with "writing as a method of inquiry" (Richardson 2000) when writing early drafts of reports or articles, even if the rules of their disciplines may not allow them to publish texts that include the combinations of academic and creative writing suggested by the authors of this volume.

The volume is divided into two parts. In Part One, *The Politics of Writing Differently*, exercises and suggestions for writing strategies are provided to accompany and illustrate the theoretical, methodological, ethical and political reflections on intersectional writing. The chapters in this section discuss the textual implications of intersectional approaches, and the exercises and suggested writing strategies exemplify what these approaches may mean in terms of exploring strategies of writing differently. In Part Two, *Learning to Write Differently*, the practical how-to focus takes the front seat: the sequence of chapters guides readers through the key moments of an academic writing process—from finding your topic, mobilizing your resources for writing, writing an introduction, and finding ways to construct "meaningful" objects of study, through engaging with theories, keywords, and stuck places, to the final stage of publishing your research.

Part One opens with a chapter by Dutch and US feminist scholar Kathy Davis, *Intersectionality as Critical Methodology*. It highlights the genealogies of the concept of intersectionality that was developed in the work of feminists of colour in the US (Crenshaw 1989, 1991) in order to address the fact that the experiences and struggles of women of colour fell between the cracks of both feminist and anti-racist discourse. Davis emphasizes that intersectionality has today become a central theoretical paradigm for conceptualizing multiple identities, multilayered workings of power in social relations, institutional arrangements and cultural imaginaries, and for deconstructing the ethnocentrism of "First World" feminist scholarship. In particular, she takes issue with the problem that, despite the undisputed appeal of the concept of intersectionality, it is not always clear what it means for a feminist inquiry to work from an intersectional perspective. In other words, how does one actually go about "thinking, working and writing intersectionally"? What does it mean to "do an intersectional analysis"? Without pretending to provide a full-fledged methodology, Davis proceeds from the (deceptively) easy procedure of "asking the other question", which was initially proposed by critical race theory scholar Maria Matsuda (1991). Davis elaborates on this question in the form of three strategies that can help get readers started in doing intersectional analysis: situating one's self, complicating gender and exploring blind spots, near-sightedness and other myopias. The chapter concludes with an exercise, constructed to inspire readers to put the three strategies to work in their own writing.

In Chapter 2, *Passionate Disidentifications as an Intersectional Writing Strategy*, Danish-Swedish feminist scholar Nina Lykke brings the question of intersectional writing to bear on the question of writing from subject positions located in intersectional in-between spaces between monolithic and normative categorizations in terms of gender, race, ethnicity, sexuality, geopolitical positioning, etc. The chapter draws specific attention to the notion of disidentification as it has been used by, among others, Chicana feminists (Alarcón 1991), queers of colour (Muñoz 1999) and third-wave feminists (Tuin 2011) to carve out speaking positions that allow for reflections on internal difference and multilayered intersectional positionings within feminist and queer movements. Building on Judith Butler's theorizations (1993) of the necessary breakdown of unifying political signifiers ("woman", "queer", etc.), Lykke points out that disidentification refers to a discursive operation by which critical subjectivities are constituted in a passionately political double move of identification with and critical distancing from identity-political discourses. Via a textual analysis of the writing strategies of two key texts—one from the postcolonial turn in feminist theory, Chandra Mohanty's "Under Western Eyes" (1988), and the other from the queer turn, Sandy Stone's "The 'Empire' Strikes Back" (2006), Lykke illustrates how disidentificatory writing strategies can be productive. She ends the chapter with an exercise that was created to inspire readers to explore a strategy of passionate disidentification as a motor for writing.

In Chapter 3, *Writing the Place from Which One Speaks*, Indian scholar Suruchi Thapar-Björkert and Estonian feminist scholar Redi Koobak, both based in Sweden, pose the question of intersectional writing and the articulation of the multilayered subject positions from which one writes, with a particular focus on intersections of national identities and geopolitical positioning. The two authors build their argument through personal stories about how complex national identities and geopolitical locations came to play a decisive role in their choice of research topics, project designs and definition of research problems. In this way, Thapar-Björkert and Koobak demonstrate the importance of the feminist epistemological and ethical tenet that researchers must make themselves accountable for the situatedness of their scholarly knowledge production. Via nuanced analyses of the ways in which the dis/similarities of their personal stories mirror each other, Thapar-Björkert and Koobak convincingly show how their complex national and geopolitical positionalities constructed them both as outsiders within, in relation to the institutional contexts in which they did their research as well as in relation to their research "objects". They also show how conscious reflections on these complexities were a vital and necessary part of the ways in which they framed their research. The chapter includes a warning not to allow the tenet about situated knowledge and politics of location to merely congeal into a lining up of fixed intersections and categorizations. On the contrary, Thapar-Björkert and Koobak emphasize the importance of considering the issue of intersectionally situated knowledge production as a question of reflecting concretely and continuously on the specific role of intersecting positionalities for project design, gathering of empirical material, writing processes, etc. in the making of the particular research. They recommend that such reflections should always be embedded in the research and writing process, and they follow up this recommendation with exercises that may lead the readers to reflect on their own positions in relation to their research.

Chapter 4, *Whiteness and Affect: The Embodied Ethics of Relationality*, written by Australian feminist scholar Anne Brewster, focuses on the ways in which ethical issues are entangled with questions of intersectional research and writing processes. Framed within the field of Critical Whiteness Studies, Brewster draws examples from her own cross-cultural feminist research on the literature of Australian indigenous people, in particular the work of feminist poet Lisa Bellear (1996). Brewster unpacks the issues of whiteness and cross-cultural research through a discussion of the role of relationality, the body and affect. In what might be called a "relational turn" in current cross-cultural research, Brewster foregrounds the primacy of relationality and the premise that the *encounter* between subjects is ontologically prior to the process of becoming of the individual subjects who encounter each other. Bodies and their affective responses to others are examined as sites for the exercise of power and of whiteness. Following feminist scholar Gail Weiss (1999), Brewster emphasizes that ethics are always corporeally enacted. Inspired by poststructuralist theorist Julia Kristeva's (1991) discussion of the anger and resentment that are often vented on "the foreigner", as well as the philosopher Emmanuel Levinas' (1985) reflection on the ethics of the encounter with the other, exercises are suggested which encourage readers to reflect on the intercorporeal and affectively laden zone in which they encounter "others", including their research subjects, materials and locales.

The last chapter in Part One, Chapter 5, *Feminist Crime Fiction as a Model for Writing History Differently*, shifts the focus to the writing of history from intersectional perspectives. Here, Hungary-based feminist scholar Andrea Pető reflects on crime fiction as a form of creative writing that may help to question traditional gender divisions in their intersections with constructions of national identities and nationhood and to deconstruct monolithic understandings of historical "truth". Pető argues in favour of using creative writing to conceptualize history as an "unfinished project". More specifically, she explores how the genre of crime fiction works with historicity as a key element. Against this background, she presents an exercise and suggests a writing strategy that step by step allows readers to develop crime stories that explore meeting points between feminist theory, literary theory, violence, historiography and popular culture and that may be used to challenge positivist historical canons that ignore gender as well as its intersections with other power differentials. The aim of the exercise is to create a vocabulary appropriate for telling gender- and intersectionality-sensitive narratives about the past. Pető introduces techniques for making competing truth claims visible in the narratives. She also discusses processes of evaluation and the ways in which the ambiguity of the genre of crime fiction can be useful for opening up space for pedagogical discussions.

Part Two, *Learning to Write Differently*, further develops the hands-on dimensions of the writing process. The pivot here is suggestions for writing strategies and exercises that are offered as inspiration and help for authors in various stages of the academic writing process. Part Two starts with a so-called writing-story (i.e. a story about the process of writing; Richardson 1997). Chapter 6, *Six Impossible Things before Breakfast: How I Came across My Research Topic and What Happened Next*, is written by Redi Koobak. Taking inspiration from Richardson's (2000) approach to "writing as a method of inquiry", Koobak offers a writing-story about her quest for a PhD research topic as an example of how exploring an unfinished collection of thoughts, inspirations and references in the shape of writing a story about/around them can provide a way to open up creative thought and face the challenges of finding and sticking to a research topic and methodology. Through exposing the specificities of a beginning researcher's uncertainties, biases and vulnerabilities, Koobak's writing-story makes visible how important it is to attend to the rhizomatic character of your points of entry into the "field" you are studying. With the help of six quotations from Lewis Carroll's *Alice's Adventures in Wonderland* (1865) and *Through the Looking Glass and What Alice Found There* (1871) that structure the writing-story, Koobak shows that critical self-reflexivity, i.e. questioning the self at the beginning of (and throughout) the research process, can become a key to unravelling the important questions one needs to keep in mind in order to arrive at and eventually "inhabit" a research topic.

Chapter 7, *The Infinite Resources for Writing*, written by Norwegian feminist scholar and fiction writer Sissel Lie, is concerned with the many resources that are at your disposal while you are developing an academic project. Lie argues that one way to mobilize these resources for thinking is just to start writing. Free writing is stressed as a useful strategy, and Lie argues that sometimes it is important to let chaos reign and be confident that you will end up finding a way through. Lie also emphasizes the importance of discussing the unfinished manuscript with others. Peers and supervisors are important readers, but it can be a very fruitful strategy to consult many different readers, who can function as midwives. Readers need to be generous, they may have questions and suggestions for changes, but they should never try to destroy the writer's motivation with a criticism harsher than the writer can take. Lie points out that it is useful to reflect on where and when you like to write, and that it is necessary to make space for writing. It is also stressed that other texts are important to help you think, that you should listen carefully to the questions the material poses and reflect on the genre in terms of finding solutions for how to structure the text. Lie emphasizes that it is necessary to be aware of the style that is required to make the text comprehensible and pleasant to read. She also underlines how personal writing-stories, like the one told by Redi Koobak in the previous chapter, can help authors come to grips with their own texts, and how perhaps the most important resource of all is the author's feeling about her or his writing, the frustrations she or he fights against and the pleasures she or he gets when writing comes easily to her or him. Serendipity, fun and making sure to really enjoy magical moments when they spontaneously occur during the writing process are key recommendations.

Lie is also the author of Chapter 8, *From an Empty Head to a Finished Text: The Writing Process*. Here she describes a writing course that she has developed over the years, at times in cooperation with colleagues. In this chapter, she recommends a range of specific exercises in relation to the different areas explored. She is concerned with writing not only as a way of getting to know oneself but also as a resource for empowerment and for an exploration of one's own experience and latent knowledge. Since writing is a fundamental part of the research process, particularly in the humanities and social sciences, Lie argues that it becomes especially urgent for humanities and social science scholars to ask whether new thoughts need new writing strategies. Free writing is one of the strategies she underlines as a useful tool for generating ideas during the research process as well as having an exchange with readers during the writing process. Overall, the chapter focuses on the ways in which authors think *about* writing, the ways in which they can think *through* writing and different ways of developing a text through *discussion and rewriting*.

Chapter 9, *The Choreography of Writing an Introduction*, written by Nina Lykke, presents a sequence of exercises as a guide to writing introductions for academic texts of all kinds. The exercise sequence is based on a choreography of six moves which together can guide readers through the writing of an academic introduction. Drawing on her experience of many years of teaching feminist courses in academic and creative writing at both undergraduate and postdoctoral levels, Lykke has reworked a sequence of moves that was originally suggested in a study of opening sections of scholarly articles (Swales 1983), revising them within a feminist and intersectional epistemological framework. In the first part of the chapter, this sequence of moves is presented, and its relevance and applicability are illustrated via a textual analysis of the introduction to a key feminist text on intersectionality, Critical Race Studies theorist Kimberlé Crenshaw's "Mapping the Margins" (1991). The second part of the chapter is made up of a writing-an-introduction exercise based on the six moves. A cluster of exercises is suggested for each move, and readers who want to practise writing an introduction can work their way through the six moves while doing the clusters of exercises indicated under each move. In each cluster, exercises aimed at opening up to creative processes alternate with exercises for structuring and systematizing for academic purposes. In line with Lie's discussion in Chapter 8 on the importance of recruiting early-draft readers, the potential of shifting between individual work and collaboration with critical *and* generous partners is also explored as part of each move. The exercise sequence as a whole leads readers step by step through the various stages of writing an introduction, but the individual exercises can also be used independently of the sequence.

In Chapter 10, *Politics of Gendered Remembering: Feminist Narratives of "Meaningful Objects"*, Andrea Pető presents an exercise which is designed to create an understanding of how narratives dealing with the past are formed. Pető is concerned about the development of research and writing practices that not only "transmit" historical facts and canonized narratives but attend to the processes through which different "pasts" are formed. The exercise is based on Petö's teaching of gender and history in various national and international settings. It involves the writing and analysis of various types of descriptions of a "meaningful object", for example, an object relating to the life of a foremother, i.e. a woman whose life you find interesting to explore as a "site of remembering" (Petö and Waaldijk 2006). You are encouraged to gather information on the object and write about it in different genres and from different viewpoints (e.g. an ethnographic note for a museum display, a letter to a friend, an illustration in a history textbook for secondary schools, etc.). The exercise helps readers to navigate in between academic and creative writing practices and is designed to inspire you to develop new outlooks regarding your research materials and historical narratives about them.

In Chapter 11, *Making Theories Work*, Kathy Davis suggests writing strategies that may help to make theory become a more personal, passionate and creative enterprise. A starting point for Davis' recommendations is the fact that, from graduate students writing their dissertation to seasoned academics working on their latest book, all academics employ other people's theories in their research. This raises a crucial question: How can you engage with these theories in such a way that you do not simply reproduce the ideas of others? How can theory become something that enables scholars to take risks, embark on unexpected paths and, in so doing, command their audience's full and appreciative attention? Obviously, there is no simple solution to writing (about) theory. However, in this chapter, Davis provides a modest suggestion—one that may help scholars to engage with theories more personally, creatively and adventurously. This engagement will provide a starting point and some of the building blocks for transforming Feminist Theory (writ large) into the writer's own theoretical story. The strategy that Davis proposes is drawn from the practices employed by many qualitative researchers of keeping a research journal, and it resonates with the more mundane practice of keeping a personal journal to make sense of one's own life experiences. It involves recording, exploring and working through responses to a particular theory or theories, engaging with the theory in a personal, creative and critical way. The aim is to appropriate theory and make it work for you. Concrete suggestions are provided for how to get started in keeping a theory journal, what to write (and what not to write) and how the journal might be used in research.

From the issue of making theories work in personal, passionate and creative ways, Chapter 12 turns to the question of language and key ideas. *Making Language Your Own: Brainstorming, Heteroglossia and Poetry* is the title of this chapter. Here, Anne Brewster reflects on writing strategies designed to re-examine the key terms that are central to one's research. Two issues are brought into focus: (1) how key terms in your field of research are always laden with the authority bestowed by other people and (2) how scholars can challenge that authority and discover new meanings for these key terms and open up new perspectives in their thinking. Two exercises are introduced which aim to show how you can re-examine the key terms that are central to your research. The exercises are framed by a discussion of language as social and therefore laden with socio-ideological value. To make the point, Brewster draws on the work of literary scholar Mikhail Bakhtin, who points out that each person's use of language always involves a process of making it over to suit their own purposes, and who is interested, among other things, in the ways in which "tendentious" or authoritative discourses can be destabilized and "carnivalized" (Bakhtin 1981). The exercises introduced in this chapter encourage you to recognize that key terms are often imbued with an authority that others have given them. Recognizing this authority and testing it against the author's own ideas is an important part of writing practices, and the exercises are constructed to inspire you to explore new writing terrains, turning to other genres for brainstorming key terms and trying your hand at exploring theoretical ideas through collage and poetry.

As mentioned at the beginning of this editorial introduction, most scholars and students know that the processes of writing do not always run smoothly. You may get stuck in your writing process. In Chapter 13, *Writing in Stuck Places*, Redi Koobak addresses the common problems of facing "stuck places" in the research process or wrestling with writer's block. As these moments of stuckness are often frustrating and likely to slow down the writing process or, in the worst-case scenario, make one give up altogether, Koobak explores strategies to overcome them. She suggests that new potentials can be mobilized when authors confront and consciously attempt to write in (or with) stuck places. Drawing on the work of Patti Lather (1998, 2007), who describes a "praxis of stuck places" as a strategy of purposefully seeking out and focusing on stuckness and insecurities of meaning as a way to keep moving and managing the uncertainties, Koobak argues that much can be learned from breaks, ruptures and failures in the research process. Using examples from her own PhD research, she examines dead ends, false starts and other stuck places in an attempt to situate the experience of impossibility in writing as "an enabling site for working through aporias" (Lather 2007, 16). In addition, she suggests some exercises and strategies for thinking through and writing in stuck places.

Chapter 14, *Publish or Perish: How to Get Published in an International Journal*, written by Kathy Davis, confronts the problem of publishing an article in a scholarly journal—a problem that remains an endeavour fraught with uncertainty, difficulties and—in some cases—outright suffering, no matter how long and venerable one's career as an academic might be. The chapter tackles some of the ins and outs of getting published, based on Davis' own experiences as author, journal editor and reviewer. The chapter focuses specifically on getting published in what are called peer-reviewed journals. To this end, Davis addresses several issues: how to write a journal article, how to find a journal, the review process, and the process of revising

12   *Nina Lykke et al.*

an article. She then provides a brief look behind the scenes of a scholarly journal with a peer-review system—a journal of which she is co-editor—in order to give some insight into how things look "on the other side of the fence". Finally, she touches briefly on the more general issue of evaluating the work of one's colleagues—that is, the dos and don'ts of giving and receiving criticism—since this is often one of the aspects that makes the process of getting published both painful and rewarding.

The book ends with a short example of an experimental text that merges a poetic and an academic reading of French philosopher Gilles Deleuze, written by Australian feminist scholar Susanne Gannon. Moreover, the group of authors offer the readers a collection of aphorisms on writing, exchanged as part of their collaborative work on the volume.

REFERENCES

Alarcón, Norma. 1991. "The Theoretical Subject(s) of *This Bridge Called My Back* and Anglo-American Feminism." In *Criticism in the Borderlands: Studies in Chicana Literature, Culture and Ideology*, edited by Héctor Calderon and Jose David Saldivar, 28–43. Durham: Duke University Press.
Bakhtin, Mikhail. 1981. *The Dialogic Imagination*. Edited by Michael Holtquist. Translated by Caryl Emerson and Michael Holtquist. Austin: University of Texas Press.
Bellear, Lisa. 1996. *Dreaming in Urban Areas*. St Lucia: University of Queensland Press.
Butler, Judith. 1993. *Bodies That Matter: On the Discursive Limits of "Sex"*. London: Routledge.
Carroll, Lewis. 1865. *Alice's Adventures in Wonderland*. London: Macmillan.
Carroll, Lewis. 1871. *Through the Looking Glass and What Alice Found There*. London: Macmillan.
Crenshaw, Kimberlé. 1989. "Demarginalizing the Intersection of Race and Sex: A Black Feminist Critique of Antidiscrimination Doctrine, Feminist Theory and Antiracist Politics." *University of Chicago Legal Forum*, 140: 139–67.
Crenshaw, Kimberlé. 1991. "Mapping the Margins: Intersectionality, Identity Politics, and Violence against Women of Color." *Stanford Law Review* 43 (6): 1241–99.
Kristeva, Julia. 1991. "Toccata and Fugue for the Foreigner." In *Strangers to Ourselves*, translated by Leon S. Roudiez, 1–21. London: Harvester Wheatsheaf.
Lather, Patti. 1998. "Critical Pedagogy and Its Complicities: A Praxis of Stuck Places." *Educational Theory* 48 (4): 487–97.
Lather, Patti. 2007. *Getting Lost: Feminist Practices toward a Double(d) Science*. Albany: SUNY Press.
Levinas, Emmanuel. 1985. "The Face." In *Ethics and Infinity*, translated by Richard A. Cohen, 85–92. Pittsburgh: Duquesne University Press.
Matsuda, Maria. 1991. "Beside My Sister, Facing the Enemy: Legal Theory out of Coalition." *Stanford Law Review* 43 (6): 1183–92.
Mohanty, Chandra T. 1988. "Under Western Eyes: Feminist Scholarship and Colonial Discourses." *Feminist Review* 30: 49–74.
Muñoz, José Esteban. 1999. *Disidentification: Queers of Color and the Performance of Politics*. Minneapolis: University of Minnesota Press.

Petö, Andrea and Berteke Waaldijk, eds. 2006. *Teaching with Memories: European Women's Histories in International and Interdisciplinary Classrooms*. Teaching with Athena. Utrecht: Utrecht University.

Puar, Jasbir. 2007. *Terrorist Assemblages: Homonationalism in Queer Times*. Durham: Duke University Press.

Richardson, Laurel. 1997. *Fields of Play: Constructing an Academic Life*. New Brunswick: Rutgers University Press.

Richardson, Laurel. 2000. "Writing as a Method of Inquiry." In *Handbook of Qualitative Research*, 2nd ed., edited by Norman K. Denzin and Yvonna S. Lincoln, 923–48. London: Sage.

Stone, Sandy. 2006. "The 'Empire' Strikes Back: A Posttranssexual Manifesto." In *The Transgender Studies Reader*, edited by Susan Stryker and Stephen Whittle, 221–35. New York: Routledge.

Swales, John. 1983. "Developing Materials for Writing Scholarly Introductions." In *Case Studies in ELT*, edited by R.R. Jordan, 188–202. London: Collins ELT.

Tuin, Iris van der. 2011. "Gender Research with 'Waves': On Repositioning a Neo-disciplinary Apparatus." In *Theories and Methodologies in Postgraduate Feminist Research: Researching Differently*, edited by Rosemarie Buikema, Gabriele Griffin and Nina Lykke, 15–29. New York: Routledge.

Weiss, Gail. 1999. *Body Images: Embodiment as Intercorporeality*. London: Routledge.

Part One

The Politics of Writing Differently

1 Intersectionality as Critical Methodology

Kathy Davis

"INTERSECTIONALITY" AS FEMINIST BUZZWORD

"Intersectionality" has become something of a buzzword in contemporary feminist theory (K. Davis 2008). Originally coined by Kimberlé Crenshaw (1989, 1991), "intersectionality" was intended to address the fact that the experiences and struggles of women of colour fell between the cracks of both feminist and anti-racist discourse. Crenshaw argued that theorists need to take both gender and race on board and show how they interact to shape the multiple dimensions of black women's experiences. "Intersectionality" provided a short-hand term for a more comprehensive and complex per-spective on identity—one which would take into account the ways in which individuals are invariably multiply positioned through differences in gender, class, sexual orientation, ethnicity, national belonging and more. Crenshaw may have introduced the term, but she was by no means the first to address the issue of how black women's experiences have been marginalized or dis-torted within white feminist discourse. Nor was she making a particularly new argument when she claimed that experiences had to be understood as multiply shaped by race and gender. Black feminists on both sides of the Atlantic and Third World feminist scholars had already produced numerous critiques of how the experiences of women of colour had been neglected in white feminist discourse and had already underscored the importance of theorizing multiple identities and sources of oppression.[1] Intersectionality was part of a growing body of feminist scholarship which was looking for more sophisticated and dynamic ways to conceptualize how socially con-structed differences and structures of power work at the level of individual experiences, social practices, institutional arrangements, symbolic repre-sentations and cultural imaginaries. Intersectionality addressed the concern about what was increasingly perceived as the ethnocentrism of white, First World feminist scholarship, offering the promise of a much-needed corrective.

Intersectionality, while not in and of itself new, brought together two of the most important strands of contemporary feminist thought that have been, in different ways, concerned with the issue of difference. The first strand has been devoted to understanding the effects of race, class and gender on women's identities, experiences and struggles for empowerment. It has been especially concerned with the marginalization of poor women and women of colour within white, Western feminist theory. Initially, this strand of feminist theory adopted a "triple jeopardy" approach to class, race and gender (King 1988) by exploring how, with the addition of each new category of inequality, the individual becomes more vulnerable, more marginalized and more subordinate. Gradually, however, the focus shifted to how race, class and gender interact in the social and material realities of women's lives to produce and transform relations of power (Anthias and Yuval-Davis 1983; Yuval-Davis 1997; Anthias 1998; Collins 2000). Intersectionality seemed ideally suited to the task of exploring how categories of race, class and gender are intertwined and mutually constitutive, giving centrality to questions like how race is "gendered", and gender "racialized", and how both are linked to the continuities and transformations of social class.

While intersectionality is most often associated with US black feminist theory and the political project of theorizing the relationships between gender, class and race, it has also been taken up and elaborated by a second important strand within feminist theory. Feminist theorists inspired by postmodern theoretical perspectives viewed intersectionality as a welcome helpmeet in their project of deconstructing the binary oppositions and universalism inherent in the modernist paradigms of Western philosophy and science (Brah and Phoenix 2004; Phoenix 2006). Critical perspectives inspired by poststructuralist theory—e.g. postcolonial theory (Mani 1989; Mohanty 2003), diaspora studies (Brah 1996) and queer theory (Butler 1989)—were all in search of alternatives to static conceptualizations of identity. Intersectionality fit neatly into the postmodern project of conceptualizing multiple and shifting identities. It coincided with popular Foucauldian-inspired perspectives on power that focused on dynamic processes and the deconstruction of normalizing and homogenizing categories (Staunæs 2003; Knudsen 2006). Intersectionality seemed to embody a commitment to the situatedness of all knowledge (Haraway 1988), promising to enhance the theorist's reflexivity by allowing her to incorporate her own intersectional location in the production of self-critical and accountable feminist theory (Lykke 2010).

Given its ability to address issues which are of central concern within different strands of feminist thinking, it is not surprising that many feminist scholars today are convinced that intersectionality is a useful—and indeed essential—concept for feminist analysis. It has been the subject of conferences and special issues of journals. Courses on intersectionality abound in master's programs in Gender Studies. The term increasingly pops up in a whole range of fields (philosophy, social sciences, humanities, economy, law), theoretical perspectives (phenomenology, structuralist sociology, psychoanalysis, deconstructionism) and political persuasions (feminism, anti-racism, multiculturalism, Queer Studies, Critical Disability

Studies, Transgender Studies). It has been heralded as a perfect helpmeet for investigating anything from individual biographies, to media represenations, governmental policies and scientific discourse, to the histories of racism and colonalism in different parts of the world.[2]

BUT HOW DO WE USE IT?

While the appeal of intersectionality shows no signs of abating, it is not always clear what the use of the concept might actually mean for feminist inquiry. In other words, how does one actually go about thinking intersectionally? What does it mean to do an intersectional analysis? As an illustration, let me recount an experience I had during a recent stint in Germany as a visiting professor. I offered a two-day seminar on the subject of intersectionality. My initial intention was to draw in a small group of Women's Studies students and introduce them—briefly—to one of the more exciting developments in contemporary feminist theory. To my surprise, however, the seminar drew interest not only from a few enthusiastic undergraduates (as I had expected) but also from PhD candidates, researchers and professors from cities throughout the region, all prepared to sacrifice their weekend and put aside their language difficulties in order to participate in my seminar. In fact, not only did I have to institute a waiting list, but many of the participants ended up having to sit on the floor. Many who were not able to attend approached me later asking whether I might be prepared to give the seminar again so that they could attend it.

Obviously, this interest was gratifying, both personally and because it seemed to confirm what I myself believe—namely, that intersectionality is where it's at when it comes to contemporary feminist theory. However, it was also puzzling. While most of the participants were convinced that intersectionality was absolutely essential to feminist theory (and they had no intention of missing the boat), at the same time, they did not know how it might actually be used with regard to their own fields of inquiry. They had lots of questions. For example, many wanted to know which categories belonged to an intersectional analysis.[3] As feminist scholars, they assumed that gender would *always* be part of an intersectional analysis, but beyond that they weren't sure how to decide. Were some categories more relevant than others—for example, gender, race and class—or was it simply a matter of adding on new differences, depending on the context or the specific research problem? Many were also worried about being essentialist (a cardinal sin in Women's Studies), so, how, they wondered, could they use categories without getting into even more serious theoretical trouble (from the frying pan into the fire)? But, of course, their main concern was *how* to actually analyze the intersections once they had decided which ones were relevant. And, last but not least, they wondered exactly how their use of intersectionality was sufficient to make their research critical/

cutting-edge/subversive or whether additional theoretical tools were necessary. Taken together, these questions indicated that the participants were struggling with uncertainties concerning the meanings of intersectionality.[4] They wanted to know how to apply it to their own research concerns. In short, they wanted a methodology.

METHODOLOGY

Initially, intersectionality as methodology was encompassed by the (deceptively) easy procedure of "asking the other question", described by Maria Matsuda:

> The way I try to understand the interconnection of all forms of subordination is through a method I call "ask the other question". When I see something that looks racist, I ask, "Where is the patriarchy in this?" When I see something that looks sexist, I ask, "Where is the heterosexism in this?" When I see something that looks homophobic, I ask, "Where are the class interests in this?"
>
> —(1991, 1189)

I say "deceptively" because, as anyone knows who has tried to employ this procedure, it merely marks the beginning of the analysis. Many feminist scholars have faced the problem of what to do *after* asking the other question. The hard work of making sense of the connections between categories of difference and interpreting them in terms of power is precisely what has yet to be done.

In 2005 the US feminist scholar Leslie McCall addressed the issue of developing a methodology for doing intersectional research for the first time. She argued that the concept would be considerably more useful if it was accompanied by more stringent methodological guidelines concerning where, how and to what end it could be used in feminist inquiry. While McCall acknowledged that intersectionality could be used to reveal the complexity of categories (as has been the case within feminist poststructuralism) or to examine the crossing categories of identity among specific groups (as Crenshaw and others have done with regard to women of colour), she also believed that an intercategorical approach to intersectionality would provide possibilities for a more sophisticated methodology. She therefore advocated moving away from the almost exclusively qualitative approaches to intersectionality which had been given priority so far and proposed instead a more rigorous quantitative methodology which would focus on "the complexity of relationships among multiple social groups within and across analytical categories" (McCall 2005, 1786) rather than on single groups, single sites or single categories. The subject of intersectionality would then become multigroup and multicomparative (ibid.).

While this call for a quantitative methodology seemed to provide a solution to many of the uncertainties I have described above, it also introduces a host of new problems. For example, it relegates intersectionality to the realm of the social sciences, thereby discounting much of the interesting work which can be done within the fields of literary criticism or Cultural Studies. Furthermore, it omits the use of single case studies which has been so productive for studying intersectionality in the past from further methodological refinement. But—and this is my main concern—the equation of better methodology with quantitative research seems to put an end to intersectionality as a creative methodology—a methodology which is ideally suited to looking for new and often unorthodox ways of doing feminist analysis.

Methodologies are not written-in-stone guidelines for doing feminist inquiry, a kind of one-size-fits-all recipe for feminist research. Methodologies should—and here I agree with McCall—provide help in doing research. I certainly appreciate her desire to develop the promising concept of intersectionality in ways which will actually help feminist scholars do better research. However, better research is not just about more complexity and more stringent procedures. Methodologies should also stimulate the researcher's curiosity and creativity. They should not produce straightjackets for monitoring research, but rather tantalize scholars to raise new questions, engage reflexively and critically with previously held assumptions and explore uncharted territory. Above all, they should mitigate against premature closure.

To this end, I want to propose a rather different strategy. It is a strategy which takes the procedure of asking the other question and elaborates it in ways which could help us do better—that is, more comprehensive, more complex, more interesting feminist research, as McCall has advocated. It is not intended as a recipe, nor as a solution to the uncertainties which plague us when we begin thinking and writing intersectionally. Instead, it is meant as a series of suggestions that could help would-be intersectional researchers to think of their analysis as a process, a journey towards more creative and critical feminist analysis.

SOME STRATEGIES

To this end, I have chosen several strategies which might help you to get started doing intersectional research. These strategies are not intended as a recipe. Nor is the list by any means exhaustive. In fact, I would hope that they would stimulate you to think of your own strategies. They can be done at any stage of the research process: prior to beginning the research, or at any point after the research has been started, or even after-the-fact in order to think of ways to recycle or rethink the work you have already done. They can also be used as a more general writing strategy to encourage a critical self-reflexivity, which is part of the process of engaging in feminist scholar-ship more generally. I have drawn my examples and illustrations—selectively and idiosyncratically—from my readings of other feminist scholars as well as from my own research.[5]

Situating Yourself

One of the ways to start thinking intersectionally is to begin with your own multiple positionings as a researcher in terms of gender, class, ethnic, sexual and other social identities. The idea is that locating yourself at the outset of your inquiries will avoid what Donna Haraway has called the god-trick—"the conquering gaze from nowhere" (1991, 188)—enabling instead the production of feminist knowledge which is accountable, reflexive and admittedly partial. While few feminist scholars today would take issue with situating one's self as an epistemological stance, in practice, it is sometimes implemented by providing a list of the researcher's identities—e.g. "as a white, middle-class, heterosexual woman, I . . .". Judith Butler has called this the "embarrassed etc. clause", that endless list of predicates that "strive to encompass a situated subject, but invariably fail to be complete" (1989, 143). Indeed, the differences are endless. However, aside from highlighting the *fact* of multiple identities, such a list does not do much work and may, ironically, even end up becoming an excuse for *not* doing the necessary anal-ysis of situating one's self.

A more intersectional strategy would not entail a list of identity cate-gories, but rather involve developing a narrative about how your specific location shapes or influences you (your thinking, theoretical preferences, intellectual biography) in specific ways—ways which will be relevant with respect to the research you are doing (see also Brewster, Chapter 4, this vol-ume, for further discussion). Ruth Frankenberg (1993), who is one of the founders of Critical Whiteness Studies, developed an interesting way to do this. She was interested in problematizing whiteness as an unmarked, racial-ized identity, and to this end she developed a methodology which she called writing one's "social geography of whiteness". She had her US white infor-mants write biographical narratives in which they described the presence or absence of people of colour in the various contexts of their everyday lives. They were asked to pay attention to the kinds of interactions that occurred across racialized boundaries within these contexts. They reflected on situ-ations where they were aware of whiteness and what it meant to them to be white (see also Brewster, Chapter 4, this volume, for a similar exercise). For example, one of the common features of whiteness turns out to be never having to think of one's self as having a race. It also means feeling at home in certain kinds of public spaces and endangered or at risk in others. The notion of writing one's social geography could, of course, easily be applied to any number of identity markers (sexual orientation, class background, able-bodiedness, national belonging).

A second step would be to select some of these geographical narratives and explore how they could be relevant to the research you are doing or planning to do. The assumption is that your social location will inevitably shape the ways you look at the world, the kinds of questions you ask (as well as the questions you haven't thought of asking), the kinds of people and events that evoke sympathy and understanding (as well as those that make you feel uncomfortable or evoke avoidance). In my own work on a US feminist grassroots organization grappling with issues of racism, I described my own discomforts and complicities as a white woman talking to other white women about racism (K. Davis 2007, 2010). I used my positionality as a white feminist to critically engage with ways that both my informants and I as researcher were—as I put it—"avoiding the R-word". I used whiteness to analyze the (unwitting) participation of white feminists in the structures and ideological discourses of racism as well as the ways my own complicities as a white feminist researcher shaped the research process.

Complicating Gender

Intersectionality was, among other things, developed in order to complicate gender as the theoretical mainstay of feminist research. The assumption was that gender can never be treated as a stand-alone category but is always and everywhere related to other differences and mutually constituted by these differences.

One way to test this assumption is to begin with an example which seems to be "about gender". Most of us have no trouble identifying some examples. They can include anything from a newspaper article about women's "double-burden" in the workforce and as caretakers to an ad promoting breast augmentations to a particular nasty case of domestic violence. Examples are everywhere and can take nearly any form: a photograph, a film, a TV program, a scientific text or a personal experience. I know that the example is "about gender" because a kind of internal red light begins flashing, a warning to be on the alert, even before I have figured out what the problem is.

Once you have found an example, the first step is to describe it and explain what makes you think it is "about gender". (This is, parenthetically, the way many of us started feminist research to begin with—something which was initially a sense of unease or a suspicion that something was not quite right went on to become a full-fledged research topic, sometimes even culminating in a dissertation or scholarly book!)

Having done this, the second step is to complicate the example and, along with it, hopefully your analysis. Intersectionally speaking, this entails asking the other (and then another and another) question. This could start with writing down three additional markers of differences. You should make a few notes after each about why you chose it and how you think—at first glance—it might provide some interesting insights into your example. For example, if you have chosen one of those ubiquitous advertisements which show a group of long-legged young women of different ethnic backgrounds, all wearing sexy underwear, you might decide that age, ethnicity and heteronormativity could be relevant or might offer additional critical insights into the example. Remember: you are not just asking another question because you like to ask questions. You are interested because you hope that by introducing additional complexity, you are going to have a better—i.e. more interesting and more critical—analysis.

The third step is to choose one of these markers of difference and proceed to do a more detailed description of the example, along with an account of why this example seems to be about age, or ethnicity, or heteronormativity. Remember to give this step at least as much attention as the first step, drawing, again, on intuitions, experiences, theoretical knowledge. Do not stop writing until you have completely run out of ideas!

The fourth step is to place the two narratives next to one another (literally) and compare them. Where have your descriptions been different? Where are the resonances and parallels in the way you analyzed the example as about gender or about age, or ethnicity or heteronormativity? In what ways are these analyses different? What were you not able to talk about in the second round that you were able to talk about in the first, and vice versa? How would you explain the resonances and the differences in the narratives?

The fifth step is to go back to your first narrative (this is about gender) and re-read it. Write down what has changed in your thinking about the example. What do these changes tell you about gender, more generally? What insights does this exercise give you into what is missing from the version of feminist theory you first applied and/or how it could be elaborated?

EXERCISE 1: ASK THE OTHER QUESTION

1. *Find an example which seems to be "about gender". Describe it and exemplify why.*
2. *"Ask the other question", thinking of three additional differences (like race, ethnicity, class, sexual orientation) which could be relevant to your example.*
3. *Choose one of these differences and write down how and why the example is "about" this difference.*
4. *Compare the narratives. Where are the resonances, and where are the differences? What can you talk about in one narrative but not in the other? Why?*
5. *Return to your first narrative and explain what insights you now have about gender.*

Blind Spots, Near-Sightedness and Other Myopias

One of the most important contributions that intersectionality has made in feminist scholarship is that it helps identify the inevitable blind spots that every researcher has when doing her or his research. Whether because of our experiences or social locations, our theoretical perspective or our political orientations, we are often unable to see what our material has to offer us. Such blind spots can subvert even our best intentions to do research which is comprehensive and critical.

A good example of such a blind spot can be found in Valerie Smith's analysis of narratives of passing—that is, stories of "characters who are 'legally' black yet light-skinned enough to live as white" (1998, 35). Such stories can be found in racially bifurcated societies like the US and apartheid South Africa. Using intersectionality as a strategy of reading, Smith reconsiders these narratives as stories which—while constructed in racial terms— are often motivated by class considerations, and whose consequences are differentially distributed due to gender (women in passing narratives are invariably punished for passing, while men are not). Her analysis highlights omissions in critical race and feminist theory, which have focused on passing primarily as a product of racism, as well as resisting the equation of passing with the desire to be white.

A simple way to look for possible blind spots is to consider a difference which seems totally irrelevant to the topic at hand and apply the exercise described above. Sometimes you are already aware of your blind spots and will want to put them automatically to the test. This is the case, for example, with whiteness, which has been taken as something requiring constant critical interrogation by many white researchers. However, many blind spots fall in the category of never-thought-about-that-before. In these cases, it can be useful to venture a bit farther afield, to go beyond the usual suspects of intersectional analysis (gender, race/ethnicity, class) and consider differences which, at first glance, seem to have nothing to do with your inquiry. For example, what could the consideration of able-bodiedness and disability possibly tell you about issues of citizenship in the EU? Or what does religion/ secularity have to do with experiences of dislocation or sedentariness? The consideration of such differences can, of course, culminate in the realization that this is really not the track you want to be on in your particular inquiry. Or it can open up new vistas for inquiry which you could not have imagined before. However, in any case, it will alert you to the possibility of new directions and make you more flexible in your encounters with your material.

A final word about a specific kind of blind spot—the near-sightedness which is almost endemic in academic research in the so-called First World. Despite the best intentions, many feminist scholars in North America or Western Europe tend to position themselves as being able to speak for women in other parts of the world. This occurs simply by virtue of the fact that they do not contextualize their research in terms of their local context or make clear the connections between their work and scholarship in other parts of the world. In contrast, scholars in other parts of the world are compelled to contextualize their work—this is often called making their work more internationally accessible.

Intersectionality can be a helpmeet here. For example, research which is centred in the US or which draws exclusively on theories produced in the US might re-examine its assumptions, questions, methods and findings through the lens of nation or national belonging or geopolitical location. (There are other names for this; the idea is to find something which will decentre universalistic assumptions which may be lurking unnoticed within one's research and/or to find ways to make global connections between here and there.)

One of my own favourites is Uma Narayan's (1997) *Dislocating Cultures*, in which she problematizes the ways so-called Third World women are represented in First World feminism. She was particularly concerned about US feminist discourse on widow burning (*sati*) in India. In order to criticize the assumptions behind the "death by culture" feminist discourse around *sati*, she compared it to another example of violence against women—namely, US domestic violence. After pointing out many of the similarities between the two, she shows how domestic violence, which is usually treated as a problem of *gendered* inequalities, might look if read through the lens of culture. For example, domestic violence could be linked to "American culture" with its Christian doctrines, myths and practices. Christian values about women's sinful nature, Eve's role in the Fall or the sanctity of heterosexual marriage could be cited as "typically American", analogous to the way *sati* in India is linked to Hinduism (Narayan 1997, 114). The fact that this reading would jar the sensibilities of many US feminist readers, who would probably argue that it just does not "feel plausible", paves the way both for contextualizing the issue of domestic violence in a broader framework and also for uncovering universalist assumptions underlying First World feminist discourse.

CODA

While I hope that the reader has been encouraged in her path toward finding ways to do intersectional analysis, I want to stress that she or he should be open to possibilities which have not been mentioned here at all. To this end, let me conclude my chapter with an example taken from a summer school in which students who had, for the most part, little understanding of what intersectionality was before they arrived taught me about intersectionality as a methodology. As part of their final exam, the students were divided into small groups and asked to devise a performance which would demonstrate what they had learned from the course. This is what one of the groups came up with:

After brainstorming about a series of everyday situations where women and men are often confronted with differences in identity and inequalities of power (for example, job interviews or walking along a city street at night or embracing one's partner in a public space or wearing a marker of one's religious affiliation), they assembled a list of relevant categories of difference—that is, differences that made a difference. They then made signs which were attached by cords around the students' necks. One student had a sign which read GENDER; another was CLASS, and still another was RACE. In addition to the usual suspects, there were signs bearing the words SEXUAL ORIENTATION, ETHNICITY, NATIONAL BELONG-ING, (DIS)ABILITY and RELIGION.

One student was chosen as leader. Her task was to read out descriptions of the everyday situations which had been assembled during the brainstorm-ing exercise, making sure to end on a note where it was clear that some inequities of power were involved. When she was finished, the students who felt that their category was relevant sprang to the front. Those who did not feel spoken to remained behind.

This exercise was interesting because of the visually evocative way it demonstrated how you can begin an intersectional analysis. It gave an imme-diate sense that in nearly any situation multiple differences would be involved. And yet, at the same time, these differences would not be equally involved, nor would every conceivable difference be relevant for a particular situation. The performance ended there, with all of us clapping with appreciation. However, it caused me to consider how this exercise could be expanded in ways that would develop it into an intersectional methodology. For example, the students who came forward could be asked to engage with one another in conversations, conversations which would make clear how different cate-gories made different aspects of the situation relevant. They could be encour-aged to explore common ground or get into arguments about which had more to say about the situation at hand. The students who were hanging out in the back could be asked to explain why they had *not* come forward. They might find reasons to change their decision. Ultimately, the goal would be a group discussion in which everyone—participants and onlookers—would return to the situation and consider what we had all learned, what had changed in our perceptions of what was going on and what we would want to look into as critical feminist researchers. It is this kind of conversation—open-ended, tan-talizingly ambiguous and yet irresistibly compelling—which is what makes interesectionality a critical methodology and a creative writing strategy.

NOTES

1. It is impossible to do justice to this writing, but here are some of the most well-known and frequently cited works: A. Davis 1981; hooks 1981; Carby 1982; B. Smith 1983; Moraga and Anzaldúa 1984; Ware 1992; Zinn and Dill 1994; Collins 1990.
2. For a good look at the range of disciplines, topics and perspectives which have employed intersectionality, the reader is referred to a special issue of the

European Journal of Women's Studies, edited by Ann Phoenix and Pamela
Pattynama (vol. 13, no. 3, August 2006).

3. Helma Lutz (2002) has provided a list of no less than fourteen lines of difference (gender, sexuality, race or skin colour, ethnicity, national belonging, class,
culture, religion, able-bodiedness, age, migration or sedentariness, property
ownership, geographical location and status in terms of tradition and development). The list is, however, potentially much longer.

4. In K. Davis 2007, I explain how many of these uncertainties are inherent in
the term itself—paradoxically part of its very popularity and success.

5. It goes beyond the scope of this particular chapter to expand on this point.
However, the reader is urged here to collect her or his own favourite examples
of how other scholars employ intersectionality in their own writings. These
examples can be analyzed for the kinds of strategies that are used—strategies
which one can "borrow"—or, as Sissel Lie says, "steal" (Chapter 7, this
volume)—and elaborate for one's own inquiry.

REFERENCES

Anthias, Floya. 1998. "Rethinking Social Divisions: Some Notes towards a Theoretical Framework." *Sociological Review* 46 (3): 557–80.

Anthias, Floya and Nira Yuval-Davis. 1983. "Contextualizing Feminism: Gender,
Ethnic and Class Divisions." *Feminist Review* 15: 62–75.

Brah, Avtar. 1996. *Cartographies of Diaspora: Contesting Identities.* London:
Routledge.

Brah, Avtar and Ann Phoenix. 2004. "Ain't I a Woman? Revisiting Intersectionality." *Journal of International Women's Studies* 5 (3): 75–86.

Butler, Judith. 1989. *Gender Trouble: Feminism and the Subversion of Identity.*
New York: Routledge.

Carby, Hazel. 1982. "White Woman Listen! Black Feminism and the Boundaries of
Sisterhood." In *The Empire Strikes Back: Race and Realism in 70s Britain,* edited
by the Centre for Contemporary Studies, 212–35. London: Hutchinson.

Collins, Patricia Hill. 1990. *Black Feminist Thought: Knowledge, Power and the
Politics of Empowerment.* Boston: Unwin Hyman.

Collins, Patricia Hill. 2000. "It's All in the Family: Intersections of Gender, Race,
and Nation." In *Decentering the Center: Philosophy for a Multicultural, Postcolonial, and Feminist World,* edited by Uma Narayan and Sandra Harding,
156–76. Bloomington: Indiana University Press.

Crenshaw, Kimberlé. 1989. "Demarginalizing the Intersection of Race and Sex: A
Black Feminist Critique of Antidiscrimination Doctrine, Feminist Theory, and
Antiracist Politics." *University of Chicago Legal Forum* 140: 139–67.

Crenshaw, Kimberlé. 1991. "Mapping the Margins: Intersectionality, Identity Politics, and Violence against Women of Color." *Stanford Law Review* 43 (6):
1241–99.

Davis, Angela Y. 1981. *Women, Race, and Class.* New York: Random House.

Davis, Kathy. 2007. *The Making of Our Bodies, Ourselves: How Feminism Travels
across Borders.* Durham: Duke University Press.

Davis, Kathy. 2008. "Intersectionality as Buzzword: A Sociology of Science Perspective on What Makes a Feminist Theory Successful." *Feminist Theory* 9 (1):
67–86.

Davis, Kathy. 2010. "Avoiding the 'R-Word': Racism in Feminist Collectives."
In *Secrecy and Silence in the Research Process: Feminist Reflections,* edited by
Róisín Ryan-Flood and Rosalind Gill, 147–60. London: Routledge.

Frankenberg, Ruth. 1993. *White Women, Race Matters: The Social Construction of Whiteness*. New York: Routledge.

Haraway, Donna J. 1988. "Situated Knowledges: The Science Question in Feminism as a Site of Discourse on the Privilege of Partial Perspective." *Feminist Studies* 14 (3): 575–99.

Haraway, Donna J. 1991. *Simians, Cyborgs, and Women: The Reinvention of Nature*. London: Free Association Books.

hooks, bell. 1981. *Ain't I a Woman: Black Women and Feminism*. Boston: South End Press.

King, Deborah. 1988. "Multiple Jeopardy, Multiple Consciousness: The Context of a Black Feminist Ideology." *Signs* 14 (1): 42–72.

Knudsen, Susanne V. 2006. "Intersectionality: A Theoretical Inspiration in the Analysis of Minority Cultures and Identities in Textbooks." In *Caught in the Web or Lost in the Textbook?*, edited by Èric Bruillard et al., 61–76. Caen: IARTEM, Stef, Iufm.

Lutz, Helma. 2002. "Zonder blikken of blozen: Het standpunt van de (nieuw-) realisten." *Tijdschrift voor Genderstudies* 5 (3): 7–17.

Lykke, Nina. 2010. *Feminist Studies: A Guide to Intersectional Theory, Methodology and Writing*. New York: Routledge.

Mani, Lata. 1989. "Multiple Mediations: Feminist Scholarship in the Age of Multinational Reception." *Inscriptions* 5: 1–24.

Matsuda, Maria J. 1991. "Beside My Sister, Facing the Enemy: Legal Theory out of Coalition." *Stanford Law Review* 43 (6): 1183–92.

McCall, Leslie. 2005. "The Complexity of Intersectionality." *Signs* 30 (3): 1771–1800.

Mohanty, Chandra T. (2003) *Feminism without Borders: Decolonizing Theory, Practicing Solidarity*. Durham: Duke University Press.

Moraga, Cherrie and Gloria Anzaldúa, eds. 1983. *The Bridge Called My Back: Writing by Radical Women of Color*. New York: Kitchen Table Press.

Narayan, Uma. 1997. *Dislocating Cultures: Identities, Traditions, and Third World Feminism*. New York: Routledge.

Phoenix, Ann. 2006. "Editorial Intersectionality." *European Journal of Women's Studies* 13 (3): 187–92.

Smith, Barbara, ed. 1983. *Home Girls: A Black Feminist Anthology*. New York: Kitchen Table/Women of Color Press.

Smith, Valerie. 1998. *Not Just Race, Not Just Gender: Black Feminist Readings*. New York: Routledge.

Staunæs, Dorte. 2003. "Where Have All the Subjects Gone? Bringing Together the Concepts of Intersectionality and Subjectification." *Nora* 11 (2): 101–10.

Ware, Vron. 1992. *Beyond the Pale: White Women, Racism and History*. London: Verso.

Yuval-Davis, Nira. 1997. *Gender and Nation*. London: Sage.

Zinn, M. Backa and B. Thonton Dill, eds. 1994. *Women of Color in US Society*. Philadelphia: Temple University Press.

2 Passionate Disidentifications as an Intersectional Writing Strategy

Nina Lykke

To do research and write from intersectional subject positions that cross-cut monolithic and bounded categories such as gender, ethnicity, race, class, sexuality, age, dis/ability, geopolitical positioning, etc. involves starting points other than identity politics, and in particular identity politics based on only one category. The diverse critiques that have characterized feminist debates on intersectionality for years share an urge to push the theorizing and politics of feminist and other social movements beyond monocategorical standpoints. Such critiques have been driven by an urge to transgress standpoints based on only one identity-political category, for example, an undifferentiated understanding of "women's perspectives" related to a universalizing notion of "women" that ignores differences between women in terms of ethnicity, race, class, sexuality, age, dis/ability, geopolitical positioning, etc. In a poststructuralist vein, many of these critiques have also spelled out the need to understand subject positions as mobile and multiple rather than founded on fixed categories which confirm what ought to be problematized and deconstructed. Queer feminist theorist Judith Butler's attack (1990) on "woman" as the subject of feminism is a case in point.

In this chapter, I shall reflect on the bearing that these critiques may have on writing processes. My aim is to explore what it means to write from subject positions based on intersections of feminist, postcolonial, queer or other critical stances. How can we establish the position from where the text is narrated, the position of enunciation or "I"-position of the text, in multiple and mobile locations rather than in fixed standpoints? What strategies are appropriate for driving the narrative of an intersectionally located text forward?

In the exploration of these questions, I shall focus on *disidentification* as a critical intersectional writing strategy and mobile politics of location. This focus is motivated by the ways in which the concept of disidentification has proved useful in discussions of critical identity-political processes related to a movement beyond monocategorical standpoints and hegemonic versions of identity politics.

In recent years, the concept of disidentification has been used as a theoretical tool to grasp intersections of gender and generation and to critically conceptualize political tensions among different feminist "waves" (Henry 2004; Dean 2008; Tuin 2011). This concept has also been related to intersectional processes of de/colonialization (Fuss 1995) and to Marxist-inspired critiques of ideologies (Pêcheux 1982). Cuban-American Performance Studies scholar José Esteban Muñoz' work on disidentification deserves special mention in the context of the discussion of creative writing processes in this volume because of his comprehensive reflections on disidentification as a driving force in artistic processes. In his book *Disidentification: Queers of Color and the Performance of Politics* (1999), Muñoz discusses the positionality of queers of colour, illustrated by analyses of the work of contemporary queer African-American and Latino performance artists. The focus of Muñoz' book is to highlight the "worldmaking power of disidentificatory performance art" (ix).

I draw inspiration from Muñoz and the above-mentioned authors. Theoretically, however, I shall align my argument in particular with Butler's discussion of disidentification as a theoretical tool to both understand and negotiate internal differences within identity-political movements (1993, 219–22). Moreover, I will draw on Chicana feminist contributions: Norma Alarcón's (1991) reflections on disidentificatory writing strategies of radical women of colour, as well as the notion of "differential consciousness", coined by Chicana feminist scholar Chela Sandoval (2000), which resonates with the concept of disidentification.

The chapter is structured so that I first make myself accountable for my working definition of "disidentification". Second, I reflect on some examples. I take a look at the disidentificatory rhetoric of a couple of texts that have been received by broad audiences as key political and performative moments of resistance to monocategorical versions of standpoint feminism. The texts I shall analyze are postcolonial feminist scholar Chandra T. Mohanty's article "Under Western Eyes" (1988) and transgender theorist Sandy Stone's article "The 'Empire' Strikes Back" (2006). Finally, I shall suggest a writing exercise that I created in order to inspire readers who want to try out how strategies of disidentification can be turned into productive writing methodologies.

THE CONCEPT OF DISIDENTIFICATION: A THEORETICAL OVERVIEW

Theoretically, the concept of disidentification has been located within different frameworks. However, they have the common denominator that disidentification is conceived as a subject position that is located in between identification and counter-identification (the latter understood in the sense of active non-identification). Disidentification is taken to signify a "dialectic of identification and counter-identification" (Dean 2008, 4). However, beyond this overall commonality, disidentification is defined rather differently within different theoretical frameworks and contexts.

To contextualize the concept of disidentification, I shall give a brief overview of three different theoretical contexts which have played a role in determining how disidentification became linked to the construction of political identities and subject positions within feminist and other critical studies.

In a psychoanalytic vein, the in-between position of disidentification was explored by feminist theorist Diane Fuss in her book *Identification Papers* and related to an ambivalent disavowal of "an identification that has already been made and denied in the unconscious" (1995, 7). As an example of this kind of disidentification, Fuss refers to Butler's discussion of the ways in which homophobic reactions may be interpreted as based on a fear of the return of a disavowed and unconscious identification with the abjected homosexual position (Butler 1993, 112).

Another frame of reference is based on French Marxist Louis Althusser's theories of ideology and locates the concept of disidentification rather differently. Within this framework, disidentification does not refer to feared, unconscious identifications but rather to a conscious political point of departure for critical opposition. Building on Althusser's theorizing of dominant ideologies and the possibilities of opposing them politically, French linguist Michel Pêcheux (1982) developed a theory of disidentification that is referenced in critical queer feminist and postcolonial work (Alarcón 1991; Muñoz 1999). In Pêcheux' framework, disidentification is understood as a political position in between identification and counter-identification with dominant ideologies. Instead of either accepting these ideologies or positioning oneself in total opposition to them, a strategy of disidentification is one that "tries to transform a cultural logic from within", working both "on and against a dominant ideology" (Muñoz 1999, 11).

A third theoretical context for critical interpretation of the concept of disidentification shares with the Althusserian one a focus on political resistance but shifts the perspectives from Althusser's Marxism to Foucauldian theories of discursive power regimes and resistance. Considered in this way, disidentificatory strategies are not to be understood in terms of opposition to dominant ideologies, but of resistance to hegemonic and normativizing discourses. This discourse-theoretical context for a feminist and queer theoretical conceptualization of disidentification is also strongly influenced by Butler, as is the psychoanalytic approach.

In this chapter, I shall in particular link up with the third—discourse-theoretical—context. Here I am in line with Muñoz (1999), who, despite elaborate references to both the psychoanalytic and the ideology-critical framework, takes his overall point of departure in a Foucauldian and Butlerian approach which defines discourse as polyvalent and sees power and resistance as working in a decentred way. On the following pages, I shall consider the ways in which disidentification can be used as a motor for writing, and in so doing I shall elaborate on the third context.

THE NECESSARY BREAKDOWN OF THE UNIFYING SIGNIFIER: A DRIVING FORCE FOR DISIDENTIFICATORY WRITING

The third—discourse-theoretical—context for understanding disidentification as a political subject position is closely linked to Butler's reflections on the construction of subjectivities and political identities through discursive processes of (mis)recognition and failure of identification (1993, 219). Butler illustrates her reflections on disidentification with reference to the political identities of "woman" and "queer" (219, 221). Referring to cultural critic Slavoj Zizek's (1989) reflections on the performativity of unifying political signifiers, Butler describes how imagined communities of political movements or groups who gather under the banner of a category, be it "woman", "queer", etc., must always fail to establish the unity they promise. According to Butler (and Zizek), the performative political signifier can never capture the complex web of intersectional social relations in which participants in political movements are always already embedded. Participants will always be socioculturally more diverse than indicated by the singular category under which they organize. This means that dimensions of the participants' diversity will always be excluded by the unifying signifier:

> The "failure" of the signifier ["woman", "queer", etc.] to produce the unity it appears to name is . . . the result of that term's incapacity to include the social relations that it provisionally stabilizes through a set of contingent exclusions.

> —(Butler 1993, 220–21)

The consequence of this necessary failure is a sort of catch-22, an aporia, a situation of undecidability. The movement's participants commit themselves to it because they are interpellated by the unity that the signifier ("woman", "queer", etc.) promises. But when the signifier of necessity fails to keep its promise, it leaves the participants with an "uneasy sense of standing under a sign to which one does and does not belong" (Butler 1993, 219). The unease that this situation generates is, according to both Butler and Zizek, what produces disidentification—a disidentification which, against this background, is defined as the ambivalent feeling of belonging and not-belonging at the same time.

But how can we deal with the situation? While Zizek argues that such unease of necessity leads to political immobilization, Butler is more optimistic. She asks about "the possibilities of politicizing *dis*identification" and suggests that "the failure of identification" may become "the point of departure for a more democratizing affirmation of internal difference" (1993, 219). Butler opens up the possibility that the necessary "internal difference"—or, in other words, the intersectional diversity of the movement's participants, which was excluded by the unifying signifier—can be articulated in the process of reiteration of the signifier. Normativizing discourses, in this case the ones defined by the unifying signifier, are, according to Butler, endlessly repeated, but never mimetically. In a Foucauldian spirit, Butler understands discourses as polyvalent: they are instruments of hegemonic and normativizing power, but also of resistance. This means that if the necessary incompleteness and failure of the unifying signifier ("woman", "queer", etc.) are not disavowed, but recognized and negotiated within the movement, it can lead to a process of self-reflection and a democracy-enhancing negotiation of internal differences and intersectionalities—a process which, according to Butler, should be ongoing in order to ensure democracy in the movement:

> These exclusions [the exclusions of the intersectional diversity of a movement's participants] need to be read and used in the reformulation and expansion of a democratizing reiteration of the term [the unifying signifier "woman", "queer", etc.]. That there can be no final or complete inclusivity is . . . a function of the complexity and historicity of a social field that can never be summarized by any given description, and that, for democratic reasons, ought never to be.
>
> —(1993, 221)

While Butler suggests that the failure of the unifying signifier, and the disidentificatory processes it entails, can be a starting point for a democratic negotiation of internal difference and intersectionality, I shall bring the argument to bear on writing processes. I shall suggest that the disidentificatory processes that are initiated by the failure of the unifying signifier can be an important driving force for creative as well as academic writing and theorizing.

Here, I align my argument with Muñoz. The idea that disidentificatory processes can be a launching pad for creative processes and for the production of critical cultural and social analysis is in line with Muñoz' reading of the performance art of queers of colour. He characterizes the disidentificatory processes to which the analyzed performance artists are committed as a combination of "a hermeneutic, a process of production, and a mode of performance" (1999, 25). He argues that their work combines a mode of critical cultural reception, which interprets and unpacks hegemonic discourses (the hermeneutic aspect), and a mode of cultural production, which twists these discourses into performances with a worldmaking political power to make a performative difference.

In an interpretation of the writing strategies of the Chicana feminist classic *This Bridge Called My Back: Writings by Radical Women of Color* (Moraga and Anzaldúa 1981), Norma Alarcón (1991) makes a parallel point about disidentificatory writing. She, too, sees disidentification as a road to a productive negotiation of difference, diversity and contradictions within political identities and subject positions. She reflects on writing as a strategy for the unfolding of disidentificatory processes, emphasizing the diverse genres and styles (essays, poems, tales, testimonials, letters, etc.)

which characterize *This Bridge*, as well as the ways in which the book consciously and reflexively fleshes out difference, diversity, conflicts and contradictions in the subject positions of radical lesbian women of colour. Alarcón wants to break with a unified "gender consciousness" which only takes into account gender relations, excluding, among other things, discussions of interracial and intercultural relations as well as intersections with class and sexualities. From the perspective of Alarcón, the disidentificatory writing of *This Bridge*, which makes a point of differences rather than unity, stands out as a tool for the enabling of such a break. To borrow a concept coined by Sandoval, disidentificatory writing replaces a monocategorical "gender consciousness" with a "differential consciousness" (Sandoval 2000, 57–63), a consciousness that works on many levels and cuts across different kinds of divisions between feminist strategies. Sandoval uses the metaphor of the clutch in a car to characterize the ways in which the "differential consciousness" of US Third World feminism works "between and among" the classifications of oppositional feminist consciousness developed by white feminists (liberal, socialist, radical, etc.) (2000, 57).

Both Muñoz and Alarcón use the term *disidentification*—the former related to performance art, the latter to the mixed genres of *This Bridge*, where the borders between poetic and academic genres are blurred. I shall take the point about disidentification as a writing strategy to bear on *academic writing*. I shall make the claim that disidentificatory processes can not only be the motor of performance art and mixed genres, as stated by Muñoz and Alarcón, but can also be seen as a core activity of feminist, postcolonial, queer, transgender and intersectional academic writing. I shall spell this out via analyses of two examples, which are chosen for their status as texts that, seen from a genealogical—i.e. retrospective—perspective, embody a couple of key moments in Intersectional Gender and Transgender Studies, moments where disidentifications were articulated forcefully and with great effect. I shall analyze the writing strategies of these texts with disidentification as my interpretative lens, focusing on the ways in which the narrators' positions and the narrative dynamics of the articles can be read as informed by disidentificatory processes.

DISIDENTIFYING WITH THE COLONIZING WESTERN GAZE

My first example is US-Indian scholar Chandra T. Mohanty's famous article "Under Western Eyes: Feminist Scholarship and Colonial Discourses", first published in 1984 and later reprinted many times.[1] I have chosen this particular text because of the huge impact it has had on the postcolonial turn in feminist theorizing. It is my claim that this text can be read as an example of a disidentificatory process. Mohanty does not use the term "disidentification", but when I read her article from the perspective of the notion of disidentification, based on Butler, Muñoz and Alarcón, it stands out as a good example. Read through this lens, the textual strategies of the article spell out how a disidentificatory process can be transformed into an excellent political and scholarly analysis.

So what is the disidentificatory project of Mohanty's article? Through which textual strategies is it articulated?

The aim of the article is to contribute to carving out a platform for "Third World feminisms" (1988, 51). In accordance with the overall task of a disidentificatory process, which, in line with Muñoz (1999), I shall define as an unpacking of existing hegemonic discourses and a making of new worlds, Mohanty outlines precisely these two tasks in relation to the conditions for an unfolding of "Third World feminisms". What is needed, Mohanty claims, is (1) "the internal critique of hegemonic 'Western' feminisms" (i.e. the unpacking of existing hegemonic discourses) and (2) a "formulation of autonomous, geographically, historically, and culturally grounded feminist concerns and strategies" (i.e. taking steps towards the making of new worlds; 1988, 51). Mohanty delimits her aim, as far as the present article is concerned, to deal with the first of these tasks: the unpacking of the problems of hegemonic "Western" feminisms.

In order to address the first aim, Mohanty introduces what she sees as the main problem with some Western feminist discourses. In accordance with what I, with reference to Butler, have stressed as a key point of departure for disidentificatory processes—the failure of a unifying signifier—Mohanty puts her finger on exactly this problem.

The unifying signifier that Mohanty sets out to criticize is the Third World Woman (singular). Against this background, the main part of the article is a meticulous documentation and analysis of ways in which influential and hegemonic Western feminist discourses construct "the 'third world woman' as a singular monolithic subject" (1988, 51). The textual material that Mohanty uses to make her point consists of a number of textual examples from the Zed Press *Women in the Third World* book series. She shows how the discursive construction of the Third World Woman in the Zed Press texts is characterized by an erasure of the heterogeneity and diversity of the specific situations of women in the so-called Third World. The diversity of situations of Third World women (in the plural) is replaced by an abstract image of the Third World Woman (singular), Mohanty argues. She sustains her argument with meticulous close readings of the Zed texts. Through these close readings, she shows how the unifying signifier, the Third World Woman, fails to grasp the specific and diverse situations of women in different Third World situations. She demonstrates how the majority of the Zed texts reproduce a homogenized, universalized and essentialized image of the Third World Woman (singular) instead of producing useful analyses of the specificities of diverse and intersectional relations of power and sustainable local strategies to work against and resist them. Mohanty shows how the Zed texts do not undertake political, economic or cultural analyses of specific situations, conditions and subjectivities but simply present the essentialized Third World Woman as victimized and dependent on the political agency of others, for example, the Western sisters. Mohanty also points out how this homogenizing and essentializing construction represents a discursive act of colonization insofar as it matches and is complicit with other—economic and political—acts of structural domination and colonization:

> [C]olonization almost invariably implies a relation of structural domination, and a suppression—often violent—of the heterogeneity of the subject(s) in question.
>
> —(1988, 52)

To disidentify with and demonstrate the collapse of the unifying signifier—in casu: the signifier Third World Woman—as a relevant and politically appropriate "object of study" makes up the main textual strategy of Mohanty's text. But it is also important to look at the ways in which the disidentificatory process works on the level of textual self-presentation or enunciation. At this level, two questions must be raised: (1) How does Mohanty interpret the implications of the homogenizing construction of the Third World Woman for the subject positions articulated in the Zed Press texts? (2) From what kind of alternative subject position does Mohanty narrate her own text?

As far as the first of these questions is concerned, Mohanty criticizes the way in which the Zed texts implicitly present their authors as discursively located in a position opposite to that of the Third World Woman. She underlines how a majority of the Zed texts are marked by a "we"/"they" relationship. She adds that not all feminist texts produced in the "West" take this we/they stance, but she indicates that textual strategies are commonly used which "codify Others as non-Western and hence themselves [i.e. their own authors and narrators] as (implicitly) Western" (1988, 52). The dichotomized we/they-based enunciation, combined with the explicit textual characterization of the Third World Woman as victimized, backward, ignorant, controlled by patriarchal relations, without agency and in this sense dependent on the political agency of others, makes the textual narrators stand out as the opposite of this. They are implicitly characterized as liberated, modern, autonomous subjects, capable of political analysis and action on behalf of their backward, non-Western sisters. Mohanty disidentifies with this position of enunciation.

Furthermore, she underlines the ways in which this Western feminist ethnocentrism in many ways matches the general ethnocentrism of Western humanism, which again ties in with larger processes of colonization:

> However, in the context of the hegemony of the Western scholarly establishment in the production and dissemination of texts, and in the context

of the legitimating imperative of humanistic and scientific discourse, the definition of "the third world woman" as a monolith might well tie into the larger economic and ideological praxis of "disinterested" scientific inquiry and pluralism which are the surface manifestations of a latent economic and cultural colonization of the "non-Western" world.

—(1988, 74)

In sum, Mohanty underlines that the Zed texts' position of enunciation, their we/they rhetoric and their lack of reflection on their own situatedness, makes them complicit in hegemonic discourses with colonizing effects. According to Mohanty's analysis, these texts take up a position that works seriously against the forming of strategic coalitions and instead serves "to distort Western feminist political practices, and limit the possibility of coalitions among (usually white) Western feminists and working-class feminists and feminists of color around the world" (1988, 53).

But what about Mohanty's own position of enunciation? In contrast with the narrators of the Zed texts, she cuts across the binary we/they relation. Instead of appearing as a Western "we" talking about "Third World others" from the elevated position of the godlike and apparently disinterested knower of traditional science, she locates herself and her text, acknowledging her own embeddedness and entanglement in her "object" of study, i.e. her "implication and investment in contemporary debates in feminist theory" (1988, 52). She states that she speaks from a position which is defined by the explicit political aim of establishing a mode of framing the analysis that will facilitate "strategic coalitions across class, race, and national boundaries" (52–53). In this way, she constructs a position of enunciation for herself, based on a politics of location (Rich 1986) and situated knowledges (Haraway 1991). This is a position which is clearly demarcated from and disidentifying with the subject positions of the Zed texts. But Mohanty also avoids the position of ventriloquist and self-declared spokesperson for the Third World Woman, which would have repeated the colonizing act of essentialization and homogenization from the reverse position.

TRANSGENDERISM: BETWEEN PASSING AND DISIDENTIFYING

My second example is transgender scholar Sandy Stone's article "The 'Empire' Strikes Back: A Posttranssexual Manifesto", first published in 1991 and later reprinted many times, among others in the *Transgender Studies Reader* (Stryker and Whittle 2006).[2] This article is also chosen because of its iconic status in the field. In the *Transgender Studies Reader* Stone's article is presented as "pathbreaking" (Stryker and Whittle 2006, 221) and genealogically crucial for the emergence of Transgender Studies. But how does this text fit into a discussion of feminist disidentifications?

I shall claim that critical Transgender Studies make up an important part of Intersectional Gender Studies and that the disidentifications of feminists embarking on a political transgender trajectory (such as Stone as well as the editors of the *Transgender Studies Reader*, Susan Stryker and Stephen Whittle, who all started out as sex-positive feminists) should be taken into account as part of the queer turn in feminist theorizing.

Like Mohanty, Stone does not use the term "disidentification" hirself. So I am the one to interpellate hir text into this context in order to close-read it with the concept of disidentification, based on Butler, Muñoz and Alarcón, as my tool. In this case, too, I shall claim that the text spells out how a disidentificatory process may generate a politically strong and scholarly sophisticated analysis.

So let me here, too, take a look at the disidentificatory project of the article, and the textual strategies through which it is articulated.

The title of Stone's article is a response to US feminist scholar Janice Raymond's book *The Transsexual Empire* (1979), which attacks transsexualism from a strongly anti-queer and anti-sex position, claiming that transsexuals, in particular politically radical male-to-female transsexuals, are undermining the feminist movement when they participate in all-women projects. In the book Raymond explicitly refers to Stone as an example, and to the controversy around Stone's employment (1974–78) as a sound engineer by the famous 1970s US feminist recording company Olivia Records. The controversy can be understood against the background of the so-called US feminist sex wars, where sex-positive feminists clashed with anti-sex feminists engaged in various kinds of activism against the sexual exploitation of women in pornography (Duggan and Hunter 2006).

The main title of Stone's article, "The 'Empire' Strikes Back", refers directly to Raymond's book and articulates Stone's aim to resist and disidentify with Raymond's absurd transphobic version of feminism and her interpellation of politically radical transsexuals as a sort of patriarchal fifth column within the feminist movement. But the subtitle, "A Posttranssexual Manifesto", refers more broadly to two other disidentifications which characterize the governing logic and textual strategy of the article.

One is a disidentification with the constructions of transsexual identities in the popular genre of trans-(auto)biographies. Stone analyzes several (auto)biographical texts of m-t-f transsexuals, among others the story (Hoyer 1931) of the Danish painter and transperson Einar Wegener/Lili Elbe, who around 1930 had sex reassignment surgery performed in Germany. The surgeons included the famous sexologist and writer Magnus Hirschfeld, who for many years had acted as a spokesperson for sexual and in particular homosexual rights. Stone points out how the storylines of these trans-(auto)biographies oscillate around the event of sex reassignment surgery, which is presented as a point of no return within the framework of a polarized, heteronormative model of sexual difference, allowing only the "pure" positions of "Man" or "Woman". The model implies that the person undergoing surgery is supposed to erase her/his past life in order to pass within her/his new gender identity. Stone disidentifies strongly with these narratives of transfiguration and erasure of past messiness in favour of a new, "pure" identity as "true Woman". In the analysis, ze emphasizes the absurdities and silences of the (auto)biographies. Ze pinpoints, among other things, how cultural environments that allow only two positions, Man or Woman, and create high stakes in the act of passing, require the narrators of the trans-(auto)biographies to reconstruct the transition from one gendered position to the other as one of total transfiguration.

One more disidentification is spelled out in Stone's text, i.e. a disidentification with the medical framing of transgender health issues. Stone describes how the diagnosis of Gender Dysphoria Syndrome was developed and ascribed to transsexuals as part of the work of the Stanford Gender Dysphoria Program. This programme was started in 1968, and for many years it was the academic focus of Western studies of transsexualism. According to the definition and diagnosis developed by the surgeons and psychologists who staffed the Stanford programme, transsexualism is a gender identity disorder. Stone summarizes the discourses of the programme as follows: The clinical understanding is inscribed in constructionist discourses and a definition of sex and gender as separate phenomena. Against this background, transsexuals are defined as individuals who mistakenly blur the distinction between sex and gender, "confusing the performative character of gender with the physical 'fact' of sex" (Stone 2006, 222). An individual diagnosed with this "disorder" "identifies his or her gender identity with that of the 'opposite' gender" (222), or, in other words, she/he perceives herself/himself to be in the "wrong body". According to the Stanford programme, transsexuals are thus confused and mistaken, but their syndrome can, at least in some cases, be corrected via sex reassignment surgery, followed up by constructive identity and behaviour realignment with the gender that matches the surgically reassigned sex. Or, in other words, the programme requires that m-t-f transsexuals, in addition to surgery, must learn to pass as "real" women. As Stone critically emphasizes, the Stanford programme did not just aim to produce "anatomically legible females, but women . . . i.e. gendered females" (228).

Stone's critical and disidentificatory analysis makes it clear that the gender dysphoria programme operates within precisely the same problematic binary system as the trans-(auto)biographies. The constructionist approach of the programme is established within the framework of a rigorous two-gender model, within which individuals will have to take up positions as either Woman or Man. The Stanford programme is shaped as an "apparatus of production of gender" (Stone 2006, 228). Stone ironically points out that this apparatus of gender production was, to a large extent, founded on the stories of transsexuals who wanted surgery and therefore tried keenly to comply with the gender norms and positions they assumed would convince the surgeons and psychologists that they should be granted an operation.

According to Stone, what was totally silenced vis-à-vis doctors and psychologists was, for example, a "secret tradition" of penile masturbation before surgery, named "wringing the turkey's neck" (228). To report penile sensations and pleasures would have disqualified the individual from passing as a "true" Woman-in-becoming, and therefore put hir at risk of being denied the desired operation. So everybody kept their mouths shut as far as this tradition was concerned.

As a conclusion to the acts of disidentification that Stone undertakes in the article, ze produces what ze calls "a posttranssexual manifesto" (2006, 230–32). The purpose of this manifesto is to carve out a position of enunciation for the transsexual subject, who, according to Stone's analysis, is objectified and denied a speaking position in all three kinds of analyzed discourse (the feminist, the medical-psychological and the autobiographical). While Raymond denies transsexuals any kind of subjectivity beyond the status of abject monsters, the trans-(auto)biographies and the medical-psychological discourses both require that the transsexual in the postoperative situation erases hir "dissonant" and "impure" transsexual past in order to take up a "pure" gender identity. In other words, the postoperative transsexual is supposed to try to pass unambiguously as the gender that matches the sex of the reassigned body. According to Stone, this is an act of symbolic violence and colonization, which denies the transsexual the right to be visible as a transsexual.

What Stone's manifesto claims and carves out is therefore precisely a position of enunciation which allows hir to speak as a permanently visible transsexual, to speak all the dissonances and complexities of bodies and desires beyond the gender binary. Or, as Stone phrases this position, to speak as a posttranssexual is to speak as a multiply embodied subject who is permanently in transit and visibly performing mobile in-between positions (2006, 232), and not just someone who accidentally ended up in the "wrong" body waiting for a "correcting" medical-technological fix.

FROM PASSIONATE DISIDENTIFICATIONS TO DIFFERENTIAL CONSCIOUSNESS

Both Mohanty's and Stone's texts have been influential. The Mohanty text gave impetus to a postcolonial turn in feminist theorizing and politics, while the Stone text was part of the queer turn. Against this background, I want to suggest that the history of intersecting feminisms can, perhaps more than anything else, be read as a story of disidentifications and passionately disidentificatory moments. Moreover, both texts make it clear that disidentificatory processes are, indeed, borne by affective investments and carried by deeply felt political and personal passions. Finally, these texts share a passionate commitment to acts of disidentification which, according to my close readings, can be understood as the driving forces of writing processes.

Each of the texts echoes the feelings of rage and powerlessness that you, as an embodied and intersectionally situated subject, experience when you and the group with which you identify are denied a speaking position within the framework of the overarching movement under whose banner you signed up in order to actually let your critique of present societal conditions be heard. To be relegated to the position of a mute object because parts of your intersectionally situated identity are foreclosed and denied the space to unfold is, of course, in the context of social movements, extremely painful and causes a lot of rage that is added to the already-existing feelings of pain and rage vis-à-vis unjust societal and cultural conditions, which are what led you to the movement in the first place.

When reading Mohanty and Stone, you can feel the passionate desire to undo the muted and objectified position (of the essentialized Third World Woman in the case of Mohanty, and of the transsexual who complies with gender norms and erases hir messy past in the case of Stone) resonating throughout the texts. To speak and write in the name of disidentification can be described as a carving out of positions of enunciation, where foreclosed and/or denied aspects of your intersectionally situated and embodied identity can unfold, and this process of undoing and constructing new positions is to be considered passionately pleasurable and cathartic. While it is rage-provoking and painful when the movement you desired to be part of denies aspects of your identity, it is conversely a great pleasure and cathartic relief when you get to claim a platform for disidentifying and for speaking these stories that "resist telling" (Crenshaw 1991, 1242). The combination of rage and pain, on the one hand, and the catharsis and pleasure at voicing the previously unspeakable position in a critically hermeneutic and performative, "world-making" act of disidentification (Muñoz 1999, ix), on the other, must clearly be understood as the force that energizes and drives the writing of these texts.

Borrowing from Chicana feminist Chela Sandoval (2000), I shall also suggest that what is generated in the disidentificatory writing process is a position of enunciation which is based on "differential consciousness"; i.e. a position that allows for resistance, but without fixing this resistance within a monocategorical standpoint and a one-dimensional ontology. The speaking positions of both Mohanty and Stone are constructed as cross-cutting and mobile and might, in Sandoval's terms, be understood as differential.

Mohanty speaks from a position as a committed feminist who wants coalitions between intersecting feminisms. But she does not identify with one monocategorical standpoint. Her disidentification with the we/they construction of the Zed texts does not lead her to fall into the trap of re-essentialization. She avoids speaking as a ventriloquist on behalf of a mono-categorically homogenized Third World Woman. Stone, too, constructs a cross-cutting and mobile position of enunciation. Ze avoids the position of just giving voice to "the transsexual". Instead, ze claims a posttranssexual speaking position which allows for mobility, fluidity and a cross-cutting of the fixed and dichotomous two-gender model.

DISIDENTIFICATORY WRITING

To let readers try out for themselves whether and how disidentifications can work as a productive writing strategy, I shall end with an exercise in disidentificatory writing.

EXERCISE 2: DISIDENTIFICATORY WRITING

1) *Think of a politically unifying signifier that is important to you and your identity. Use the word "political" in a broad sense to make sure that you find a signifier that you really have something to write about. Examples: feminism(s), anti-racism(s), queer, a political party, an NGO, your discipline, your profession, etc.*

2) *Try to recall a memory of a particular place, space, moment in time and scene that gave specific meaning to the signifier for you and positive/pleasurable feelings of identification and belonging.*

3) *Try to recall yet another memory of a particular place/space/ moment/scene, related to the signifier, but this time one that you remember as being entangled with less positive, ambivalent or directly negative feelings.*

4) *Write down brainstormed keywords to help you recapitulate both the positive and the more negative memory. Use these keywords as a point of departure for writing two separate freestyle texts— one on the positively and one on the more negatively remembered place/space/moment/scene. Make sure that you involve your senses and your feelings in both texts. What do you hear, see, smell, touch and taste when you think about each of the two places/spaces/ moments/scenes? What positive and/or negative feelings are related to the memories of each of the two places/spaces/moments/scenes? Try to be specific about the feelings and relate them to the sensual description.*

5) *Compare the two texts. Try to reflect on the reasons for the positive feelings you connect to the first memory and the more negative ones you link to the second memory. Try out whether it makes sense to analyze the two memories with the notions of identification/ disidentification as a lens. Reflect on this process and whether or not it works to use this analytical framework.*

6) *Write a synopsis for an article on the political community to which your chosen unifying signifier relates.*
   A. *If it made sense for you to analyze the two memories with the notions of identification/disidentification as a lens, build your synopsis against this background: for example, first discuss the identifications and afterwards the disidentifications (or counter-identifications) at stake for you.*

> B. *If it did not make sense for you to analyze the two memories with these notions as a lens, revisit each of the two places/ spaces/moments/scenes and try to imagine what would happen if, for example, your gender/sex, sexual orientation, skin colour, mother tongue, age, able-bodiedness and/or other categorizations were changed. Build your synopsis against this background: discuss, for example, first your own identifications and afterwards the potentials or delimitations of the unifying signifier to attract and appear inclusive to groups of individuals located in intersectionally different ways from yourself.*

POSTSCRIPT

Passionate disidentifications as a critical intersectional writing strategy have meant a lot to my own writing as well. I shall end with an account of this in order to locate myself in the discussion as well as to illustrate how disidentificatory strategies for doing intellectual work and critical writing can function on a personal level. I shall try to take disidentification as a genealogical lens for a brief overview of some of the main themes in my scholarly work since I started publishing in the mid 1970s.

I have often started out with an embodied feeling of unease vis-à-vis theoretical discourses to which, on the one hand, I felt attracted because of the explanatory power they seemed to me to hold in terms of giving plausible and critical accounts of important power differentials, but which, on the other hand, seen from my point of view, also lacked an understanding of other power differentials that I felt were important. Along with other socialist feminists, I began my academic career as a critical feminist intellectual, disidentifying with the exclusive Marxist focus on class relations. This disidentification led me to contribute to feminist Marxist theorizings of intersecting power differentials based on gender and class (Lykke 1993). Along with other queer feminists, I disidentified with the heteronormative two-gender model, which has sometimes been uncritically reproduced even in feminist research, and, from a point of departure in this disidentification, I have done queer readings of psychoanalysis and literature (Lykke 1993, 1994). Along with other posthumanist feminists, in more recent years I have disidentified with the exclusive and anthropocentric focus on human affairs in much feminist theory and politics and have contributed to the inclusion of cyborgs, "earth others" (Plumwood 1993) and other non-human agencies in the discussion of the intersecting power differentials that need to be taken into account in feminist theorizing and politics (Bryld and Lykke 2000). Along with other post- and transdisciplinary feminists, I have also disidentified with feminist endeavours to anchor feminist research exclusively within the frameworks of the disciplines—and have tried theoretically as well as politically to go against the policing power of the disciplines, carving out spaces for the unfolding of Feminist Studies as the oxymoron of a postdisciplinary discipline (Lykke 2010). These and other disidentifications that have characterized my life as a critical feminist intellectual have been productive for my writing processes. I wrote this chapter because I hope that disidentification as a conceptual tool for reflecting on writing strategies can also work for others.

NOTES

1. Cf. Mohanty, Chandra T. 1984. "Under Western Eyes: Feminist Scholarship and Colonial Discourses." *Boundary 2* (special issue): "On Humanism and the University I : The Discourse of Humanism," Vol XII: 3/Vol XIII, 1: 333–58. The quotes in the following analysis are from the reprint in Feminist Review (Mohanty 1988). The text can be downloaded from http://blog.lib.umn.edu/raim0007/RaeSpot/under wstrn eyes.pdf (accessed 29 November 2012).
2. Cf. Stone, Sandy. 1991. "The 'Empire' Strikes Back: A Posttranssexual Manifesto." In *Body Guards: The Cultural Politics of Gender Ambiguity*, edited by J. Epstein and K. Straub, 280–304. New York: Routledge. The quotes in the following analysis are from the reprint in Stryker and Whittle 2006, 221–35. The text can be downloaded from www.actlab.utexas.edu/~sandy/empire-strikes-back (accessed 2 September 2012).

REFERENCES

Alarcón, Norma. 1991. "The Theoretical Subject(s) of *This Bridge Called My Back* and Anglo-American Feminism." In *Criticism in the Borderlands: Studies in Chicana Literature, Culture and Ideology*, edited by Héctor Calderon and Jose David Saldivar, 28–43. Durham: Duke University Press.

Bryld, Mette and Nina Lykke. 2000. *Cosmodolphins: Feminist Cultural Studies of Technology, Animals and the Sacred*. London: Zed.

Butler, Judith. 1990. *Gender Trouble: Feminism and the Subversion of Identity*. London: Routledge.

Butler, Judith. 1993. *Bodies That Matter: On the Discursive Limits of "Sex"*. London: Routledge.

Crenshaw, Kimberlé. 1991. "Mapping the Margins: Intersectionality, Identity Politics, and Violence against Women of Color." *Stanford Law Review* 43 (6): 1241–99.

Dean, Jonathan. 2008. " 'The Lady Doth Protest Too Much': Theorising Disidentification in Contemporary Gender Politics." *Working Paper in Ideology in Discourse Analysis* 24. London: Gender Institute, London School of Economics.

Duggan, Lisa and Nan D. Hunter. 2006. *Sex Wars: Sexual Dissent and Political Culture*. New York: Routledge.

Fuss, Diana. 1995. *Identification Papers*. New York: Routledge.

Haraway, Donna. 1991. "Situated Knowledges: The Science Question in Feminism and the Privilege of Partial Perspective." In *Simians, Cyborgs and Women: The Reinvention of Nature*, 183–201. London: Free Association Books.

Henry, Astrid. 2004. *Not My Mother's Sister: Generational Conflict and Third-Wave Feminism*. Bloomington: Indiana University Press.

Hoyer, Niels. 1931. *Fra mand til kvinde: Lili Elbes bekendelser*. København: Hage & Clausen. English translation by James Stenning, *Man into Woman: The First Sex Change* (Blue Boat Books, 2004).

Lykke, Nina. 1993. *Rotkäppchen und Oedipus. Zu einer feministischen Psychoanalyse*. Vienna: Passagen Verlag.

Lykke, Nina. 1994. "Between the Scylla of the Early Mother and the Charybdis of the Fatherlaw." *Psychoanalysis and Contemporary Thought* 17 (2): 287–325.

Lykke, Nina. 2010. *Feminist Studies: A Guide to Intersectional Theory, Methodology and Writing*. New York: Routledge.

Mohanty, Chandra T. 1988. "Under Western Eyes: Feminist Scholarship and Colonial Discourses." *Feminist Review* 30: 49–74.

Moraga, Cherríe and Gloria Anzaldúa, eds. 1981. *This Bridge Called My Back: Writings by Radical Women of Color*. New York: Kitchen Table: Women of Color Press.

Muñoz, José Esteban. 1999. *Disidentifications: Queers of Color and the Performance of Politics*. Minneapolis: University of Minnesota Press.

Pêcheux, Michel. 1982. *Language, Semantics and Ideology*. Translated by Harbans Nagpal. London: Macmillan.

Plumwood, Val. 1993. *Feminism and the Mastery of Nature*. London: Routledge.

Raymond, Janice. 1979. *The Transsexual Empire: The Making of the She-Male*. New York: Teachers College Press.

Rich, Adrienne. 1986. "Notes toward a Politics of Location." In *Blood, Bread and Poetry: Selected Prose 1979–1985*, 201–31. London and New York: Norton.

Sandoval, Chela. 2000. *The Methodology of the Oppressed*. Minneapolis: University of Minnesota Press.

Stone, Sandy. 2006. "The 'Empire' Strikes Back: A Posttranssexual Manifesto." In *The Transgender Studies Reader*, edited by Susan Stryker and Stephen Whittle, 221–35. New York: Routledge.

Stryker, Susan and Stephen Whittle, eds. 2006. *The Transgender Studies Reader*. New York: Routledge.

Tuin, Iris van der. 2011. "Gender Research with 'Waves': On Repositioning a Neo-disciplinary Apparatus." In *Theories and Methodologies in Postgraduate Feminist Research: Researching Differently*, edited by Rosemarie Buikema, Gabriele Griffin and Nina Lykke, 15–29. New York: Routledge.

Zizek, Slavoj. 1989. *The Sublime Object of Ideology*. London: Verso.

3 Writing the Place from Which One Speaks

Redi Koobak and
Suruchi Thapar-Björkert

> I have been working to change the way I speak and write, to incorpo-
> rate in the manner of telling a sense of place, of not just who I am in
> the present but where I am coming from, the multiple voices within
> me . . . I refer to that personal struggle to name that location from
> which I come to voice—that space of theorising.
>
> —bell hooks (hooks 1990, 146)

We first started thinking together about our location, the literal and metaphorical places from which we speak and write, when we became inspired
to write a paper (Koobak and Thapar-Björkert 2012) as a result of our
extended discussions on visibilities and invisibilities in our experiences as
migrant women—Suruchi comes from India and Redi from Estonia—living
and working in Sweden. This further led to reflections on the politics of
location and the ways our geopolitical location informs how we position
ourselves in our research and writing. Arguably, not only did our postcolonial and postsocialist positioning give us an analytical tool to resist hegemonic practices in largely white Western academia and everyday life, but it
also foregrounded the importance of intersectionality in the way we write.
Our shared perception of being both "similar" and "different" in our positioning vis-à-vis the Swedish context enabled us to bring the commonalities
between us into sharper focus and brought us together to reflect on the
ever-shifting sense of identity and place. Like bell hooks in the quotation
above, we found that our outsider/insider location was a "space of theorising" and for articulating multilayered subject positions. It was not just "the
present" but where we were "coming from" and the constant shaping of
one through the other that was important to us.

In this chapter, we aim to locate feminist debates on the politics of
location in relation to writing and provide examples from our own research,
along with some writing prompts to suggest ways in which to position yourself in your collective and individual writing projects. We reflect on the dialogue between us that generated a new consciousness of the significance of
context and the ways in which the dynamics of where we are and how we are
positioned affects our viewpoint and production of knowledge. Although

there is no dearth of literature on the importance of location and situating yourself within your research within Feminist Studies, there is still a lack of understanding of how to translate this theoretical knowledge into practice among students and more experienced scholars alike who struggle with this question. While we cannot offer any universal blueprint here since every project is embedded in its own context, we suggest some starting points and questions to consider when writing the place from which one speaks.

"WHERE ARE YOU FROM?"

In sharing and writing about our similar yet very different experiential accounts and affiliations with "difference" and "otherness" in everyday life, we created a collective voice, a sense of agency for ourselves, and made space to loosen some of the rigidity that is often attributed to identity categories (Koobak and Thapar-Björkert 2012). Like Chandra Mohanty's invocation of location, ours is also "symptomatic of large numbers of migrants, nomads, immigrants, workers across the globe for whom notions of home, identity, geography and history are infinitely complicated" (Mohanty 2003, 125). While the markers of a "different" ethnicity are more clearly apparent for Suruchi than for Redi, it was our shared experience of exclusion that nurtured a sense of community where none was easily found in the context within which we live (Mohanty 2003, 128; see also Pratt 1984). Sometimes, we feel that we straddle two cultures. At other times, we fall between the two (see also Rushdie 1991).

What came to frame our discussions of location was the recurring question "Where are you from?" which was almost always posed to Suruchi because of her visible difference but rarely to Redi in the same way. This question brings up the notion of home, which for both of us is "a shifting construction, contingent upon temporal, spatial and affective investments in place and relations" (Rowe 2005, 40). For Suruchi, home is also a complex and politicized issue. In India, home meant her parents' home, but in Sweden, normative notions of home are dislocated as she lives and works in a different city from her children and partner of Swedish ethnicity. Although Redi is privileged through her whiteness and the fact that she passes as a Swede, she does not identify with Swedishness. Rather, she identifies with the experience of her partner and friends who look visibly different from the implicit unmarked white Swedish norm. As a result, she often tends to make her foreignness clear from the outset by stating that she is not Swedish.

Reflecting on these personal experiences together evoked new questions about the self and the subject as well as the subject's location. Not only are our narratives contextual, but they also enable us to understand the changing nature of identity, often shaped through social interactions. One of the pitfalls of voicing these shifts in identity construction, however, is that talking about issues of being "othered" reaffirms one's marginal position, whereas some people may not be so willing to accept that position. They prefer to "fit in" rather than claim a voice from a position of marginality. For example, when living in the UK, Suruchi knew many native Indians who preferred to have only British friends, always responded in English when spoken to in Hindi and culturally did everything that the British do. Similarly, Redi met a person from Estonia living in Sweden who has gone to great lengths to "pass" as a Swede, from meticulously perfecting his accent in Swedish to changing his last name to a Swedish one, thus making a conscious effort to conceal where he is from. For us, none of these strategies were acceptable because they do not leave space for questioning why "fitting in" by denying one's cultural roots becomes so important. Outsiderness will always be a limitation, for instance, when it comes to the expectation that one will fit in. These limitations should not necessarily be seen as negative as they create openings for new meanings to emerge, although not everyone finds it easy to occupy a position on the margin. Arguably, then, our writing process is inextricably intertwined with who we are both in the present and in the past, as denying one would be denying the other.

EXERCISE 3: GEOPOLITICAL LOCATION AND IDENTITY

How has your geopolitical location shaped your identity? Consider the intersecting dimensions of gender, sexuality, race, ethnicity and class. How does your identity shift when you cross national and geographical boundaries?

WRITING THE POLITICS OF LOCATION

The issue of locatedness, of naming the place from which one speaks, has become one of the epistemological foundations of feminist theory and gender knowledge during the past few decades. Since its inception, the concept of a "politics of location" (Rich 1984/1986) has been aimed at fostering reflection on and responsibility for how feminists know and act within the locations they inhabit, reproduce and transform. Focusing on the politics of location has emerged as a strategy to think beyond constructing simplistic essentialist positions, for both individuals and collective feminist subjects. As Mary Eagleton states,

> There is a move from the encouragement to claim an "I", a subjecthood, certain rights; to an awareness of difference, how one person's rights might be the next person's further exploitation; to a position where any collective identity as "women" is radically questioned.
>
> —(2000, 301)

This has a bearing on how we write and produce knowledge as feminists.

Since Simone de Beauvoir (2010), who laid out the theoretical premise for "political sisterhood" and provided a critique of bourgeois-patriarchal ideology, the politics of location and experience with a privileged focus on the embodied self has served as the anchoring point and ground of validation for feminist theory. In her often-cited piece "Notes toward a Politics of Location" (1984/1986), Adrienne Rich takes this idea further by considering the experiences of women of colour and lesbians within feminism. She argues for the importance of "[r]ecognizing our location, having to name the ground we're coming from, the conditions we have taken for granted", in particular taking her own "whiteness as a point of location" for which she "needed to take responsibility" (219). By deconstructing the hegemonic use of the word "woman", Rich simultaneously questions the effects of racism and homophobia inherent within the women's movement in the US. In doing so, she highlights that although white women can be marginalized as women, they also marginalize others. For Rich, "a struggle to keep moving, a struggle for accountability" (211) is embodied and material and thus has to begin with the body—the body which has "more than one identity" (215), that takes us away from "lofty and privileged abstraction" (213), back to specificity, "to reconnect our thinking and speaking with the body of this particular living human individual—a woman" (214). Rich's framework of analysis extends the foundational category of "experience" by emphasizing diversity and multiple power locations. Importantly, attention to the politics of location then brings into focus differences between women despite sharing common situations and experiences and cautions feminists against the perils of speaking "for" other women from any universalist "we" perspective. However, on a more critical note, Caren Kaplan points out that "[a] politics of location is not useful when it is construed to be the reflection of authentic, primordial identities that are to be reestablished and reaffirmed" (1994, 139). Thus, she questions conventional oppositions between global and local, Western and non-Western, that Rich's formulations uphold and argues that Rich conflates Western and white, reinscribing the centrality of white women's position within Western feminism.

These discussions on the politics of location are paralleled by the writings of Donna Haraway (1988, 1991), who argues that scientific and scholarly knowledge is not value-neutral and disinterested but needs to be understood as embedded in its contexts of production, which include the researcher subject's location in time, space, body and historical and societal power relations as well as the research technologies as part of the research process. In short, "[f]eminist objectivity is about limited location and situated knowledge" (Haraway 1991, 188), which allows for a multiplicity of viewpoints. "Situated knowledges" are marked knowledges that produce "maps of consciousness" reflecting the various categories of gender, class, race and nationality of the researcher (111). This perspective not only enables and encourages feminist researchers to bring their own particular location

nd position into the research but demands that they do so before any dis-
ussion of another's reality can be brought in.

Understanding repression and resistance as dialectical, bell hooks empha-
izes the necessity of material displacement for rethinking one's location in
hifting power relations, albeit from the point of view of marginality rather
han centrality. She highlights the political and productive potential of mar-
ins, which she refers to as "this space of radical openness", "a profound
dge", a site of political resistance to hegemony (hooks 1990, 149). As she
uggests, there are no fixed meanings attached to specific locations; nothing
s intrinsically positive or negative, inside or outside, because centres and
nargins have been historically produced. Like hooks, Mohanty speaks from
marginalized position which for her "forces and enables specific modes of
eading and knowing the dominant" (1995, 82). She uses the term "politics
f location" to refer "to the historical, geographical, cultural, psychic and
maginative boundaries which provide the ground for political definition
nd self-definition for contemporary US feminists" (68). She articulates the
mportance of recognizing the multiplicity of locations and modes of know-
ng and knowledges that arise from them.

While the notion of the politics of location has undergone a series of trans-
ormations, it has become so commonplace that it is seen as a self-evident
s well as self-explanatory part of doing feminist research. This has some-
imes led to programmatic and abstract formulations that simply state
;eneric identity categories without taking into account the fact that one can
peak of one's location only through mutually constitutive intersectional
ocial relations. For example, writing "as a [name the category]" locks the
esearcher into an a priori position that can override the changes and chal-
enges that the research process brings. Distinctions such as family history,
thnicity, geopolitical positioning, sexuality, dis/ability, religion and oth-
rs are important but should not be considered obvious or as fixed points.
Rather, they should be understood as multiple, fluid and contingent on temporal and historical shifts that emerge in the contiguous processes of doing
and writing research.

In trying to relate these feminist conversations on the importance of the
politics of location to processes of writing, we are faced with the imperative of "transparent reflexivity" in search of positionality (Rose 1997).
As Gillian Rose claims, transparent reflexivity is bound to fail because "it
depends on certain notions of agency (as conscious) and power (as context),
and assumes that both are knowable" (1997, 311). In other words, it relies
on the notion of a visible and knowable landscape of power in which the
researcher has an obligation to make herself accountable. In their research
on non-Western contexts, Richa Nagar and Susan Geiger frame the discussion around two questions which complement their understanding of
reflexivity. First, they pose the question: How can feminists use fieldwork
to produce knowledge across multiple divides (of power and geopolitical
and institutional locations) in ways that do not reinscribe the interests of

the privileged? Second, they ask: How can the production of knowledge be tied explicitly to a material politics of social change favouring less privileged communities and places? Nagar and Geiger argue that there is "little discussion of how to operationalize a 'speaking with' approach to research that might help us work through negotiated and partial meanings in our intellectual/political productions" (2007, 271).

Furthermore, feminist and postcolonial scholars have tried to bypass the problem of representation in writing and research through turning to self-representation as a more ethical alternative. The logic of this alternative is rather simple: when one cannot represent others without always being suspected of a lack of valid representational delegation and therefore of sexual, racial or class discrimination, should one only represent oneself? On a more critical note, however, Rey Chow (2001) points out that while one can find many possibilities in self-representation, there are also several limits to self-referentiality. The assumption that the act of referring to oneself is direct and unmediated means that self-representation is paradoxically thought to be non-representational and becomes equated with the expression of truth and transparency, or what Foucault describes as confession, "the infinite task of extracting from the depths of oneself, in between the words, a truth which the very form of the confession holds out like a shimmering mirage" (1980, 59–60). Self-referential speaking is in fact a symptom of a collective subjection, "to represent, to examine, to confess about oneself are compulsive acts that imagine the self as a refuge outside power—an alibi from representation, so to speak—when the self is merely a rational systematization and a relay of institutional forces at the individual level" (Chow 2001, 46). While an insistence on the marginal, the local, the personal and the autobiographical—on the supposed liberation of ourselves from subordinating powers through representing ourselves—may seem radical and empowering, all this may in fact allow such powers to work even more effectively.

EXERCISE 4: YOUR MOTIVATIONS AND PERSPECTIVES

How does your gender, sexuality, race/ethnicity, class or nationality (or any other important identity category) affect your motivation for and/or perspective towards your project?

REDI'S STORY

Parallel to the discussions above, there has been a long-standing concern in feminism about "knowing" and "doing" research. The process of doing research could bring up its own sets of issues in relation to contextuality. Inevitably, the Western academy equips us with methodological tools that are often not entirely applicable to specific historical contexts. It is some of these challenges that I explore in my research story below, paying particular attention to the process of how I came to my project and how it kept shifting. Making the process part of the end product, showing the messy side of the journey, is a way to locate and situate your shifting subjectivity and anchor your knowledge claims.

One of the most surprising twists that my project took towards the middle phase of my PhD studies was that I realized that I was in fact deeply drawn to working with the Estonian context. It seems that initially I did everything possible to avoid having to engage with feminism in the Estonian context—or with the supposed lack thereof. It did not seem to fit with my theoretical aspirations, as I felt there was not much going on in Estonia. Throughout the years since I first became interested in feminism I kept hearing, time and again: There is no real feminism in Estonia. There are feminists, sure, but many of them feel that the frameworks "we" have learned through theories from the West do not always seem to match the local specificities, and thus feminism in this context feels fraught with tension and ambivalence. "We" are "lagging behind". There is a particular imaginary, a particular understanding that has been formed around what feminism is and should be, an image that has stuck, an image of feminism with a Western, Anglo-American face, an image that "we" in Estonia always seem to fail to live up to. Thus it felt that the only way to avoid being subsumed under only one category, my nationality, and the "failure" or "lag" it brought with it, was to focus on theory in all its abstractions and universalisms. I wanted to be one of the theorists, not just standing in for my particular context, just another case study. I wanted to be a producer of knowledge and not just a transmitter of knowledge produced by those at the centre.

I started off my PhD project with an interest in self-portrait photography and the notion that being in charge of one's own image yields agency and thus serves as a form of women's empowerment and provides a space for evoking social change. This idea seemed provocative, both simple and complex at the same time. The use of self-portraiture by feminist artists to challenge and pose questions about women's identity and subjectivity and their role in society has been well documented in the West, and it seemed that to some extent women's issues and self-portraiture were almost inextricably linked and that this link had been almost naturalized. But, as I felt from early on, this work has often relied on simplistic notions of what representation and photography are and what they do, and what identity or subject-based politics is and does.

In July 2009, I participated in a summer workshop, [PROLOGUE] EST, on the north coast of Estonia, which became a turning point for my thesis. This workshop brought together feminist artists, curators and art critics but also Gender Studies scholars and government officials, who were all invited there to talk about gender, art, society and politics, articulating and exploring feminist ideas about gender from Eastern and Western European perspectives. My role at this workshop, the reason I was invited there, was to represent the academic and theoretical side of feminism, a role I was used to playing mostly in academic contexts with their own rules, discourses and boundaries. But I also had my own agenda: to do fieldwork for my thesis and interview Mare Tralla, who is often credited as the first Estonian feminist artist, about her self-portraits.

Already on the bus on the way to the location of the workshop, I felt strongly that the art world seemed like something else altogether, at least in this embodied, material, moving space that was taking us across bumpy country roads closer to several days of discussing feminist art and politics, sharing a space for talking, sleeping, eating. I felt strangely alienated, although this bus-full of women and I had a number of concerns in common: we were interested in the position and viability of feminism and feminist art in post-Soviet Estonian culture, still perceived as "lagging behind" feminist discourses in the West—and we were also there to discuss the position of feminism in Europe and the world more widely. The latter, curiously, was largely thanks to the presence of some international artists and curators, who kept reminding us to look at the bigger picture when the discussion shifted to concerns about how little was happening in feminism in Estonia. Was my feeling of alienation a result of the sense of betrayal I always felt when asked how my PhD studies in Sweden were coming along? Was it the burden of expectation when questioned about whether I was planning to return to Estonia? *Estonia needs you! We have a shortage of people in this field. You have to come back!* I was certainly confused in terms of coming "home" to do my fieldwork, juggling a sense of belonging and unbelonging at the same time.

As I quickly resorted to taking notes to maintain a sense of my academic self, I was trying to jot down the feeling of the eerie, in-between state of being simultaneously awake and asleep in which I found myself, drifting without any concrete constants to hold on to. Against the background of the jittery chit-chat of the women from the local arts scene, some of whom I only knew by name, or not always even that, I gradually felt I was turning into Theory, the one that is often directly opposed to Practice, the one that belongs to the realm of Academia where arguably feminism slouches without sharp teeth to bite back. I was an outsider here and did not really fit in comfortably. They all seemed to project a sharp division between feminism in art and feminism in academia. Where theory is powerless in its abstractions and trapped in institutionalized structures, art potentially emerges as fire that stings, as a wake-up call that initiates *real* change. Or so it seemed right then and there. The Estonian feminist art world did not *really* exist for me until this very moment when it suddenly materialized in the form of a lively, noisy, critical, chaotic and closely interconnected crowd. Yet when I overheard women discussing Estonian art as provincial, feminism as a Western import, the local context as entirely different from a wider European context, something struck a chord. Feelings of provincialism and certain incompatibilities between feminist theories that I had become well versed and the local context of "back home" were not entirely absent from my usual academic experience in various Western contexts.

It was during the round of presentations at the introductory seminar that I first met Anna-Stina Treumund. She presented herself as a lesbian/feminist-identified artist and photographer who is interested in exploring the question of why there are no openly lesbian artists in Estonia. Although she appeared frail and somewhat uncertain in her body posture and gestures, I sensed passion and determination in how she expressed what she wanted to do. There was one important point that triggered my initial interest in her project: the question of visibility and representation in relation to identity. Familiar from countless discussions in Gender Studies classrooms and feminist books, conferences and workshops, I was still struck by how much the issue of visibility seemed to matter to her. What is this need for visibility she is talking about? Why is it important? What are the underlying assumptions of visibility? Does making someone, e.g. the lesbian community, visible automatically make them recognizable and therefore acceptable? Does making oneself visible equate to becoming acceptable? Why does she voluntarily want to bring down on herself that storm of nasty homophobic comments that will surely follow? Can a photography exhibition change minds and attitudes? Can art make a difference? *There has been no such exhibition in Estonia before, and I just have to do it*, she said, convinced and convincingly. This was before I knew she was working with self-portrait photography, the medium I had chosen as my site of research to explore questions of identity, representation and feminist politics.

Over the course of the next few days, I became interested in Anna-Stina's passion for her project, which seemed to deploy and contest various conceptions of the self/subject and its representation in relation to notions of gender and sexuality in her queer political photographic artwork. I became especially intrigued by the way in which the discussions she is picking up in her work relate to discussions of Eastern European feminism and queer politics, as well as questions of the politics of visibility. My encounter with Anna-Stina in the midst of my theoretical ambivalences and queries eventually brought up the possible connection between the artist's feelings of alienation as a lesbian woman in Estonia and my own unreflected feelings of alienation within Feminist Studies in a Western context as a woman from postsocialist Eastern Europe. I was completely struck by these connections, and I ended up abandoning all my previously chosen case studies.

The affinity between the experiences of the artist and myself inspired me to try and focus productively on various aspects of this sense of being an outsider within and to consider the ways in which visual arts—engaging with visual images situated in a specific geographical and temporal context—could reconfigure feminist imaginaries and push feminist theory in particular to be more mindful of and accountable to geopolitical difference. I became interested in how and to what extent the desire for transformation through representation materializes in and through the work of an artist who is located in postsocialist Estonia. What does it mean to be a feminist, a queer subject in the fluid yet sometimes dangerously fixating formations of postsocialist space? Can artistic practices help us to grasp the experience of the self in these changing times? How much of the artist's location and situatedness in postsocialist space seeps into her work, and into our inter-pretations of her work?

Anna-Stina's work challenged me to contest the general assumption that Eastern European feminist discourse is merely derivative of that in the West and is all about "catching up", getting rid of the "lag", and I was thus able to address far more localized and contextual questions that were important for me than my initial theoretical interest in concepts would have allowed.

EXERCISE 5: WHAT BROUGHT YOU TO YOUR PROJECT?

What brought you to your project? Can you trace when you first became interested in this subject/your research question? Why is this project important to you? Go deep.

SURUCHI'S STORY

Writing about the concepts of location and position through our mutual conversations, thinking one through the other, led me to draw on perspec-tives that are embedded in specific Western and non-Western contexts, and while my story appears to be different from Redi's, the analytical tools that we share arise from our mutual conversations. How the same analytical tools can generate such different stories in itself reflects the fluidity of our location and position.

Receiving a prestigious PhD grant always brings with it its own pres-sures, especially the pressure to demonstrate your ability to the rest of the academic world and show that you are somehow "clever" and competent and thus worthy of the grant. Typically, your worthiness is tested every step of the way. When I came to the Faculty of Oriental Studies (!) at Cambridge University in September 1990 as a Nehru Centenary Fellow, my competence was subject to an unfamiliar scrutiny. During the first academic introduc-tion in the manicured gardens of Clare College, complete with strawberry canapés and champagne cocktails, I was asked a question by a white male British historian and member of the Senior Common Room: "So what is your methodological approach?" If asked the same question now, I would take a sip of my cocktail, look into the eyes of the bearer of the question and give an articulate, nuanced answer. But at that point I was not able to articulate anything impressive and instead said, "I have not thought that through yet!" Before I got a chance to explain further, the next question came hurtling along: "Will you be doing archival research?" When I replied that documenting women's oral histories was important, he looked perplexed. Maybe he thought that I was not a true historian or that it was not important to document women's lives or that collecting oral histories was methodologically flawed? This interrogation on the soundness of my methodologies triggered another concern: How was I to position myself in the Western academy as a non-Western researcher who was about to embark on a project about understanding women's historical narratives in India? Was I nervous because I was the only non-Western researcher in an overwhelmingly white college or because I was located in a traditional history department where it was difficult to find anyone interested in Gender or Women's Studies during the early 1990s? My initial nervousness was further accentuated when I also had no choice but to work with the only lecturer who was interested in questions of gender. This lack of choice of supervisors opened up new dimensions of power since she was able to shape what I wrote, how I wrote and thus how I thought about my PhD. What I learned from this experience was that I always speak from my position, my context and my place irrespective of its categorization as a centre or a margin within my discipline. I say this because it was often implied that my topic, the nationalist movement in India, was already "over-researched" and not "sexy" enough.

After receiving my MPhil from Cambridge University, I completed the next three years at the Centre for the Study of Women and Gender at the University of Warwick. The next challenging moment came when I was about to embark on my field trip and decided that it would be for a period of nine months. "Why should it take you so long?" many of my colleagues asked as they tried to make sense of the length of research time I had calculated for myself. The Women's Studies department was an interdisciplinary centre but everybody retained their academic ties with their own departments. Perhaps it was because I was seen as a historian and such a query would not be raised for an anthropologist? Or because I was an Indian who was going to research "my" own context, which would not require so much time? Although it is important to be self-reflexive about how we locate ourselves as "researchers" in relation to research projects at "home", this self-reflexivity should not discourage us from researching specific contexts in relation to our location. There is still an uneasy tension between one's location and the context one is researching. This leads us, among other things, to familiar refrains that Western researchers cannot research non-Western contexts or that non-Western researchers can conduct research most effectively in their own countries.

My colleagues' inquiry into the length of my research period was immediately followed by the question: "Have you combined a holiday period with it as well?" and "Wouldn't it be *so* nice to be back home?" There are inherent assumptions embedded within these questions that link back to the debates on the production of feminist knowledge and feminist methodologies on the location and position of the researcher and the ways these facilitate data collection. It was assumed that since I was of Indian origin it would be fairly "easy" for me to interview women of the same origin. What is still taken for granted is that interpersonal conversation patterns between women, particularly of similar background, are unproblematic. Thus, the question "Why so long?" was in many ways justifiable.

Familiarity with one's context can be exploited at specific moments in different locations. For example, the expectation of familiarity can obliterate the dilemmas, anxieties and contradictions one may feel, even in known contexts. During my tenure at Bristol University in the UK, I was often called on by the Violence against Women Research Group to "mingle" with invited academics from India. At first, I thought that it was like any other ordinary invitation, but in fact it was laden with assumptions. Here the unifying signifier "Indian woman" subsumed multiple subjectivities and internal differences between Indians, in this case academics from India (see, for example, Lykke, Chapter 2, this volume). Furthermore, while I felt like an Indian ambassador on these occasions, expected to share my cultural capital, the scientific merits that one gains from international collaborations were retained by my white female colleagues from the research group. Often white Western academia has the privilege of setting patterns of inclusion and exclusion: inclusion when convenient, exclusion when not.

My PhD research investigated how the nationalist movement shaped the lives of ordinary middle-class women in India from 1930 to 1942. My main objective was to challenge the dominant historical narratives of both Indian and Western scholars, who have inevitably focused on elite Indian women as central actors in the nationalist project. Having grown up in a family with its own nationalist genealogies, I was convinced that this was not a complete portrayal of women's participation in the movement. Moreover, I wanted to disrupt the class hierarchy in the dominant narratives by focusing on "ordinary" middle-class women. I wanted to present these women as "subject(s) with . . . (their) own location . . . (their) own stories to tell" (Borsa 1990, 37). I wanted to use fieldwork to produce knowledges that do not reinscribe the interests of the privileged.

It became apparent to me that there were bound to be limitations in writing about "Third World women" from a location in a Western country. There were times when I was faced with the problem of being positioned as "other" by my respondents because I was a researcher based in the UK and had what was perceived as the advantage of being able to return (to the UK) to write about my investigations. My nationality was subordinate to my social position (Thapar-Björkert 1999). Furthermore, there were continuous shifts in the ways in which I was positioned by the respondents. Some respondents were surprised that an Indian woman working in a foreign country was still interested in Indian women. These women wanted to relate to me as an Indian first and as a scholar from the West later. They would say, "Tum bahut mahan kam kar raye ho," which means "You are doing work for a great cause". Other respondents were impressed when they realized that I was doing my research degree in the UK. This might have worked to my disadvantage had the respondents tried to project a "glamorous" picture of their participation and not mentioned their "real" experiences as nationalist activists. I had to make a concerted effort to convince them that, instead, I wanted to produce an account of their anxieties, their problems in their family lives and, more important, their distinct experiences as women in the nationalist movement. I had a torn consciousness of being both the "other" (as a researcher from Britain), and one of those "others" whose history has often been misrepresented by dominant cultures, in this case Britain. To a certain extent, I was in an advantageous position because I could draw on both these perspectives.

Thus, as Geiger argues, positionality is not fixed but relational, a "constantly moving context that constitutes our reality and the place from which values are interpreted and constructed" (1990, 171). How one is positioned may influence aspects of the study, such as the types of information collected or the way in which it is interpreted post-fieldwork. Although issues of gender, religion, class or race have been viewed as characteristics or as "ready-to-wear" products of identity politics, they can be incorporated in the research narrative "only if they are not left self-evident as essentialized qualities that are magically synonymous with self-consciousness, or, for that matter, with intellectual engagement and theoretical rigor" (Robertson 2002, 790). The dynamism of positionalities in time and through space renders the insider/outsider boundary highly unstable. The insider/outsider distinction is more difficult to sustain if one recognizes that the researcher is continuously and simultaneously an observer and a subject in the research process (Soobrayan 2003). Knowledge is thus co-created and not unidirectional.

For whom one is writing, and from which context, shapes the writing process and the written product. For example, the categories of analysis used in feminist research were under constant negotiation in my project. Most of the "ordinary" middle-class women I interviewed could not relate to the notion of class consciousness or gender inequality. There will also always be a gap in my perception of the respondents' experiences as there is a possibility that I could have failed to fully perceive the complexities of these women's lives. At the same time, they could not perceive the complexities of my own life.

EXERCISE 6: POWER AND PRIVILEGE IN RESEARCH

When thinking about your project, consider carefully your role as the researcher. What power and privileges do you bring to your research project? What might you be taking for granted in terms of access to information, certain research methodologies or insider/outsider status?

CONCLUSION

Our conversations arose from our friendship and shared experiences of living in Sweden as "non-Swedes", disidentifying with Western feminist academia (cf. Nina Lykke, Chapter 2) through our specific postcolonial and postsocialist positions. These discussions generated a productive dialogue on the methodological and epistemological dilemmas that are endemic to research work. Our particular geopolitical positionings raised the question not only of how our location positions us but also of how we position our "objects" of study.

The individual narratives that we have explored in this chapter converge because we disidentify with the existing Western feminist academic paradigms from the perspective of our specific geopolitical positionings. Our narratives reveal the productive potential of challenging hegemonic transnational feminist discourses from the margins. What was important in our conversation was that often the dialogue between the First and the Third World is foregrounded at the cost of excluding perspectives from the former Second World, the postsocialist countries of former Eastern Europe. Juxtaposing our individual stories allows us to highlight our critical stance on the "lagging-behind" discourse that is attributed to the Second World in much the same way as to the Third World, which problematically cements the binary between the Global North and the Global South. In writing our stories, we were able not only to reflect on the problematic categories of East/West and North/South but also to stress the importance of the local in relation to global hierarchies.

Our personal stories brought about the complex intersections of national identities and geopolitical locations and the role they play in the choice of research topics, project designs and definition of research problems. We want to underline three themes in particular. First, our institutional contexts are intertwined with the national and geopolitical positionalities that inform our everyday lives as well as the way we do our research. Second, our stories highlight that it is important to articulate the multilayered nature of the positions from which we write in order to make ourselves accountable for the situatedness of our knowledge production. Third, it is of utmost ethical and political importance to reconfigure the geopolitics of locatedness as an axis of difference that matters for contemporary feminist theorizing. To conclude, we want to emphasize that the politics of location is important not only for minoritized subjects—such as ourselves—who challenge hegemonic paradigms from the margins but also for those who occupy sites of privilege.

REFERENCES

Beauvoir, Simone de. 2010. *The Second Sex*. London: Vintage Books.
Borsa, Joan. 1990. "Towards a Politics of Location: Rethinking Marginality." *Canadian Women's Studies* 11 (1): 36–39.

how, Rey. 2001. "Gender and Representation." In *Feminist Consequences: Theory for the New Century*, edited by Elisabeth Bronfen and Misha Kavka, 38–57. New York: Columbia University Press.

agleton, Mary. 2000. "Adrienne Rich, Location, and the Body." *Journal of Gender Studies* 9 (3): 299–312.

oucault, Michel. 1980. *The History of Sexuality, Vol. 1: An Introduction.* New York: Vintage Books.

eiger, Susan. 1990. "What's So Feminist about Women's Oral History?" *Journal of Women's History* 2(1): 169–182.

Iaraway, Donna. 1988. "Situated Knowledge: The Science Question in Feminism and the Privilege of Partial Perspective." *Feminist Studies* 14 (3): 575–99.

Iaraway, Donna. 1991. *Simians, Cyborgs, and Women: The Reinvention of Nature.* London: Free Association Books.

ooks, bell. 1990. *Yearning: Race, Gender and Cultural Politics.* Boston, MA: South End Press.

aplan, Caren. 1994. "The Politics of Location as Transnational Feminist Critical Practice." In *Scattered Hegemonies: Postmodernity and Transnational Feminist Practices*, edited by Inderpal Grewal and Caren Kaplan, 137–51. Minneapolis: University of Minnesota Press.

oobak, Redi and Suruchi Thapar-Björkert. 2012. "Becoming Non-Swedish: Locating the Paradoxes of In/visible Identities." *Feminist Review* 102: 125–34.

Aohanty, Chandra. 1995. "Feminist Encounters: Locating the Politics of Experience." In *Social Postmodernism: Beyond Identity Politics*, edited by Linda Nicholson and Steven Seidman, 68–86. Cambridge: Cambridge University Press.

Aohanty, Chandra T. 2003. *Feminism without Borders: Decolonizing Theory, Practicing Solidarity.* Durham: Duke University Press.

Jagar, Richa and Susan Geiger. 2007. "Reflexivity and Positionality in Feminist Fieldwork Revisited." In *Politics and Practice in Economic Geography*, edited by Adam Tickell, Eric Sheppard, Jamie Peck and Trevor Barnes, 267–78. London: Sage.

ratt, Minnie Bruce. 1984. "Identity: Skin, Blood, Heart." In *Yours in Struggle: Three Feminist Perspectives on Anti-Semitism and Racism*, edited by Elly Bulkin, Minnie Bruce Pratt and Barbara Smith, 11–63. New York: Long Haul Press.

Rich, Adrienne. 1986. "Notes toward a Politics of Location." In *Blood, Bread and Poetry: Selected Prose 1979–1985*, 201–31. London and New York: Norton.

Robertson, Jennifer. 2002. "Reflexivity Redux: A Pithy Polemic on 'Positionality'." *Anthropological Quarterly* 75 (4): 785–92.

Rose, Gillian. 1997. "Situating Knowledges: Positionality, Reflexivities and Other Tactics." *Progress in Human Geography* 21 (3): 305–20.

Rowe, Aimee Carrillo. 2005. "Be Longing: Toward a Feminist Politics of Relation." *NWSA Journal* 17 (2): 15–46.

Rushdie, Salman. 1991. *Imaginary Homelands: Essays and Criticism, 1981–1991.* New York: Penguin.

oobrayan, Venitha. 2003. "Ethics, Truth and Politics in Constructivist Qualitative Research." *Westminster Studies in Education* 26 (2): 107–23.

Thapar-Björkert, Suruchi. 1999. "Negotiating Otherness: Dilemmas for a Non-Western Researcher in the Indian Sub-continent." *Journal of Gender Studies* 8 (1): 57–69.

4   Whiteness and Affect
The Embodied Ethics of Relationality

Anne Brewster

In this chapter, I want to draw attention to our intersectional, intersubjective, intercorporeal and interaffective relations to our research subjects, materials and locales, and to the ways in which they shape our research. I shall argue that a recognition of these relations may set the stage for the unfolding of an embodied ethics of relationality, and I suggest that you explore and reflect on these concerns via embodied writing. To illustrate my points, I will take my own cross-cultural research on Australian Aboriginal literature as an example and focus on the particular issues it raises for me regarding whiteness and the ways in which my research is framed by my location as a white middle-class woman. As a located and embodied writing is central to my argument I will present three writing exercises which I hope will inspire you to reflect on your relations to your research materials, subjects and locales; the first one deals with the last of these.

EXERCISE 7: WRITING ABOUT PLACE

Think about the sites at which your research materials or subjects are/ were located. This may include the places where you conduct your research. It may be a library or domestic space. It might be a school room, shop, prison, archive, sports field, courtroom, laboratory, museum or art gallery. It might be the national space mapped out by governmentalities or border crossings that transect nation spaces. It might be a televisual, cinematic, multi-media or electronic space. It might be a garden, desert or swamp land or a footpath, boat, bus, cable car or highway.

If possible and appropriate, go to this place; sit or walk for a while, and observe your bodily and affective reactions to it. Don't analyze; just allow your body to absorb the "vibrations" of the place and of the other people who have been there. The events or people you are thinking about in this space may have been there in the distant past. Allow yourself to "connect" with those events and those people, however distant temporally or spatially they may be.

Write a short paragraph in response to the following questions:

- *What kind of relationship do you have with this place?*
- *What kind of relationship does it have with you?*
- *Is it hospitable or excluding? Is it familiar or unfamiliar? What is the nature of this hospitality or exclusion, this familiarity or unfamiliarity? To whom is it hospitable/excluding or familiar/ unfamiliar?*
- *What events have taken place here?*
- *Are there any significant objects here (or no longer here)?*
- *What other people have lived in, passed through, avoided or been denied access to this place?*
- *How does their relationship with this place differ from yours?*
- *What kinds of feelings and sensations are you experiencing?*
- *Are you waiting for or unconsciously anticipating something? What?*
- *What would you like to see happen here?*

You can do this exercise by yourself or in a group. If you are doing the exercise in a larger group, get into small groups of three to discuss your responses to the questions. Everyone should read out their paragraphs and comment on each other's work. If you are part of a larger group, it should reconvene so that everyone can summarize the main points of discussion.

THE MEANING OF RELATIONALITY IN MY RESEARCH ON AUSTRALIAN ABORIGINAL LITERATURE

I was initially drawn to do research on Australian Aboriginal literature because, as a fifth-generation white (in my case, Angloceltic) Australian, I was conscious of my embeddedness within the colonial history of the nation. Although my family were not pastoralists who invaded large tracts of land, they did nonetheless, as urban people, occupy Aboriginal land, and continue to do so, and are thus the beneficiaries of the dispossession of Aboriginal people. Aboriginal literary subjectivities which are being produced through an emerging literature seem to me to be initiating a dialogue, inviting response and responsibility. I want to examine the ways in which this literature interpellates me as a white reader and the ways it critiques whiteness.[1] In my research I explore the ways that I am rhetorically addressed as a white person by Aboriginal literature, taking my own responses to Australian Aboriginal literature as one index of Australian whiteness. I am interested in the *bodily* aspects of reading and the various *affects* (for example, anger, grief and guilt) that inform my perceptions of and relationship with indigenous people.[2]

Affects and embodiment are constitutive not only of individuals' subjectivity but of collective identifications; they shape sociality and communities. They also impinge on and shape research. As far as my own research is concerned, I reflect on my methodology in order to take account of the affects that inform the dominant white Australian culture in which I work. I think about how I am positioned bodily and affectively within this dominant culture. I also think a lot about the ethics of my research and its bodily and affective aspects. Feminist theorists have challenged the liberal humanist notion that ethical imperatives are determined primarily by abstract reasoning, that they are divorced from the body. Gail Weiss (1999), for example, argues that ethics are corporeally enacted: it is through and in our bodies that we feel the effects of moral judgements and practices.

In this chapter, the explanation of my research on Australian Aboriginal literature and the particular issues it raises for me regarding whiteness and ethics is designed to illustrate and contextualize my argument about the importance of addressing intersubjective, interaffective and intercorporeal relations to our research subjects, materials and locales. Against this background, I shall give a snapshot of my research and analyze a poem by Aboriginal writer Lisa Bellear. Through this analysis, I shall demonstrate how Critical Whiteness Studies enable me to examine the power relations in which I and my research are embedded. I undertake a reading of this poem in order to contextualize the issue at the heart of this chapter, namely, the fact that conventional understandings of research elide the impact of researchers' bodily location and affective dispositions on their research and writing practices. For example, I have found that I have been able to analyze and understand my own implicatedness in whiteness only by recognizing the complexity of the ways in which I, as a writer, am bodily and affectively embedded in it.

The way in which I conceive of the various topics I discuss in this chapter is shaped by my own location within the dominant culture. In broad terms I would say that my research is framed by my location as a white middle-class woman. However, the moment I invoke this location, I am aware that the formulation is not straightforward or unproblematic. There are multiple further fissions within the categories "white", "middle-class" and "woman" (such as able-bodiedness, religion, sexual preference, generation and nationality). I cannot, therefore, speak for all women within the category "white middle-class woman", nor can I assume that my experience is representative of the category. What I aim to do, therefore, is to articulate my own specificity while allowing for a multiplicity of subject positions (see Riggs 2006, 2007). But I also want to suggest that sometimes we reach a point in our research where that specificity strikes us in its irreducible bodiliness. This is the experience that I want to plumb in the writing exercises which I present alongside the discussion. Through the writing exercises, I want to inspire you to pay attention to the dual orientation of the body in the process of writing, that is, the way it turns both inward (towards itself) and outward (towards the other), as well as to think about your own relationality to the subjects and materials of your research.

I draw on Critical Whiteness Studies because they seek to open up the cultural reproduction of whiteness and the white subject to scrutiny.[3] Whiteness Studies in Australia has had a strong affiliation with Aboriginal Studies and scholarship because it has been championed by Australian Aboriginal scholar Aileen Moreton-Robinson and her foundational study, *Talkin' Up to the White Woman* (2000). Whiteness Studies argues that whiteness has traditionally been resistant to questioning, occupying as it does the norm to which racialized identities are compared and found to be inferior. As the norm it has been invisible (at least to white people) and therefore had not, until the advent of Critical Whiteness Studies, been identified as a topic of analysis. In focusing on whiteness, critical whiteness theory prompts us to study the historical, cultural, discursive and institutional processes by which whiteness is produced and by which white authority and power are maintained.

CONTACT ZONES

To help you to recognize your affective connections with the people and materials of your research, here is a short exercise that will remind you of your body and the ways you inhabit it. It will reintroduce you to the inter-corporeal zone in which we encounter our others (whoever they may be). Feminist theory reminds us to situate ourselves in bodily proximity with the people and objects of our research. This exercise will take you back into this realm of intersubjectivity and intercorporeality where you may encounter not only your others but also the edges of your own bodily and psychical being. It is along these edges that we make contact with the other. This contact influences the way we understand our others but also the way in which we understand ourselves and our research.

EXERCISE 8: AT THE BORDER OF SELF AND OTHER

This exercise is best done with a stranger or else with someone you do not know very well. (It would also be interesting to do it with someone with whom you are physically intimate, for example, a family member, friend or lover, and consider how these results differ from those produced with a stranger.) You can do this exercise either with just one other person or in a group. An exemplary environment for this is the classroom because there many people may not know the person sitting next to them.

- *Turn to the person next to you. Both of you raise your arms so that your hands are at chest level. Spread your fingers and gently place your fingertips against your neighbours' fingertips. Then close your eyes. Hold this pose for 1.5 minutes. At the end of the 1.5 minutes open your eyes. Look into the eyes of your partner for a short time (about 10 seconds). (Don't do either of these actions for much longer than the time I suggest; otherwise, thoughts intrude and the bodily awareness is dispersed. Thoughts will, of course, intrude during the 1.5 minutes, but the body awareness remains fresh.)*
- *The point of this exercise is to encourage you to observe your feelings and bodily reactions. Keep your awareness on the bodily contact. Be prepared to initially feel a bit shy or embarrassed. If you are in a group some people may giggle and chat as they prepare to put their fingers together. People may move about in their seats as they find a comfortable position. Don't be disconcerted by this; it's simply a way for people to move into the exercise. Be patient for a moment or two, and the laughter and talk will subside. It is important to create an environment of mutual trust and to allow people to prepare physically and mentally to shift into a different kind of awareness.*
- *If you are leading the group in this exercise and you need to direct people, speak slowly and softly in order not to disrupt the meditative mood that they will now be in. The basic ground rule for an exercise like this is no talking, either during the exercise or afterwards while people are writing. This may distract other people in the group. If you explain this to the group they will understand the need for silence.*
- *When you stop, take 10 minutes to write down your feelings and sensations. Reflect on your bodily reactions within the "contact zone". This zone of physical touch immerses us in a range of sensations and affects. Can you feel how effervescent and volatile this zone is? It is as if your awareness of the other person and of yourself is flickering in and out, on and off. The light touch of the other person sparks moments of anticipation and feeling which have their own momentum and their own trajectories. They mingle in your mind with fragments of memory, thoughts and random associations. All these things flash in and out of your awareness. You are open, awaiting and receiving but not holding onto or directing these sensations.*
- *After writing, people can be invited to get into groups of two for 10 minutes, to read their work and discuss the ideas and feelings that have arisen. After this the larger group should reconvene,*

and people can read their responses out and talk about them with the group. This is an important part of the exercise as it is instructive for everyone to see a range of different responses to the exercise. If it is a big group there may be too many people for everyone to read their pieces, and three or four will suffice. If anyone is reluctant to share what they have written at any stage of the exercise they can "pass". That should be made clear at the outset. This will maintain an environment of trust where everyone feels comfortable and privacy is respected. You will need to allow about half to three-quarters of an hour for the whole exercise (depending on the size of the group).

draw on Julia Kristeva's evocative essay "Toccata and Fugue for the oreigner" (1991) to contextualize this exercise. It provides a theoretical amework to examine—in very general terms—embodiment and affective elations with other people. You have two options as to how you can do is. You can arrange that the group members read it before the exercise f touching fingers. Following the exercise, the writing and the discussions, ike a 10-minute break. Then return to discuss the article (allow 20 minutes r more, depending on the size of the group). Alternatively, you can read the rticle some time later and meet (perhaps the following week) to discuss it.

In the essay, Kristeva addresses the issue of how members of a dominant hite group can develop ethical relations with their "others" (for example, inority groups) without either ostracizing them or demanding their assimation through the prohibition and levelling of difference. She suggests that eveloping ethical relations is a pressing issue for contemporary nations 1 an era of political and economic integration and the increased mobility f peoples across the globe. She talks about the anger and resentment that re often vented on "the foreigner" (a category which includes immigrant inorities, especially those marked by racial or ethnic difference) by the ominant group—in her case, the white majority in France. She suggests that the foreigner" is often held responsible for the "ills of the polis" (1991, 1).

Deploying a psychoanalytic rubric Kristeva suggests that, "strangely, the oreigner lives within us: [she] is the hidden face of our identity" (1991, 1). he argues that the foreigner within can be perceived at the moment vhen "the citizen-individual ceases to consider [herself] as unitary and glo-ious but discovers [her] incoherences and abysses, in short [her] 'strange-esses'" (2). Kristeva suggests that "by recognising [her] within ourselves, ve are spared detesting [her] in [her]self" (1). It is thus an ethical act when nembers of the dominant group recognize their own "otherness". Kristeva rgues that it is important for members of the dominant group, in particular, o recognize the existence within themselves of ungovernable drives, such as anger, which are easily stimulated and unpredictable because they are labile and changeable. Her thesis is that if members of the dominant culture recognize and monitor aggressive affects in themselves, they may cease venting them on "foreigners". Perhaps Kristeva's argument is overly optimistic, but it does resonate with some of the fundamental principles of Critical Whiteness Studies, which assert that, by turning the attention to whiteness and the ways in which the dominant group marginalizes and stigmatizes minority peoples, it is possible to address the issue of how white researchers might avoid reproducing these racializing structures of power in their research and writing.

Speaking (in the first-person plural) as a member of the dominant group, Kristeva argues that it is imperative that members of this group enhance their "ability to accept new modalities of otherness" (1991, 2). In my own research, "new modalities of otherness" entail a radical re-imagining of my relationality with Aboriginal people and culture. In the Australian context the recognition of Aboriginal sovereignty is a vital element in the ethical re-imagining of indigenous and white relations. Aboriginal legal scholar Larissa Behrendt, for example, asserts that "the notion of [indigenous] sovereignty goes to the heart of the restructuring of the relationship between indigenous and non-indigenous Australia" (2003, 96). Kristeva's work raises a question for me: How should I approach the otherness of Aboriginality in Australia against the background of the ways in which I am implicated in whiteness and the dominant culture? As a member of the dominant group, Kristeva, addressing this dominant group, recommends:

> Let us not seek to solidify, to turn the otherness of the foreigner into a thing. Let us merely touch it, brush by it, without giving it a permanent structure . . . Let us also lighten that otherness by constantly coming back to it—but more and more swiftly . . . An otherness barely touched upon and that already moves away.
>
> —(1991, 3)

Here Kristeva situates relations with the other within the zone of intercorporeality. I find this way of locating relations useful as it avoids the reification of difference. In the zone of intercorporeality, relationality is a mode of somatic and psychical attention and orientation.

It is the experience of this mode of relationality that I aim to reproduce in the finger-touching exercise. The exercise is designed to remind participants that they are embodied subjects, with complex and volatile somatic and psychical relationships with others.

I want to make it clear at this point that I am not recommending that researchers undertake physical contact with the people they are researching. In most cases I imagine this would be inappropriate. The point of this exercise is to be aware of the ways in which our sense of self is produced through the ways in which we as researchers relate to the materials and the ubjects of our research. The exercise is designed to encourage research-rs to recognize the volatility of what is known in Postcolonial Studies as he "contact zone" (see Pratt 1992), that is, the zone of intersubjectivity, nteraffectivity and intercorporeality in which we reside bodily. I hope the xercise can help you render your relationships with your research subjects, naterials and locales less abstract and bring them into the realm of bodily nd material immediacy. The exercise is meant to take you to the border of n encounter where the "singular self [comes] to itself in the presence of the ther" (Nancy 1991, xviii). Hopefully the exercise will recreate a scene of odily exposure to alterity, an experience that philosopher Jean-Luc Nancy lescribes as "a trembling at the edge of being" (1991, 61).

In recognizing this prickling sensation at the border of subjectivity which he exercise is meant to generate, and the point at which you engage with he other bodily and psychically, I hope you will be reminded of the volatil-ty that underlies or subtends the identities you assign both to yourself and o others. In my case, this recognition and the exploration of the contact one have, for example, enabled me to better understand the instability and nutability of whiteness.

THE FACE OF THE OTHER

The human face in particular brings us into the raw and naked contact zone with the other. Emmanuel Levinas suggests that our encounter with the oth-r's face is not one simply of perception or knowledge: "the relation to the ace is straightaway ethical" (1985, 87). He says:

> [R]elations with the face can surely be dominated by perception, but . . . cannot be reduced to that . . . the face is not "seen". It is what cannot become a content, which your thought would embrace; it is uncontain-able, it leads you beyond.
>
> —(85–87)

In leading you "beyond", the face invites you into a relationship with the other, a relationship which is characterized by "response" and "responsi-bility". As Levinas says, "before the face I do not simply remain there con-templating it. I *respond* to it" (88; my italics). It is an awareness of this *responsiveness* that enables you to develop what he describes as an "ethical" relationship with the other, and what Gail Weiss (1999), whom I discuss below, describes as the scene of "embodied ethics".

Think about how you are bodily affiliated with the imagined bodies in history, in literature, in the archive, in the media and in the other fields in which you conduct research. How does the body figure in these texts? How do you imagine these bodies? Or, to put it in another way, how do the values and ideas that inform your research field find embodiment (Foster 1995,

12)? And what is your relation to these imagined bodies? What kind of cultural histories do these bodily relations speak of?

EXERCISE 9: THE FACE

Think about the faces you have encountered in your research (either real or textual): What kind of response do they evoke in you? Can you picture them? Do they lead you "beyond"? Here is a series of writing questions about those faces:

- *How similar/dissimilar or familiar/unfamiliar is the face you are thinking of?*
- *What affects does it provoke in you? (These may include anxiety, curiosity, fear, pleasure, suspicion, desire, annoyance, resentment, concern, admiration, sadness or anger.)*
- *Does one feeling slide or segue into another feeling?*
- *Think of an occasion when you were meeting with someone from the group you are researching. How did you feel, bodily?*
- *What can you glean from these feelings? Do you experience a sense of empathy? Do you experience an awareness of difference?*
- *What do these feelings, affects or bodily reactions tell you about yourself and your relationship with the subjects, materials or locales of your research?*
- *Is there an identifiable power differential between you and the other?*

Write for half an hour in response to these questions.

You can either do this exercise by yourself or in a larger group. If it is in a larger group, break into smaller groups of three and discuss some of these questions. Reconvene as a larger group and read out some of your written responses to the questions.

This and the previous exercises aim to remind you that you have a complex and *singular* embodied relationship with your research subjects, materials and locales. As Nancy says, singularity is "always other, always shared, always exposed" (1991, 28). This relationship is bodily as well as cognitive. Knowledge is shaped by habits, memory and experience which are socially and culturally contracted. Habits, memory and experience also reside in the materiality of the body, and they are passed on through the generations in non-cognitive and non-textual ways. The writing exercises in this chapter aim to awaken in you a somatic attention to your bodily situatedness. This attentiveness is meant to remind you of the different temporality of the body and its impact on your thinking.

Knowing can never be complete or fixed because another person or another culture is never an enclosed horizon (see Marotta 2009). Boundaries are porous and osmotic; identities are co-extensive and interdependent. This interdependency is something that dominant cultures often disavow in their assignation of identities to themselves and their others. The writing exercises in this chapter aim to remind you of your own "trembling" edges. They are meant to demonstrate that we know ourselves not in the abstract or in isolation but in embodied, material relations with the people and objects around us. Hopefully you sensed something of the dynamism and volatility of these relations in doing the exercises.

RELATIONALITY AND AFFECT

So how do I link these writing exercises, and the awareness of intercorporeality, interaffectivity and intersubjectivity that they produce, to the Critical Whiteness Studies methodology that I use in my research? The idea of relationality is central to my work on Australian Aboriginal literature and my analysis of the ways in which whiteness impacts on my research and writing. Posthumanist theory and its advocacy of what might be called the relational turn have given me a vocabulary to talk about the inter-racial nature of my research. Two theorists that I have found useful, Brian Massumi (2002) and Sarah Ahmed (2000), for example, echo Levinas' (1985) insistence on the primacy of relationality. They suggest that the *encounter* of subjects is ontologically prior to the individual subject who encounters. In other words, encounter precedes identity. Our subjectivity is shaped by our intersubjective encounters with other subjects (and, I shall add, encounters with various cultural and natural landscapes and their non-human actors). Ahmed argues that the subject comes into being only through its encounters with others; its identity cannot be separated from its psychical and social interactions with them.

In my work I examine the juridico-political dimensions of relationality and the ways in which the category of the white subject and the white Australian nation are predicated on the subordination and exclusion of the racialized other. In "settler" nations such as Australia the racialized other is initially the indigenes who have been dispossessed of their land and, in many cases, their languages and cultures. In later historical moments various immigrant groups—for example, refugees—have also been positioned as racialized others within the white Australian nation and excluded from legal and cultural citizenship.

In this chapter I emphasize that it is necessary to examine not only the *discursive* significance of relationality but its interaffectivity, intersubjectivity and intercorporeality. I argue that it is important that researchers are sensitive to the ways in which they are affectively and bodily connected to the subjects and materials of their research. In my case, I am interested in the affective dispositions of contemporary Australian whiteness and the ways they are connected to a disavowed colonial history of violence. What interests me particularly is the spectrum of white affects which arise from my own late twentieth-century understanding of Australia's colonial history and its dispossession of Aboriginal people. (Much of the history, for example, of the stolen generations, had been suppressed in Australia until the 1970s.)

I use a poem by an Aboriginal Australian poet, Lisa Bellear, titled "Feelings" (1996, 13–14) to explore the issue of white affect.[4] In the poem the Aboriginal speaker challenges, in a very forthright manner, a female professor who asks her to confirm that she is Aboriginal. I see the professor's question as symptomatic of the dominant white culture's will to manage and control the identification and representation of Aboriginal people. In the postcolonial state's governance Aboriginality has historically been defined and managed through the scopic regime—in other words, by visual appearance.[5] Some Aboriginal people with light skin have had doubt cast on their authenticity. This may be the context for the exchange in the poem, where the professor's question, "are you Aboriginal?" produces an angry reaction in the Aboriginal speaker.

Feelings

Like Douwe Edberts
Freeze dry coffee
I stand motionless
But full of feelings
Gin, native, abo, coon
An inquisitive academic
Then asks "are you Aboriginal?"

Do I punch
Do I scream
Do I raise my arms
To ward off
The venomous hatred
Which institutionalized
Racism leaves unchallenged
As they collect their evidence
To reinforce their "superiority",
And our "inferiority"

Am I Aboriginal
Am I Torres Strait Islander
Am I South Sea Islander

I laugh inside, at her ignorance
I shake my head,
But how can I pity

A person who is identified
As the expert exponent on
Indigenous Australians

Eh Professor, big shot,
Big cheese, or whoever
You claim to be
You've really no idea

Love to chat sister,
But there's faxes to send
And protest letters to write

I turn and walk away
Preserving my dignity
Without humiliating hers.
        —Lisa Bellear (1996, 13)[6]

interpret the anger of the poem's "I", in part, as a reaction to the fact that the Aboriginal speaker challenges the professor's authority to question her about her Aboriginality. The poem foregrounds the power invested in the dominant group's arrogation to itself of the right to name and define Aboriginal peoples. (The poem also lists, for example, derogatory slang terms that have been used to denigrate Aboriginal people, and these demonstrate how aggressive and epistemologically violent the act of naming can be.)

Following my exploration of the notion of embodiment in the first part of this chapter, I shall analyze how this powerful poem impacts on me; how it rhetorically engages me and makes me aware of the entitlement and privilege that accrue to white academics. My reading of the poem is not definitive. The poem may perform a different kind of work and have a different significance or meaning for other readers.

Although the poem does not explicitly identify the professor as white, the "institutionalized" power and authority she embodies, along with her putative "superiority", locate her in a position homologous to that of a white academic. I therefore read the poem as describing an encounter between an Aboriginal "I" and a white professor. From my point of view, the poem rhetorically opens up a space of dialogue through its direct address. By addressing the white professor as "you", the Aboriginal speaker effectively puts me, as a white academic reader, in the white professor's shoes. The poem's first-person mode assigns the Aboriginal speaker the subject position and questions the white professor's authority to name and define her. I find myself responding empathetically—with a mixture of emotions—to the Aboriginal speaker's anger. Further, when the Aboriginal speaker addresses the white professor as "sister", this produces a charged and ambivalent moment for me, as an embodied white feminist reader. I experience my relationship with the Aboriginal "I" bodily at this point as both proximate (through empathy) and distantiated (she has turned and walked away). I read the word "sister" rhetorically as ironic in some measure. It acts to critique the universalist assumptions that characterize some aspects of white First World feminism and the concept of an all-encompassing "sisterhood". However, the tone of the address also seems to me measured (the Aboriginal speaker wants to "preserve" the "dignity" of both women). I read this as an attempt, on the Aboriginal speaker's part, to avoid reproducing the white academic's aggression.[7] It seems to me that she is endeavouring to negotiate an ethical relationship with the white professor in spite of the latter's offending question. The stanza that follows, namely, the lines:

> I turn and walk away
> Preserving my dignity
> Without humiliating hers

strikes me as an act of brokerage, an attempt to retain a cordial and ethical relationality, however attenuated, between a minoritized woman and one endowed with the privilege and entitlements accorded to white people—a relationality in which both women retain their dignity.

Indeed, although the conversation between the Aboriginal speaker and the professor within the poem is cut short because the Aboriginal speaker turns away from the professor, the Aboriginal *writer* (Lisa Bellear), in effect, reconvenes this inter-racial dialogue virtually with *me*, a white feminist reader. As a white academic I occupy a position homologous to the white professor. The poem therefore stages an inter-racial encounter with me—one which re-enacts both the embodied interaffectivity and the ethical relationship negotiated within the poem. The poem works, in my case, to "unsettle" the universalism of some aspects of white feminism. It counters any desire I might have to identify with the injury and anger articulated by the Aboriginal speaker. I am attentive to her "feelings", but I also accord them the "space" that the due respect of difference requires: she has, after all, "turn[ed] away". In doing this, I acknowledge (1) my complicity with the systemic entitlements of whiteness and a history of violence and (2) the Aboriginal speaker's difference, a key element which women of colour and minoritized women have argued is indispensable for ethical inter-racial relationships. (In the Australian context, as I argued earlier, a key index of difference is Aboriginal sovereignty.)

Without the recognition of difference I might be tempted to identify empathically (in an unconditional way) with the Aboriginal speaker, in the belief that this identification endows me with an ethical awareness that differentiates me from the white professor and exempts me from the ongoing systemic entitlements and racist assumptions of whiteness. However, in recognizing my structural homology with the professor, I acknowledge the continuation of the systemic privilege accruing to white people. It cannot be shed in a simple voluntary act on my part. I also recognize that my own white embodiment is informed with these systemic relationships of Aboriginal disadvantage and dispossession. In my reading of Bellear's poem I experience an empathetic recognition combined with what Dominick LaCapra terms "unsettlement" (1997). My experience of empathy is not an act of identification. Although I am moved (bodily, affectively) by the speaker, I am also aware of my proximity to the addressee within the internal dialogue of the poem, that is, the white professor. My reading of the poem, in effect, performs what Robyn Wiegman (1999) calls the split subjectivity of whiteness; it is an index both of my location in whiteness and of my ability to critique whiteness. Although I disidentify with the white professor's entitlement to name Aboriginal people, I cannot simply, by an act of will, step outside whiteness and its vast system of entitlements in which I am enmeshed. (See also Nina Lykke's discussion of disidentification in Chapter 2, this volume.)

CONCLUSION

In conclusion, I would argue that although the poem, in my reading of it, insists on indigenous difference, it also allows for and indeed convenes inter-racial dialogue. I read the last stanza, in its effort to preserve the dignity of both women, as being open to a potential for change in the white professor.[8] This, in turn, I would suggest, leaves me, as a white feminist reader, potentially with an ability to learn and adapt. The potential for political alliance between Aboriginal and white feminists is not foreclosed. Other readers may have a different reaction to these lines. I base my conclusion in part on a consideration of Bellear's comments on the subject of feminism. She herself did not shy away from the term "feminist", describing herself as an "urban indigenous feminist" (2000, 102). While I do not intend to imply that there is an unmediated link between the poem's poetic first-person speaker and its author, there are nonetheless parallels between the Aboriginal speaker in the penultimate stanza and Bellear's life of political activism. In this stanza,

> Love to chat sister,
> But there's faxes to send
> And protest letters to write

the poem's speaker defines her Aboriginality *politically*, that is, in terms of her activism. (Her most pressing concern is to save her energy for the necessary work of indigenous protest.) Similarly, she figures her relationship with the professor as definitively *political*, that is, subtended by the politics of whiteness. In keeping the door open for dialogue she is, in effect, laying down the foundation for a new ethics of inter-racial relationality. The onus is now on the white professor/me as white reader to develop an embodied ethics of relationality which recognizes and works to relinquish white entitlement and to acknowledge indigenous difference.

Just as Bellear's poem announces (in its title) that the topic is centrally that of her "feelings",[9] as a white reader of Aboriginal literature I am interested in how the poem engages me affectively. My relationship with the indigenous "other" is intensely informed by feelings. Massumi argues that relationality registers on the body materially, bodily and affectively before it registers cognitively or consciously. Bodily and psychical participation (in the dynamics of interrelationality) precedes cognitive understanding. What is particularly interesting about Massumi's work is that he theorizes how social change and transformation are inaugurated at the site of the body. The feelings of both individuals and larger collectives can change rapidly. Recognizing the role that affects play in collective and national identifications can also remind us of the potential for change within these identities.

Being cognizant of whiteness as a dominant racializing power formation provides the foundation for white scholars in particular to anticipate and imagine new ethical forms of intercultural relationships (Frankenberg 1993). An awareness and consideration of the bodily dimensions is thus an indispensable part of the ethics of inter-racial research. Elizabeth Grosz (1990) has argued that the body is the site of the exercise of power; it is the point where power stops being abstract. She characterizes the body as a contractual, exchanging being. Gail Weiss (1999) extends this idea of the contractual body to argue that we are never neutral in our bodily encounters with others; we experience situations through affective responses. With this in mind she points out that ethics are always corporeally enacted. She challenges the idea that moral agency is achieved only through cognition. Being mindful of the constitutive and mutually defining relationship between bodies, others and the world, it is important to investigate how we inhabit our research topics bodily. Weiss argues that writing mediates the contact we have with the body of the other. Through its stimulation of feeling it opens up a zone of relationality: reading and writing function to "connect" us to our others. They can therefore do the work of an embodied ethics.

As I mentioned at the beginning of this chapter, in my research on Australian Aboriginal literature I examine how Aboriginal literary subjectivities engage and critique whiteness through acts of inter-racial reading. My work is predicated on the idea that whiteness is unstable and that it is constantly reconfiguring itself (although it does so in ways that are not always predictable or governable). I borrow from Henry Giroux the idea that rethinking whiteness can be an exercise in both critique and possibility (1997, 295). I am mindful that in reconfiguring itself whiteness always seeks to protect its entitlements and privilege. This makes me circumspect about liberatory epistemological rhetoric and progressivist narratives, and wary lest I reproduce them in my own work. Aboriginal disadvantage and dispossession are endemic and entrenched. There are many powerful Aboriginal writers, artists, community leaders and professionals, several of whom I have quoted in this chapter. Some years ago I approached an Aboriginal colleague working in the field of critical whiteness theory for advice about my methodology. She advised me that my project should be two-pronged; that I should complement my readings and dissemination of Aboriginal literature (the latter event is vitally important to Aboriginal writers) with an examination of whiteness. I aim to think about how Aboriginal literature engages with whiteness and vice versa. This involves cultivating an awareness of my own sociocultural position within the dominant group and examining the complex set of assumptions, beliefs, hopes and anxieties in which I am embedded and which, to some extent, are indexical of Australian whiteness. There has been no simple formula to follow in identifying these contingencies, and doing so is not a "stage" in my research that I can complete and move on from. Rather, it is a dimension of my research that will continue to expand and grow throughout the entire course of my project. Rosi Braidotti argues that political transformation is generated and subtended by new forms of subjectivity. She reminds us that subjectivity does not always coincide with consciousness (1994, 149). She recommends, for example, that feminists pay attention to the presence of unconscious identifications, of desire and memory, and that they "conjugate" these with commitments to political transformation (170). She argues that new kinds of subjects (which are at once desirous and political) are not created by "sheer volition" alone; rather, they are accompanied by the transformations of psychical and bodily reality and the material conditions in which they are embedded.

I hope that this chapter might help you to situate yourself within this zone of psychical and embodied relations. In positioning you in the zone of interaffectivity, intersubjectivity and intercorporeality, the chapter aims to inspire in you what Braidotti calls "points of exit" (1994, 170) from which differently racialized feminists can destabilize the universalizing identifications of whiteness.

NOTES

1. I do not want to imply that Aboriginal people's relations are solely with white people. There are many convergences and divergences between Aboriginal and other minority groups in Australia (see, for example, Stephenson 2007), as there are racialized and ethnicized relations between white people and other minority groups in Australia (see, for example, Hage 2000).
2. My fictocritical work uses whiteness theory interwoven with anecdote and memoir to explore white affects (see Brewster 2009a, 2009b, 2009c). Publications of my research on Aboriginal literature and the way it engages whiteness include Brewster 2008a and 2008b.
3. Toni Morrison's scholarly monograph *Playing in the Dark: Whiteness and the Literary Imagination*, which was published in 1992, for example, was one of the first important texts in the field. See also Roediger 1994.
4. For a longer discussion of this poem see Brewster 2007. My discussion in this present chapter revises and reworks the reading of the poem I published in

Feminist Theory to take account of my homology with the white academic in the poem.

5. The white Australian assimilation policy (from the mid 1930s onwards, for example) aimed at the biological absorption of "half-castes" and fair-skinned Aboriginal Australian children into the white population (see, for example, Neville 1947).

6. Bellear, Lisa. 1996. "Feelings." In *Dreaming in Urban Areas*. St Lucia: University of Queensland Press, p. 13. Printed with permission from John Stewart (copyright-holder).

7. Once again, these lines are open to interpretation. Bellear has stated that, in the poem, "the indigenous person gets fed up with [the] exchange but rather than get 'agro' [aggressive] they walk away" (written correspondence with me). However, not everyone reading the poem would interpret it in this way. Moreover, I cannot fully know what Bellear "intended" the poem to mean or "do" for its readers. The fact that the poem functions pedagogically for me is a result of my own readerly predilections and not necessarily of the author's intentions. Indeed, as the text continues to circulate across a range of audiences, its meaning exceeds that intended by the author. There is no guarantee that any reader's interpretation and response will align seamlessly with the author's.

8. Bellear has said that the poem "is about not listening", that "the academic doesn't listen". With my interpretation of the poem, I express the hope that white feminists can learn precisely to "listen" to Aboriginal and minority women.

9. Another Aboriginal poet, Romaine Moreton, discusses the importance of indigenous literature in articulating and displaying, and thereby demanding recognition of, Aboriginal feelings: "[O]ne thing that has remained absent . . . throughout the history of this country anyway, is the full understanding of the emotional state of Indigenous peoples, that has not been written about. They've documented our bodies, our brain size, our leg size, how we sit and stand, but not how we feel" (Ford 2003).

REFERENCES

Ahmed, Sarah. 2000. *Strange Encounters: Embodied Others in Post-coloniality*. London: Routledge.

Behrendt, Larissa. 2003. *Achieving Social Justice*. Annandale: Federation Press.

Bellear, Lisa. 1996. *Dreaming in Urban Areas*. St Lucia: University of Queensland Press.

Bellear, Lisa. 2000. *Beyond Reconciliation*. Master's thesis, University of Queensland.

Braidotti, Rosi. 1994. *Nomadic Subjects*. New York: Columbia University Press.

Brewster, Anne. 2007. "Brokering Cross-Racial Feminism: Reading Aboriginal Australian Poet Lisa Bellear." *Feminist Theory* 8 (2): 209–22.

Brewster, Anne. 2008a. "Engaging the Public Intimacy of Whiteness: The Indigenous Protest Poetry of Romaine Moreton." *Journal of the Association for the Study of Australian Literature* 8 (special issue): 56–76. www.nla.gov.au/openpublish/index.php/jasal (accessed July 14, 2009).

Brewster, Anne. 2008b. "Humour and the Defamiliarisation of Whiteness in the Short Fiction of Australian Indigenous Writer Alf Taylor." *Journal of Postcolonial Writing* 44 (4): 427–38.

Brewster, Anne. 2009a. "Beach Combing: A Fossicker's Guide to Whiteness and Indigenous Sovereignty." In *Practice-Led Research, Research-Led Practice in the Creative Arts*, edited by Roger Dean and Hazel Smith, 126–49. Edinburgh: Edinburgh University Press.

Brewster, Anne. 2009b. "Teaching *The Tracker* in Germany: A Journal of Whiteness." In *The Racial Politics of Bodies, Nations and Knowledges*, edited by Barbara Baird and Damien Riggs, 228–44. Newcastle upon Tyne: Cambridge Scholars Publishing.

Brewster, Anne. 2009c. "Travelogue." *Outskirts: Feminisms along the Edge* 20. www.chloe.u wa.edu.au/outskirts/ or www.chloe.uwa.edu.au/outskirts/archive/volume20/brewster (accessed on July 14, 2009).

Ford, Andrew. 2003. Transcript of an Interview with Kerrianne Cox and Romaine Moreton on *The Music Show*, Radio National, 25 January. www.abc.net.au/rn/music/mshow/s751864.htm (accessed 23 January 2007).

Foster, Susan Leigh, ed. 1995. *Choreographing History*. Bloomington: Indiana University Press.

Frankenberg, Ruth. 1993. *White Women, Race Matters: The Social Construction of Whiteness*. Minneapolis: University of Minnesota Press.

Giroux, Henry A. 1997. "Racial Politics and the Pedagogy of Whiteness." In *Whiteness: A Critical Reader*, edited by Mike Hill, 294–315. New York: New York University Press.

Grosz, Elizabeth. 1990. "Inscriptions and Body-Maps: Representations and the Corporeal." In *Feminine, Masculine and Representation*, edited by Terry Threadgold and Anne Cranny-Francis, 63–74. Sydney: Allen & Unwin.

Hage, Ghassan. 2000. *White Nation: Fantasies of White Supremacy in a Multicultural Society*. North Melbourne: Pluto Press.

Kristeva, Julia. 1991. "Toccata and Fugue for the Foreigner." In *Strangers to Ourselves*, translated by Leon S. Roudiez, 1–21. London: Harvester Wheatsheaf.

LaCapra, Dominick. 1997. "Lanzmann's 'Shoah': 'Here There Is No Why'." *Critical Inquiry* 23 (2): 231–69.

Levinas, Emmanuel. 1985. "The Face." In *Ethics and Infinity*, translated by Richard A. Cohen, 85–92. Pittsburgh: Duquesne University Press.

Marotta, Vince. 2009. "Intercultural Hermeneutics and the Cross-cultural Subject." *Journal of Intercultural Studies* 30 (3): 267–84.

Massumi, Brian. 2002. *Parables for the Virtual*. Durham: Duke University Press.

Moreton-Robinson, Aileen. 2000. *Talkin' Up to the White Woman: Indigenous Women and Feminism*. St Lucia: University of Queensland Press.

Morrison, Toni. 1992. *Playing in the Dark: Whiteness and the Literary Imagination*. Cambridge, MA: Harvard University Press.

Nancy, Jean-Luc. 1991. *The Inoperative Community*. Translated by Peter Connor. Minneapolis: University of Minnesota Press.

Neville, Auber O. 1947. *Australia's Coloured Minority*. Sydney: Currawong.

Pratt, Mary Louise. 1992. *Imperial Eyes: Travel Writing and Transculturation*. London: Routledge.

Riggs, Damien W. 2006. *Priscilla, (White) Queen of the Desert: Queer Rights/Race Privilege*. New York: Peter Lang.

Riggs, Damien W. 2007. " 'Unnatural Crimes' and 'Natural' Rights: Towards an Understanding of Queer White Colonialisms." In *Historicising Whiteness: Transnational Perspectives on the Construction of an Identity*, edited by Leigh Boucher, Katherine Ellinghaus and Jane Carey (pp. 35–40). Melbourne: RMIT Publishing.

Roediger, David. 1994. *Towards the Abolition of Whiteness: Essays on Race, Politics and Working Class History*. London: Verso.

Stephenson, Peta. 2007. *The Outsiders Within*. Sydney: UNSW Press.

Weiss, Gail. 1999. *Body Images: Embodiment as Intercorporeality*. London: Routledge.

Wiegman, Robyn. 1999. "Whiteness Studies and the Paradox of Particularity." *Boundary 2* 26 (3): 115–50.

5 Feminist Crime Fiction as a Model for Writing History Differently

Andrea Pető

Every historian publishing in peer-reviewed publications with low circulation but high prestige secretly envies the astonishing success of crime fiction that explores historical events, such as *The Da Vinci Code* (2003) by Dan Brown or *The Historian* (2005) by Elizabeth Kostova—books read by millions around the globe. If feminist scholars want to move from sheer envy to useful critical appropriation of the methods and theories used by these authors to reach out to wider audiences, what can they do? This is the question I shall reflect on in this chapter. These methods of reaching out can, in my opinion, be appropriated in critically useful ways. Moreover, I also consider it pertinent to study the methods of these top-selling crime fiction writers as a way of counteracting the reluctance of some feminist scholars to engage with history out of "fear" of the positivist epistemological legacy of history writing. I will present a different entrance point to history—through the reading/writing of crime fiction (see also Pető, Chapter 10, this volume).

More precisely, the chapter will present a writing exercise that highlights the question of what feminist historiography—and, more broadly, interdisciplinary Feminist Studies—can learn from bestselling writers of crime fiction that explores historical events, and how their tricks to reach wider audiences can be deconstructed and perhaps recycled in a critical feminist mode. I shall also demonstrate how this exercise, based on creative writing as a method, can be used to reconceptualize terms like "truth", "clue" and "past", key concepts of both history writing and the sub-genre of crime fiction that explores historical events.

The writing exercise that is the focus of this chapter was developed as part of a graduate course conceived as a multidimensional meeting point between literary theory, the study of violence, writing history and popular culture. The course was called "Textual Outlaws: Feminist Historical Crime Fiction". I taught it at the Department of Gender Studies at the Central European University in Budapest, Hungary. To contextualize it, I shall not only present the exercise but also describe and discuss the course. I hope that this kind of contextualized account will inspire readers to revise and adapt the writing exercise for integration into their own teaching and learning environments.

"TEXTUAL OUTLAWS": A FEMINIST COURSE IN
CRIME FICTION EXPLORING HISTORICAL EVENTS

Students come to my Gender Studies courses from many different academic
and national backgrounds. But, independent of their background, crime
fiction as a popular genre is well liked among them. Moreover, it is also
accessible to those who have not studied literature before. In addition to
focusing on crime fiction, the multidimensionality of this course also made
it attractive to students.

To understand the framing of the writing exercise, it is important to know
in more detail how I constructed the course. Each session includes a contribution from the teacher, student presentations (submitted in writing in advance),
a film analysis and a novel analysis connected to the theoretical issues covered
in that particular session; special attention is also given to writing strategies
and creative writing exercises. In terms of format, all sessions are divided
into two parts: The first is based on a more "traditional" academic teaching
format, in which collective knowledge is developed by means of a critical
examination of historiography and relevant literature. In this part of the session, students are asked to give presentations on theoretical aspects of the
course. In the second part, the theoretical dimensions are linked to creative
writing exercises and a transdisciplinary theoretical framework is applied. In
this part, students are encouraged to write short crime stories.

Several handbooks on teaching creative writing are available (Gold-
berger 1986; Richardson 1990). The one I use is designed to help students
write short stories (Grant-Adamson 2003). During the course, we follow
the practical steps in this handbook. A key aspect of the work is to let
students discover the author in themselves, as most of them have never
experimented with creative writing before. Michel de Certeau (1984) uses
the term "appropriation" to express the process whereby even people who
are "mere" consumers do not remain passive in relation to the objects of
consumption. Along these lines, I understand the sequence of creative writing exercises in this course to be a kind of appropriation. In the exercises,
students are encouraged to experiment with different modes of writing as
appropriation: writing to learn and writing to activate their thinking and
their imagination. Through the writing exercises, historical crime fiction is
conceptualized as a component of collective memory that is open for recon-
ceptualization in a subversive way.

EXERCISE 10: DEVELOP A SHORT CRIME STORY

*The assignments are always followed by a discussion or a reading in
class. It is important to develop a supportive environment that also
makes the participants feel confident.*

1. *Introduction: Students are asked to write a short summary describing the story they have in mind and to connect it to one of the theoretical issues (race, ethnicity, class, sexuality, postcolonial theory, antifascism) discussed throughout the course.*
2. *Repeat this exercise in the next session. Ideas might substantially change and develop during the period between sessions, and thinking time is to be recognized as valuable.*
3. *As a home assignment, students write a paragraph summarizing the plot. They present their summary in class and get feedback from the other participants.*
4. *The next step is to develop the main character, the person who does the detecting. As a home assignment, students write a paragraph about her or him and present it in class for a round of feedback. If there are a lot of students, they can form groups and read their texts to each other, in order to receive feedback. If you have only a few students, individual presentations can be organized for the whole group.*
5. *As a home assignment, students are requested to write a description of one object that plays an important role in their story or that is simply present while the events are unfolding. They also present this object to the rest of the class.*
6. *The next home assignment is to develop the plot of the story: Who is where? When? Doing what? For how long?*
7. *The moment has arrived for the students to write the first draft of their story.*
8. *The students read their draft stories in a "fish-bowl" format. Two students sit facing each other (one is reading, the other commenting) while the others form a circle around them with their chairs. The person who is reading will be the commentator for the next person until everybody has read and commented. It is crucial to secure a non-competitive environment by underscoring that these are first-draft stories. If there are many students in the class, the readings can be stretched out over the whole second half of the course, with a maximum of two stories per session.*
9. *Work on the story in class: Ask the students to mark on the hard copy the characterizations of the main character in the story. Through this targeted description they can improve their writing technique.*
10. *Work on the story in class: Ask the students to highlight the descriptive parts. Organize a group discussion on the findings.*
11. *Work on the story in class: Ask the students to mark out where past and present time change during the story. Organize a group discussion on the findings.*

12. *After the submission of the stories, give feedback to the authors (never use red ink for corrections) and also offer them the opportunity to rewrite the story for final submission. Organize a public reading of the stories with volunteers from the course for a larger student community in the school; make the stories or a recording (podcast) of the readings available online if the authors give their permission. If possible, it is also a good idea to organize a festive reading for a wider audience by the end of the term.*

WHY CHOOSE THE GENRE OF CRIME FICTION FOR A WRITING EXERCISE?

The crime fiction genre, as part of popular culture, is a meeting point between politics and entertainment. As such, it is well suited for teaching purposes.

First of all, crime fiction sticks to a rather standard formula, which is known and even expected by readers. Fear and joy are produced in the readers sequentially, and in a way that makes them feel secure. When reading a crime fiction text, they know that by the end of the story the crime will be solved and the social order restored. This assumed security also serves as a red thread during the writing process. Since the formula is known to most students, it offers an easily accessible common base for future crime fiction writers.

Another reason why the crime fiction story is appropriate for this kind of writing exercise is because it is a good source for tracing the genre's transformation in different national contexts as well as for analyzing how it has developed and differentiated. The brutality and realism of North American hardboiled crime fiction distinguishes it from its British counterpart—which is even labelled differently: detective fiction. Whereas in crime fiction the investigator is a solitary hero who fights against crime on the margins of legality, in detective fiction psychological awareness and the close reading of clues replace violence. The investigator's intellectual capabilities are used to identify and reveal the perpetrator. In Hungarian, the term *krimi* covers both branches of crime fiction. During communism it was a dormant genre since detection was the monopoly of the police, who were controlled by the Communist Party. Currently, crime fiction stories from the Scandinavian countries have become very popular internationally, and it is interesting to observe that they are very different from crime stories coming from either Russian or Anglo-American contexts. In order to make students reflect on national contexts and differences, they are asked, as a part of the exercise, to map the historiography of the crime fiction of their own country or a country of their choice, and afterwards to compare their work with other students' historiographies.

The third reason why crime fiction is useful for feminist education is the genre's flexible identity structure. On the one hand, the closed nature of crime fiction's formula and the difficulty of cracking it from a feminist perspective have often been debated (Munt 1994). In the 1970s, feminist critics even labelled it the "least useful genre" for feminists to analyze (Heilbrun 1988, 1). On the other hand, the genre does indeed provide opportunities for feminist critiques of notions such as jurisdiction, power, hierarchy and law, and as my writing exercise shows, it is also very suitable for teaching academic writing differently. In early crime fiction stories, the male investigator was the privileged actor, but during the more recent development of the genre, the character of the investigator has gradually been shifting towards plurality, diversity and conflict. It is useful to follow this process in the context of a course like the one I have developed.

The crime fiction genre, which used to epitomize the male-dominated narrative in hardboiled fiction, has changed. Solving crimes requires the investigator to develop skills such as the ability to undertake historical analysis: constructing a narrative about past events and giving meaning to events. But what happens when, in lieu of a middle- or upper-class male investigator, a woman interprets the facts, reads the clues and, having broken down the linear chronology of events, retrospectively establishes an explanatory plot? The genre has come a long way since one of Agatha Christie's main protagonists, Miss Marple, relied on a "woman's intuition" and never questioned British life and its hierarchies. By now we have crime fiction stories with independent, feminist investigators as protagonists, such as the lesbian investigators of crime fiction authors Antonia Fraser and Amanda Cross (pseudonym for Carolyn Gold Heilbrun).

Female investigators are often characterized as being plagued by dilemmas caused by their position in society. These women professionals are often presented as being committed not only to solving the crime but also to making the world a better place. In these crime fiction texts, this position of the female investigator characters is again motivated by the ways in which they are represented as taking sides with the victims and as grounded in an understanding of the senselessness of violent death. Moreover, female investigators are often cast as characters who reject the role of victim, not just as women mirroring gestures of hegemonic masculinity, but also as women living their own lives.

Finally, the analysis and critical recycling of the crime fiction genre, as I have described it here, is also a fine point of departure for critical feminist teaching because it can open up the boundary between academic writing and fiction in a way that resonates with the political goal of becoming accessible to broader audiences. Crime fiction is a popular and "accessible" genre in the sense that its characters—investigators, victims and perpetrators—struggle with everyday issues. Therefore, the genre offers space for identification but also for critical distancing. It is sometimes easier to understand and empathize with fictional characters than with real ones, because the fiction nsures a certain distance between ourselves and the characters, allowing a ritical and reflexive point of view. An investigation of the violence repre- ented in the crime fiction story, moreover, can enable a discussion of stu- lents' relationship to authority or authorities.

WHY IS CRIME FICTION HISTORICAL?

eminists' relationship with canonical stories of "the past" is often ambigu- ous (Pető and Waaldijk 2011). The theoretical position on which this course s based is that the past starts right now. Therefore, it is crucial that during he writing exercise students reflect on their relationship to the past, espe- ially in step five, where they are requested to write a description of an object that is related to their story in important ways (see also Pető, Chapter .0, this volume). It is also important to take into account how the students' lifferent backgrounds (in terms of gender, class, race, sexualities, dis/ abilities, nationalities, etc.) may position them differently towards history and the past. So it is important that the teacher makes space for discussion of these kinds of differences.

This writing exercise also serves as a possible solution to the theoretical problem of rendering historical narratives sensitive to intersectionally gen- lered issues, including the memory flux that, to different degrees, perhaps characterizes all periods in history.

Today, we see a "memory boom", where private memories are ques- ioning the dominance of public memory. We may perhaps claim that the listance between professional historians and a reading audience seeking alternative popular historical works and "their own reading" of history has probably never been greater than today. An example is the overwhelming popularity of glossy history journals and websites about history while aca- lemic historians struggle to sell even 300 copies of their work. Historical ilms and documentaries, which in my own context of postcommunist Hun- ;ary, for example, were mushrooming at the beginning of the transition rom communism to capitalist democracy, represent just the beginning of his period—which has since been continued with the rewriting of historical events by means of websites about specific historical events or in a Web- oom of "second life".

On a daily basis, historians experience how the canon of historical knowl- edge is incapable of meeting the challenges of democracy, as it is not able to nclude different social groups, while technological development challenges previous forms of historical representation. Many people interpret the irre- versible changes in the mediation and transmission of historical knowledge as a crisis of historical understanding. We read fewer books, and accord- ng to current debates on the historical canon (Stuurman 2000), the "fac- ual" knowledge of the younger generation is radically reduced. In this way, 'history" itself—the history we have known since it became an "academic subject" in the nineteenth century—has been transformed. Crime fiction that explores historical events plays a crucial role in this process and feminist scholars should have a say.

The re-examination of our relationship to the past is even more pertinent in the postcommunist part of Europe, where the transformation caused by the memory boom (the personalization of past events and a broadening of the community of remembering) coincided with the transition from communism to capitalist democracy. Still, there has been little real change in the writing and teaching of history in the former communist countries since 1989. A brief period of euphoria immediately after 1989 was followed by the institutional polarization of historiography and research. Instead of questioning the canon, historians have tended to create counter-canons. In the institutions of higher education where history is taught, the Bologna process, the transformation of the European higher educational space, strengthened traditional history as a discipline as well as the associated teaching practices in undergraduate courses. Even at the master's and PhD levels, there is little room for an interdisciplinary approach; in most cases the traditional division between cultural and social history continues to prevail. The much-anticipated historical paradigm shift in Eastern Europe has not occurred.

Nevertheless, when the "new history" is being written in an intersectional way, as in my course, new questions are raised, which include issues of class, gender, sexuality, nationality, race and ethnicity. Writing crime fiction puts the very difficult enterprise of writing history intersectionally into practice. In my course we are no longer speaking of "historiography" but of "historical culture"—an umbrella term denoting the study of relationships with the past that also takes into consideration the communities of remembrance. This approach enables us to examine intersectional gender history. From our perspective, it is impossible to debate the foundation and operation of society—above all the development of the concept of nation—without considering intersectional gender. When the new approach is then interwoven into the old canon, this is no longer understood as the sole narrative determining the history of nations and democracy but reappears as just one of several effective narratives.

The rethinking of historicity and the past also requires the re-examination of what a source can be. While writing crime fiction stories, the authors feel that they are creating the sources themselves. This approach provides space for a plurality of narratives, fundamentally altering our definition of historical sources. Such a change of definition is also prompted by the exercise of writing a crime fiction story. In addition to written documents, historians may utilize pictures, sculptures, buildings, films, oral history and rituals/rites to promote an understanding of the past. Using such resources, they seek to determine their own relationship to the "past in the pasts"—and not what "really" happened. This meta-historical approach permits historians to examine the reception of historical representation and its social redistribution, in addition to scholarly analysis. The world of crime fiction can also be such a "site of remembering", to use Pierre Nora's (1989) term, a place where we may study the complexity of relationships to the past. Through their fictional characters, students can position themselves in that past and thereby determine how a source can be defined.

WHY SHOULD CRIME FICTION EXPLORING HISTORICAL EVENTS BE USEFUL FOR FEMINISTS?

Gender Studies is a self-reflexive discipline; it is critical of its own phantasmagoria. I do not use crime fiction in its most conservative narrative form but for the sake of subverting the genre for political ends (Heilbrun 1988). David Middleton and Derek Edwards defined history writing as "practices of institutional remembering and forgetting" (1990, 10). This institutionalized and collective remembering is always linked to the notion of "true" memories which various political regimes have suppressed or even denied. Various groups in society use such "true" memories to promote their own political power, and the women's movements are no exception in this regard. Thus, the demand that "true" memories should be recognized amounts, in every instance, to a hegemonic political demand. The exercise of writing a crime fiction story is an important step towards deconstructing these processes of "remembering and forgetting".

The primary reason for teaching feminist crime fiction that explores historical events with the focus on a writing exercise is to demonstrate how, in the process of remembering, memories of the past change in accordance with expectations of the present. Such expectations differ according to the intersectionally gendered situatedness of the subject who articulates them. Remembering is related to the ways in which the individual defines her or his relationship to the past and to the community. Such remembering can take place at a symbolic or metaphorical level. The feminist political struggle for social change takes place via symbolic metaphors, and these metaphors are historical as they are connected to imaginations of the past. Against this background, the writing of feminist crime fiction that explores historical events can be understood as a metaphor for reconceptualizing our own past.

Another reason for teaching feminist crime fiction which explores historical events is related to the specific relationship that many female historians have with the language of much professional history writing. There are many examples of female history students who fail to finish their PhD theses because they refuse to conform to the traditional academic narrative and language. It is also more of a rule than an exception that women academics at a certain point in their careers begin to experiment with other genres, thereby implicitly questioning the epistemic ideology of "Western" rationalism (Fleishman 1998). This ideology separates knowledge and subjectivity from each other, establishing an unbiased and context-free, objective "truth". The academic style of writing is a ritual which is necessary to gain academic recognition and to formulate "objective" truths. Doubt has been cast from two directions: first, from the perspective of poststructural historiography, which understands knowledge as contextual and where a particularistic perspective is acceptable (as being only one amongst many), and, second—in many ways related to the first—from the perspective of feminisms.

The course that provides the context for the exercise of writing a crime fiction story follows the historical development of crime fiction as a genre and illustrates how feminist theory intersects with creative writing. A first step in the critical feminist literature on crime fiction is to examine what happened when women became the writers of detective stories. Feminist literary scholars' disappointment regarding the genre of crime fiction is often motivated by the absence of a change in the formula. To demonstrate this in the course, you could, for example, look at Agatha Christie's *Death Comes as the End* (1944). Here, the female figures do not have any subversive potential. A second step could be to look at the "politics of presence" and discuss whether or not—and, if so, how—the rules of the genre change if both the author *and* the detective or investigator are women. Examples are *Total Recall* (2001) by Sara Paretsky, where private investigator Warshawski inquires into assets stolen during the Holocaust, and Barbara Neely's *Blanche among the Talented Ten* (1995), in which the investigator and protagonist Blanche is an African-American domestic worker without any formal education. The two latter examples show that the genre of crime fiction can be useful for feminists who want to question taboo topics and the elitist, white, middle-class character of the genre.

A detective/investigator is an interpreter of facts and a reader of clues (Ginzburg 1990). She or he is the one who finds the clues and analyzes them. The detective also establishes the links between cause and effect, in line with scientific requirements. Interpretation, or the creation of one single possible narrative, is the privilege and power of the detective. The detective discovers the "truth", and the genre rules normally position her or him outside of the cultural codes in which the characters are embedded. The detective represents the neutral gaze of positive epistemology, and in this sense a critical analysis of the positioning of the detective can promote an important understanding of positionality, including that of the historian. Like the detective, the historian possesses a monopoly on power and interpretation when writing a historical narrative, and it is precisely this interpretative monopoly that the exercise of writing a crime story is exposing as well as subverting.

Another reason why feminist crime fiction is a useful genre as a writing exercise for critical Gender Studies students is that, in customary crime fiction genre plots, the woman is a metaphor for mystery and sexual difference. Gender Studies critically examines the concept of "woman". The new cultural historical approach seeks to analyze the woman as an object and agent of symbolic practices and policies. The woman as the heroine of, for example, revolutionary narratives is called into question by those women who have been left out of the version of the past that has been canonized as History. Throughout my course "Textual Outlaws" the boundaries between exclusion and inclusion are examined: How are these boundaries manifested, and how do (or don't) they change if the detective/investigator/historian is a woman?

The concept of "outlaw", which I included in the title of the course, is helpful when it comes to the description of characters in the writing exercise and their relation to patterns of exclusion/inclusion (Young 1996). Breaking the law is an act that reconfirms the binary opposite of "us" and "them"—those who abide by the law and those who do not. This theme can be spelled out in the course through an analysis of, for example, *Possession* (1990), the genre classic by A. S. Byatt. In this novel the protagonist, marginalized for adhering to historians' principles, steals an unknown archival source from under the nose of the archive worker who is responsible for ensuring that the rules of the historian's profession are adhered to. By doing so, however, the protagonist breaks the "code", opening the way for an autonomous interpretation through which he can establish a new code.

WHY USE CREATIVE WRITING?

The creative writing component is one of the other attractions of this course besides the fact that nearly everybody enjoys reading crime fiction. As the pressure mounts in academia to publish in English, a writing exercise like this can contribute to the improvement of writing skills. An excursion into creative writing creates skills that are transferable to academic writing.

Since the course is taught in English, with students from all over the world, the dividing line between students with native-level proficiency and students who are studying English as a foreign language can be a problem. The course also prioritizes the Anglo-American tradition of crime fiction writing, but luckily we have more and more translated authors who originally did not write in English.

In an educational process taking place in an international environment, creative writing is a site where students' longing for "home" can be manifested (Fortier 2001). When choosing their topics, despite the Anglo-American focus of the literature on theory and practice, students still place the events in their home environments. In this way writing also becomes a reflexive processing of the fact that they are working, studying and living in an environment that differs from their home.

The writing and the style of writing can also enable students to identify utopian scopes of action. They can, for example, use the writing exercise to establish a progressive politics by means of parody, remix and a subversive style of writing. Writing can be used to unveil the "enemy"—often the internal enemy, the merciless logic of which is, among other things, a spiritual legacy of the Cold War, which fits well into the genre of crime fiction.

Feminist teaching in practice—in the dialogue that arises through reflexivity—focuses on understanding rather than passing on bits of knowledge. Students are not empty vessels into which knowledge must be poured. Instead, they have to play an active role in the production of knowledge, and the crime fiction writing exercise which requires that they become authors prompts them to be creative and active and to take responsibility for the unfolding of their stories.

Moreover, during the presentation of stories in class, anxieties and fears associated with academic writing will often surface—anxieties that also hinder creative writing ("I could never write well", "history is just so boring"). But in a reflexive classroom, these anxieties can be discussed and dealt with, and creative writing may even be used to explore, understand and finally overcome such anxieties.

However, even though the required crime story is fictional it does not seem to instil a sense of freedom to the degree I had anticipated. Even though I present the writing exercise as fiction writing, students have often been much more inclined to link the process of the story to a "real" event than I had thought they would. Students often refer to the fact that they have modelled their character "X" on "Z", a concrete person they know. They also tend to illustrate what they want to say by citing or quoting from literature—because this "describes what it was like". Even song lyrics and poetry are used to illustrate the text; in this way they link their narrative with "real" texts.

In terms of the topics and frameworks chosen by the students, violence against women and the suppression of memories related to gender-based violence, which are of central concern to feminist thinking, have figured prominently in several of the students' stories; through the crime fiction plot, they have been able to analyze such aspects using human rights discourse and critical feminist analysis of violence as theoretical frameworks. The taboo theme of sexism, violence and marginalization within the homosexual community has also featured among the topics chosen by students taking my course.

A general conclusion after three years of teaching this course, including the writing exercise, is that it has tended to be relatively difficult for many students to formulate the plot and the theoretical framework for their story. The writing exercise has proved to be particularly problematic for students coming from war and conflict zones. Students from Kosovo, Georgia, Chile, Nepal, etc. may, for example, themselves have experienced traumas, and it has been difficult for them to confront their stories, their memories and their repressed experiences, and this has posed particular challenges for the instructor.

Nevertheless, towards the end of the course, the freedom of interpretation offered to the students-historians as storytellers and detectives appears in a more vigorous form (Benjamin 1970). Historiography appears now as a system of several truths that arise in connection with a specific event, and the student-historian—the writer of history—enters the scene as interpreter within the framework of this multilayered system. Moreover, a community is created between students taking the course and participating in the development of gender-based critical interpretations of crime in literature; by becoming acquainted with each other's stories, the students also acquire a better understanding of the unfolding scripts of our lives.

CONCLUSIONS

The writing exercise which has been the pivot of this chapter ultimately examines—at symbolic levels—the historical development of the concept of cultural citizenship (Stevenson 2003). In the texts written by students, cultural asymmetry, symbolic orders and issues of marginalization and marginality receive new content, and in accordance with Judith Butler's interpretation of performativity (1990), we may even claim that the different and more diverse recollections of the past can establish a present-day reality that is new in certain respects. To approach history telling as performative, as we do in the writing exercise, may contribute to a democratization of history linking it with its audience and potentially providing democracy with a new rhetoric. A changed and more diverse historical perspective can, for example, facilitate an understanding of the norms of the heteronormative desire economy and our ability to change such norms (Sieg 2005), and generally assist in revealing unchanging cultural norms as well as contribute to cultural change.

History as an "unfinished project" with implications for the future is recast in crime fiction that explores historical events. Instead of adhering to the traditional "truth requirements" of historical research, we examine historical possibilities. But when our "past-understandings" are changed in the course of writing and analyzing feminist crime fiction, light is also shed on the ways in which projections of the future are always implied in narratives of the past.

REFERENCES

Benjamin, Walter. 1970. "The Story Teller." In *Illuminations*, 83–110. London: Jonathan Cape.
Butler, Judith. 1990. *Gender Trouble*. New York: Routledge.
Certeau, Michel de. 1984. *The Practice of Everyday Life*. Berkeley: University of California Press.
Fleishman, Suzanne. 1998. "Gender, the Personal, and the Voice of Scholarship: A Viewpoint." *Signs* 23 (4): 975–1016.
Fortier, Anne-Marie. 2001. "'Coming Home', Queer Migrations and Multiple Evocations of Home." *European Journal of Cultural Studies* 4 (4): 405–24.

92   *Andrea Pető*

Ginzburg, Carlo. 1990. "Moretti, Freud, and Sherlock Holmes: Clues and Scientific Method." In *Popular Fiction*, edited by Tony Bennett, 252–76. London: Routledge.
Goldberg, Natalie. 1986. *Writing Down the Bones: Freeing the Writer Within*. Boston: Shambhala.
Grant-Adamson, Lesley. 2003. *Writing Crime Fiction*. Chicago: Contemporary Books.
Heilbrun, Carolyn. 1988. "Keynote Address: Gender and Detective Fiction." In *The Sleuth and the Scholar: Origins, Evolution, and Current Trends in Detective Fiction*, edited by Barbara A. Rader and Howard G. Zettler, 1–11. Westport: Greenwood Press.
Middleton, David and Derek Edwards. 1990. *Collective Remembering*. London: Sage.
Munt, Sally R. 1994. *Murder by the Book? Feminism and the Crime Novel*. London: Routledge.
Nora, Pierre. 1989. "Between Memory and History." *Representations* 26: 7–24.
Pető, Andrea and Berteke Waaldijk. 2011. "Histories and Memories in Feminist Research." In *Theories and Methodologies in Postgraduate Feminist Research: Researching Differently*, edited by Rosemarie Buikema, Gabriele Griffin and Nina Lykke, 74–91. New York: Routledge.
Richardson, Laurel. 1990. *Writing Strategies: Researching Diverse Audiences*. Newbury Park: Sage.
Sieg, Katrin. 2005. "Women in the Fortress Europe: Feminist Crime Fiction as Antifascist Performative." *Differences* 16 (2): 138–66.
Stevenson, Nick. 2003. *Cultural Citizenship: Cosmopolitan Questions*. Maidenhead, Berkshire: Open University Press.
Stuurman, Siep. 2000. "The Canon of the History of Political Thought: Its Critique and a Proposed Alternative." *History and Theory* 39 (2): 147–66.
Young, Alison. 1996. *Imagining Crime*. London: Sage.

Part Two

Learning to Write Differently

6 Six Impossible Things before Breakfast

How I Came across My Research Topic and What Happened Next

Redi Koobak

ONE

> *"Begin at the beginning,"* the King said gravely, *"and go on till you come to the end: then stop."*[1]

Looking aimlessly around the store, I chanced on a notebook that spoke to me. It was a blank lined notebook with hard covers, illustrated with quotations and drawings from Lewis Carroll's Alice books. To tell the truth, I had never read them but had just seen clips from a screen adaptation (which I cannot remember much about) and heard many people praise how cute and fun and deep this children's story was. However, my resentment towards commercial products made with themes from mass-popularized stories slowly began to wear off as I leafed through the notebook. Sure, it looked childishly sweet, but the quotations spoke to me. They spoke to me softly, comfortingly, but also in the kind of demanding and challenging way I needed at that point. I was drawn to how they related to my confusion and uncertainty about my research topic. They made me smile.

It was the last day of my trip to New York. The night before, in a café just around the corner from that store, I had had a rather inspiring, yet also somewhat frustrating, meeting with a Women's and Gender Studies professor who had just recently finished writing a book on the topic I had been determined to write my PhD thesis on. She had spoken passionately about her research, and I had felt that I had no desire to continue with this topic that had been frustrating me for two years (see also Koobak, Chapter 13, this volume). I was intensely inspired by her passion and alarmed by my growing despair about the topic. This meeting became a turning point for me: I was powerfully reminded that the research process can only work if I have passion for the topic, if I find and manage to hold on to that *something* that keeps me going day and night. As the King in the notebook's pages said, I needed to begin at the beginning, and the starting point for me was finding a topic that I would be just as passionate about as this professor was about hers.

I decided that this Alice notebook was to become my research diary for my dissertation. This decision, coupled with the meeting of the night before, was what set things in motion; it pushed me towards looking for a topic I would feel strongly about and guided me on my way through the challenging search process. By chance I had found a structure to follow in a notebook themed around a children's story. It was the quotations scattered around its corners that enabled me to think through important points in developing a research project.

In that moment of feeling frustrated with my old topic and coming across a notebook that contained the questions I needed to ask myself, I also sensed intuitively that I needed a different approach to writing. The unreliability of my memory had always plagued me, leaving me perplexed at how it is possible to "lose" my thoughts, my experiences, my reflections so quickly and so definitively. Starting a research diary in which to record and keep even the smallest ideas and threads of thought seemed like a great idea.

It was not until some time later, however, that I realized I was onto something with my intuition about having to change my approach to writing. Writing can be viewed as a lot more than just recording thoughts—writing actually *is* thinking. By creating and establishing the concept of writing as a method of inquiry, Laurel Richardson (1994, 2000; also Richardson and St. Pierre 2005) has expanded the notion of writing from a mode of "telling" to one of "knowing", a way of discovering and analyzing, thereby providing a powerful critique of traditional writing practices in qualitative research. The concept of writing as a method of inquiry originally emerged out of her frustration with the "boring" style of qualitative studies, which, as she points out, "suffered from acute and chronic passivity: passive-voiced author, passive 'subjects'" since for years scholars had been taught "to silence their own voices and to view themselves as contaminants" (2000, 924, 925), accepting the omniscient voice of science as their own. Following such a mechanistic, static model of writing that fails to take into account the role of the writing itself as a creative and dynamic process results in constructing research accounts that present knowledge claims in a universalizing, authoritative manner, "in the homogenized voice of 'science'" (Richardson and St. Pierre 2005, 960).

Reading Richardson, I needed to remember that "writing is not just a mopping-up activity at the end of a research project" (2000, 923). Writing is so much more: a part of the beginning, the middle and the end, the whole process. I am not thinking properly, or even at all, if I am not writing. This very simple and important notion of writing as a way of knowing and discovering took me a surprisingly long time to figure out. Once I did, it was like magic, as Richardson and St. Pierre note:

Thought happened in the writing. As I wrote, I watched word after word appear on the computer screen—ideas, theories, I had not thought before I wrote them. Sometimes I wrote something so marvellous it startled me. *I doubt I could have thought such a thought by thinking alone.*

—(2005, 970; emphasis in original)

Holding the Alice notebook in my hand, then, on that day in that store in New York, I intuitively knew that writing had to become a part of my everyday existence as a researcher, not as something grand, something that only Real Writers do, but something casual, everyday, as common as thinking itself. This was my beginning: finding passion and writing to think, writing for the purpose of wanting to find something out, something that is not and cannot be known before writing.

TWO

"*Would you tell me, please, which way I ought to go from here?*"
"*That depends a good deal on where you want to get to,*" *said the Cat.*
"*I don't much care where—*" *said Alice.*
"*Then it doesn't matter which way you go,*" *said the Cat.*
"*—so long as I get somewhere,*" *Alice added as an explanation.*
"*Oh, you're sure to do that,*" *said the Cat, "if you only walk long enough.*"

When I began searching for a new research topic that would ultimately speak to me, I was determined to find something that I would be really passionate about. But I had no idea where I wanted to begin or where I wanted to end up. I began critically re-evaluating my interests and hobbies, and soon realized that as a person who has taken more than 5,000 images in less than a year, I must be into photos. So why not research the issues of visual representation? Although at that point I had not fully developed an academic interest in visual culture theory in general or photographic theory in particular, the topic of visual representation fit comfortably with my earlier explorations of theories of the body, subjectivity and sexual difference.

From a seemingly easy decision, several inspiring thoughts emerged. I began reading around theories of photography and visual culture, taking notes and playing with a multitude of approaches. I was intrigued by the self-portraits in the "365 days" group on Flickr, an online photo-sharing website, and used my bafflement about such widespread interest in recording the self through the camera eye as my focus. I tried out cyberethnography as my methodology as it allowed me to position myself as an active participant in the creation of "my field" together with my research "subjects" and to continue exploring my interest in taking photos at the same time.

As my research project was taking shape, I came to regard self-portraits as an important means of looking more closely at and making sense of the relationship between the subject and the representation. Self-portrait photography arguably offers a way of keeping control of one's own representation and can therefore be a potentially empowering means for the subject to see and imagine herself or himself. All the more interestingly, while photography carries with it an apparent realism, self-imaging is also decidedly performative. A self-portrait may be hastily snapped with a mobile phone camera, or it can be a carefully composed and almost theatrical performance for a digital camera lens. It can be forgetfully stored away on a personal computer or proudly shown off in photoblogs and communities on the Internet, but it is often created in a highly self-conscious mode, not necessarily reflecting the "true" self of the person behind the camera. Thus, self-portraits open up space for questions about how subjectivity is negotiated and established as well as how the human body is and can be represented.

In the initial project description that emerged out of these reflections I proposed to analyze digital self-portrait photography as a "technology of embodiment" (A. Jones 2002, 950) and identity production in cyberspace through engaging with the context of these technical and visual environments where identities are formed and negotiated. So, indeed, I had a plethora of great possible research questions lined up, including how gender, race, social class and sexuality are produced and authorized in the minute instances of everyday online/offline praxis related to self-portraits. Yet the more daily self-portraits I looked at in the group and the more self-portraits I took myself and posted online, the more ambivalent I became about the focus of my research. Browsing through hundreds of self-portraits every single day and putting my own self out there soon led me to doubt whether I wanted to participate in what seemed to me to be just a time-consuming "vanity fair". I grew tired of the triviality of the comments and the blandness of hundreds of look-alike snapshots, while also recognizing (and detesting!) in myself a certain amount of envy towards other Flickr users who from my point of view were so much better at taking photos than me thanks to their professional cameras, longer practice and just sheer creativity—all of which I felt I was lacking. I resented the narcissism and self-promotion that was taking place in "my field", and I resented the feelings that my participation in this field created in me. I was yearning to develop a truly feminist research project that would be "contextual, inclusive, experiential, involved, socially relevant" (Nielsen 1990, 6, quoted in Wolf 1996, 35) and was disappointed in the superficiality I found. How could I make my project more meaningful? How could I argue for its social, political, cultural and ethical relevance? How much further did I have to walk to get somewhere meaningful?

THREE

It takes all the running you can do, to keep in the same place.

I continued my opening-up and zooming-in writing exercises with my supervisor. Having written a first draft of the project description did not mean I was all set with the new topic. I had to keep going, keep searching, keep writing through my hesitations and frustrations. I wrote two kinds of papers for my supervisor. The ones that she called opening-up exercises consisted of more or less free writing: writing to get everything out of me, gathering all the inspirations, quotations, pictures, thoughts on things I read and saw and questioned. The next step after discussing these opening-up papers was to try to zoom in on things that seemed especially important; in other words, to pick out points to focus on and write more specifically around those.

Somewhere during this process, I found some reconciliation with my topic with the help of an article by Daniel Rubinstein and Katrina Sluis (2008). They call the "everyday" or "vernacular" photographs on social networking websites such as Flickr "networked snapshots" and emphasize that, because of the abundance of digital images and image-sharing websites, the value of a single photograph is diminished. Their argument enabled me to make sense of my frustrations and intrigued me enough to continue. The repetitious nature of a networked snapshot and its often bland and banal character condition its appearance as a non-object that is often overlooked and thus "camouflaged as a non-political, non-significant and non-ideological site" (Rubinstein and Sluis 2008, 23). Therefore, because the similar and mass-produced vernacular images so often go unnoticed, they appear normative and perpetuate "the notion of the world going about its business in a natural way" and reinforce "the sense of identity and unity which overwhelms differences and distinctions" (24). So it is precisely because of their apparently non-political and non-ideological character that these snapshot self-portraits should be studied.

Yet my negotiations around the topic took me a step further. Rubinstein and Sluis once more got me thinking:

> The self-image of the deprived, the cut-off, the bombed out, does not exist online because the rhetoric of personal photography is anchored in a sense of individual and social identity and the pathos of control over the means of image making. Within the context of the networked snapshot, this means access to the Internet, to electricity and to mobile telephone networks.

—(2008, 24)

The kind of self-reflection and self-promotion featured in the "365 days" group on Flickr is characteristic only of those who possess certain economic and social capital and have the means, i.e. expensive equipment, time and skills, and desire to compete for a certain prestige and ranking in the popularity hierarchy. For example, being featured in "Explored", i.e. the ranking of the most "interesting" photos of the day, which is based on statistics of how many times a photo is viewed, commented on or marked as a favourite, becomes a goal almost to the point of obsession. Thus, trying to make it to "Explored" is turned into a matter of lifestyle, requiring more and more intricate set-ups and tricks to produce the "most interesting" image. Although there are ways to research this phenomenon in a critical way, I could not help but be haunted by guilt: Was I perpetuating social inequalities by choosing to devote my attention to something so "vain" and "trivial" when there are much more important and serious problems to look at? Did my choice of topic have problems in terms of ethics at a more global level?

As I was struggling with my doubts concerning the choice of topic (and this struggle indeed continues), I came across an article, "Mexican Contemporary Photography: Staging Ethnicity and Citizenship" (2004) by Marina Pérez de Mendiola. She writes about a campaign that took place in Mexico before the presidential elections of 1994. In the framework of the election registration programme, people were invited to "ven y tómate la foto" ("come and take a picture of yourself"). Posing for a camera that automatically takes, develops and prints a photograph of the voter was thought to attract the disenfranchised people of Mexico (numbering ten million, mostly indigenous) to the polls. Pérez de Mendiola explains:

> The Partido Institucional Revolucionario (PRI), the party in power from 1928 to 2000, banked on the idea that the portrait, a type of self-representation, taken automatically, would be regarded as self-acting, self-regulating, and as promoting image control: the mechanical eye would capture the image as presence. These devices (the political and the aesthetic ones, as well as the automatic camera) rely on the popular conception of the self-portrait as a less threatening and more empowering means for the subject both to see and imagine him- or herself. The slogan conveys the idea that this spontaneous, mechanical portrait will bring recognition of social integration and civil identity.
>
> —(2004, 126)

What I found interesting in this case was how in a political context self-portraits acquire meanings very different from those of the self-portraits on Flickr or in art galleries and art books. The self-portraits in the Mexican election case are directly connected to ideas about power and change. I was especially intrigued by how this campaign played on the idea that the self-portrait can be empowering in comparison to, say, an automatic picture taken by an official government photographer to establish the voter's identity.

Sure, since the late nineteenth and early twentieth century photographers have often used their cameras as instruments for initiating change. By making problems literally visible, they have tried to convince the world to work towards a solution, to initiate change in the situation. One of the first so-called social reform photographers, Jacob Riis, a Danish-born journalist and author of the immensely popular *How the Other Half Lives* (1890), used photographs to illustrate his arguments about the need to reform slum life in New York at the turn of the twentieth century. Nowadays, there are numerous organizations that believe in the power of photographic storytelling and are committed to using photography in the hope of initiating social change.

Photographic action does not, of course, lead automatically to desired solutions, but photos have often worked well for raising awareness as photography has frequently been accorded special status as "truthfully" recording the world and thus providing unquestionable "evidence" of the need to bring about social change. Another thing is, of course, when those photos that are supposed to initiate social change are taken by the people who need change in their lives and not by outsiders, professional photographers subjecting the "underprivileged" to their camera's gaze. Considering the important questions in photography—Who is taking pictures of whom? Where and how are they shown? For what purpose?—self-portraits should be all the more empowering. But does giving cameras to the "underprivileged" and the "powerless" automatically result in getting more "authentic" images of their situations? Moreover, what does it mean for marginalized and minority groups to participate in self-representation?

Another aspect that troubled me was that, however noble the underlying intentions, the effect of showing the world the "truth" about the inequality that still exists in so many areas can be counterproductive. As Susan Sontag reminds me:

> The vast photographic catalogue of misery and injustice throughout the world has given everyone a certain familiarity with atrocity, making the horrible seem more ordinary—making it appear familiar, remote ("it's only a photograph"), inevitable. At the time of the first photographs of the Nazi camps, there was nothing banal about these images. After thirty years, a saturation point may have been reached. In these last decades, "concerned" photography has done at least as much to deaden conscience as to arouse it.

—(1979, 21)

So could it be that the photographs that might otherwise aspire to initiate social change have actually lost their power to evoke a moral response, to awaken and encourage people to do something about the inequality and atrocities they are called on to "witness"? How does this influence my research?

FOUR

The Caterpillar and Alice looked at each other for some time in silence: at last the Caterpillar took the hookah out of its mouth, and addressed her in a languid, sleepy voice.

"Who are you?" said the Caterpillar.

This was not an encouraging opening for a conversation. Alice replied, rather shyly, "I—I hardly know, sir, just at present—at least I know who I was when I got up this morning, but I think I must have been changed several times since then."

"What do you mean by that?" said the Caterpillar sternly. "Explain yourself!"

"I can't explain myself, I'm afraid, sir," said Alice, "because I'm not myself, you see."

Who am I now here? Where am I now? After all these wanderings and detours, how do I position myself in relation to my research? At this point, my PhD project has found its shape in three little case studies that all speak to my desire to look at the relationship between the real and the representation, in particular how the subject relates to and is established by (self-)representation. I take self-portrait photography as a keyword and intend to explore a kind of scale or gradation of self-representation. I am aware of overlaps between the three examples, and although they defy neat categorization, some tentative, or imaginary if you wish, lines can be drawn between them. These three examples are

1) the "realistic"—the so-called social change photography that seems to assume that greater visibility of marginalized/underprivileged groups leads to an increase in their power (especially if it is they themselves who are taking pictures of their situations);
2) the "in-between"—the "365 days" group on Flickr, which provides an example of daily documentation of selves with a certain amount of theatricality and performance (from quick snapshots to highly stylized professional photographs); and
3) the "artistic"—self-portraits taken by artists and exhibited as artwork. They seem to be the extreme form of self-conscious performance of selves and often problematize notions of the body, sex/gender, race, class and sexuality.

What has enabled me to weave these various cases together is inspiration from Peggy Phelan's book *Unmarked: The Politics of Performance*. Phelan brings up the question of visibility and invisibility and looks at the implicit assumptions of the so-called progressives and conservatives about the connection between representational visibility and (political) power:

Representation follows two laws: it always conveys more than it intends; and it is never totalising. The "excess" meaning conveyed by representation creates a supplement that makes multiple and resistant readings possible. Despite this excess, representation produces ruptures and gaps; it fails to reproduce the real exactly. Precisely because of representation's supplemental excess and its failure to be totalising, close readings of the logic of representation can produce psychic resistance and, possibly, political change. (Although rarely in the linear cause-effect way cultural critics on the Left and Right often assume.)

—(1993, 7)

What Phelan is trying to do, then, is to argue that "the binary between the power of visibility and the impotency of invisibility is falsifying" (6). She claims that power can be found in remaining unmarked, unspoken and unseen and calls for a more nuanced account of the power of visibility. So how does this translate into my little case studies? My examples definitely complicate the question of visibility and invisibility, which can thus serve as a kind of underlying theme that connects all these examples of visual (self-) representation. Since I have not decided on the exact materials I will be looking at for each of the case studies, I am continuously refining my focus.

Furthermore, I am always troubled by the question of positioning the self which is fundamental to any research, especially when it claims to be feminist. Clearly, my knowledge is situated, embodied and partial, and I am positioned socially, culturally, institutionally and geopolitically, which means that I need to confront and consider the politics of location very carefully. But how do I meaningfully problematize my privileged position as a researcher? How do I engage with the politics and ethics of my project? How do I take into account the position from which I am speaking? As Diane Wolf (1996, 35) points out, it has become all too common just to situate oneself instead of reflecting on broader questions of epistemology, the politics of research and writing. What does positioning myself come to mean in this context, then? What does positioning "others" mean?

FIVE

> *"How am I to get in?" asked Alice again, in a louder tone.*
> *"Are you to get in at all?" said the Footman. "That's the first question, you know."*

Sometimes getting access to the field in a useful as well as ethically responsible and considerate way seems the hardest part of conducting research. While I am troubled by my lack of knowledge as to how exactly I am to gain access to my "informants" and how I am to make myself "visible" as a researcher (and what that will really give me), I am equally wary of treating "access" as the key to a magical, neat world with clear, fixed borders and with clear, neat answers just lying around there, waiting to be discovered. Considering a cyberethnographic approach to the "365 days" group, does my being on Flickr and posting daily photos establish my insider position? Does it mean "going native"? What are other possibilities for immersing myself in the field? Furthermore, how do I define my field? Is it one, or is it three? How are the three case studies different from one another? Moreover, what about similarities between them? As Vered Amit points out:

> The notion of immersion implies that the "field" that ethnographers enter exists as an independently bounded set of relationships and activities that is autonomous of the fieldwork through which it is discovered. Yet in a world of infinite interconnections and overlapping contexts, the ethnographic field cannot simply exist, awaiting discovery. It has to be laboriously constructed, pulled apart from all the other possibilities for contextualization to which its constituent relationships and connections could also be referred.
>
> —(2000, 6)

I began the construction of my "fields" by writing my way into what I expect to encounter at various moments during my research and how I view the inevitable tension between what I think I should do in the field "out there" and what is bound to happen unexpectedly, beyond my control.

I started with exploring my social change photography case study, which takes me directly to the heart of the relations between (in)visibility, agency and power. Social change photography projects combine photography with grassroots social action, teaching marginalized groups how to use cameras with the intention of gaining insight into how they conceptualize their circumstances. As a form of community consultation and action, participatory photography projects often try to bring the perspectives of those who lead lives that are different from those of the people traditionally in control of the means for imaging the world directly into the policy-making process. It is also a response to issues raised over the authorship of representation of communities.

One specific social change photography project that has caught my attention is called ph15. It is a space created by a group of photographers in Ciudad Oculta ("Hidden City"), one of the poorest neighbourhoods in Buenos Aires, Argentina, where a group of kids from the neighbourhood are being taught and encouraged to express their personal views through the use of photography. Although I am not planning to swing into a full ethnography of ph15, I am adopting an ethnographic attitude towards all of my case studies as part of my methodology. By an ethnographic attitude, I mean the constant process of familiarizing myself with the unfamiliar and defamiliarizing the familiar, making the everyday strange and the strange everyday. I attempt to do the scaling and scoping of the different contexts I encounter in a mode of critical openness, keeping in mind that researchers tend to need a mixture of things. Sometimes methodologies that others have developed and put together will do the job; at other times these are just not good enough. Furthermore, methodologies are not fixed; they can get better with time or turn out to be altogether useless at any moment.

I want to consider a more creative approach to communicating and working with the children taking part in ph15, an approach reminiscent of participatory action research. As this photography project itself seems like an institutionalized form of participatory action research, using creative methods to promote critical self-reflexivity about the lived experiences of the participants, how can I as a feminist researcher interested in (in)visibility, agency and self-representation involve these children in my research in the most empowering and fair way? Does that mean I have to use the *same* (or at least similar) critical and creative tools as the teachers at ph15? Do I have to be *more* creative, *more* empowering? How can I possibly do *more* than the ph15 project is already doing for them? What would be my point of entry? What difference would it make to my research, considering the way in which I have set it up, if I were to actually go and experience a tiny fraction of the everyday life at ph15 rather than browse the Web for material that is put "out there"? How do I deal with my own baggage? My possibly imperialist vantage point? I am plagued by all sorts of concerns and insecurities.

I am drawn to how promising the feminist participatory action research sounds. I am attracted by how it attempts to act as a vehicle for change, democratizing the research process and pushing research to be accountable to the communities most affected by it. But I am also worried about how "participation" is sometimes overused. Most problematic are certain kinds of research practices which in the name of participation "mask realities of tokenism, reinforce social hierarchies, emphasize consensus, and reproduce the dominant hegemonic agenda" (Cahill 2007, 269). In light of these concerns, how does ph15 look as a participatory, empowering project? What does empowerment mean in this particular context? How do I disentangle the notion of empowerment from its history, "where the term was especially overused with regard to communities of colour, and young people of colour in particular, who were often simultaneously identified as powerless and threatening" (274)? In the end, who is empowering whom and for what purpose? What does it mean to be empowered, to feel empowered? Does it equate to feeling powerful (Cruikshank 1994)? In light of these questions, how does my desire to be more inclusive and empowering look? How do I even begin to conceptualize these complexities?

Moreover, when considering the immediate mental picture I have of what it might mean to go into the field "out there", I am struck by how similar it looks to the countless romanticized accounts of ethnographers going into the field, which is located somewhere "away", which is strange, distant and exotic, for which you might have to travel across the globe to get to and attempt to become (partly) part of. A field that is not "home", that is clearly separated from the protective cocoon of academia. A field that threatens to implode under the weight of the supposed answers lying around and waiting for the ethnographer to discover them. Just pack your bags and go. Is that when the fieldwork *really* starts? When does it end? Does it ever end? Has it already begun? How do I avoid regarding the categories of home and away, us and them, self and other, as static and fixed? How do I render them flexible, shifting, messy in the most productive way? How do I capture the ground on which I stand, my politics of location?

SIX

> *"There's no use trying,"* Alice said, *"One* can't *believe impossible things."*
>
> *"I daresay you haven't had much practice,"* said the Queen.
>
> *"When I was your age, I always did it for half-an-hour a day.*
>
> *Why, sometimes I've believed as many as six impossible things before breakfast."*

The journey through my messy thoughts towards my dissertation topic has come to a point where I want to open up room for the "impossible". At any point in research, space should be given to imagine the impossible, the what ifs, the elusive, the unbelievable, the fluid, the unfixed, the ambiguous places that open up your imagination and also reveal possible biases. The six impossible things can thus be, simply put, things that ought to be impossible if the so-called conventional assumptions were correct. So going into the looking-glass world and trying to imagine these impossible things as being possible would be an exercise in uncovering and thinking through the common-sense assumptions that lurk behind words and statements. Such an exercise could be viewed as something enabling, something that pushes you to critically review your thoughts, assumptions and prejudices.

Thinking about my project, I want to imagine a new DSLR camera and a course in photography to develop my photographic skills, all the books by my favourite photographer Francesca Woodman and a visit to a museum or gallery that exhibits her self-portraits, a thorough knowledge of feminist art history and art criticism, an overview of projects that have used self-portraits as an agent for social change . . . This sounds rather like a wish list and quite an achievable one at that. But considering the extent to which keeping this kind of wish list has helped me to move forward with the project, I want to continue to train myself to believe in "six impossible things before breakfast".

AFTERTHOUGHT ON "WRITING-STORIES"

"Six impossible things before breakfast" in my title refers to a "writing-story" (Richardson 1995) that I wrote as a way of "arriving at" and "inhabiting" my PhD research topic. Even though in the end I abandoned two of the case studies that came out of this quest and elaborated on just one (see also Koobak and Thapar-Björkert, Chapter 3, this volume), writing in this format was an important step forward for me. The six parts of my writing-story, which at the time of writing seemed utterly impossible, evolved into a project that kept shifting and surprising me, yet the six Alice quotations always remained in place, always reminding me of the important steps in research. They helped me remember the difficulties of starting off and how crucial it is to keep going, to keep asking myself the same questions over and over again to make sure I stay on track. They helped me not to forget to ask myself how I position myself and my topic in a larger context, how I gain access to the field and how I should always imagine and strive for the impossible.

Richardson (1995) notes that "writing-stories", or stories of how our texts are constructed, emerge out of this context of becoming, and she suggests that we regard writing as a method of inquiry. Also, these narratives that extend reflexivity in research to the study of our writing practices draw on autoethnographic methods that attempt to connect the personal to the cultural, placing the self in the social context (Ellis and Bochner 2000; Reed-Danahay 1997). As Stacy Holman Jones highlights:

> Autoethnography works to hold self and culture together, albeit not in equilibrium or stasis. Autoethnography writes a world in a state of flux and movement—between story and context, writer and reader, crisis and denouement. It creates charged moments of clarity, connection, and change.
>
> —(2005, 764)

The lure of autoethnography thus lies in the fact that it attempts to incorporate the "I" of the writer into a commentary on the world without making any grand scientific or totalizing claims about it but remaining uncertain, tentative and speculative, and hence ultimately also more honest. Autoethnographers "ask their readers to feel the truth of their stories and to become coparticipants, engaging the storyline morally, emotionally, aesthetically, and intellectually" (Ellis and Bochner 2000, 745).

Similarly to autoethnographic accounts, writing-stories are highly personalized and revealing texts that enable us to situate our writing in other parts of our life and to show "how contexts, social interactions, critiques, review processes, friendships, academic settings, departmental politics, embodiedness, and so on have affected the construction of the text" (Richardson 1995, 191). These accounts of our contexts and pretexts for writing evoke new questions about ourselves and our subject, open up new points of entry to our field and serve as a reminder that our texts are grounded and rhizomatic. In her *Fields of Play: Constructing an Academic Life*, Richardson retrospectively contextualizes ten years of her sociological work in order to raise questions about "finding or creating spaces that support our writing so we can keep writing, developing a care for the self, despite conflict and marginalization" (1997, 5). She shows how writing-stories alert us to the consequences that our writing can have and underlines the poignancy of ethnographic representation through her personal narratives. While her writing-stories were written after she wrote the texts that she is contemplating, she also points out that writing-stories can be useful for thinking through and writing about research experience, or even "as alternative or supplement to the traditional methods chapter" (2000, 932). Or, as St. Pierre suggests, "one might treat one's writing about a project as additional data, another fold in the research process" (2002, 58).

What makes writing-stories attractive, then, is the fact that they offer critical reflexivity about the writing self in different contexts as a valuable creative analytical practice. Reflexivity is not something that happens and should be kept separate from the research process, just as writing is a method of inquiry. Writing and reflexivity go hand in hand. Being reflexive strengthens the research. Inspired by Richardson and St. Pierre, I have come to realize that thought happens in its most vigorous form during the process of writing. The static model of writing, favoured in the Anglo-American academic context, that I practised and polished for years, first as a student and later as a lecturer at the Department of English Language and Literature at the University of Tartu, Estonia, forced me to think through all my points before writing them down and in many ways froze creativity into a rigid frame, often creating a writer's block that took days to overcome. I am enchanted by the simplicity of the thought that writing can in fact be an empowering methodology.

Through writing this "writing-story" I became more aware of my underlying worries about the rigidity of academic writing forms and styles and the loss of the "I" that I had implicitly carried with me. I was striving for more creativity, for a more personal voice as I came to acknowledge that the illusion of an omniscient and omnipotent epistemologist can no longer be sustained. I rejected the sense that the researcher is an innocent bystander, a neutral someone who just happens to be reporting on a certain topic, going out of her way to cite all the important knowers in the field to lend support to her arguments and protect herself against potential criticism.

The lessons I learned cannot and should not be erased. The writing practices polished over years are crystallized within me, and all I could do was to unlearn their stiffness and break their apparently symmetrical and ordered form. I attempted to invent them anew. I wanted to breathe new life into my texts by making myself and my research subjects visible, by expanding the notion of academic writing and what it means for me, and by experimenting with form and style, with voice and the process of writing.

Unlearning the learned without complete erasure requires a break, a rupture, a disruption, often deliberate and sometimes rehearsed multiple times in the head before materializing it on paper. At the risk of sounding

ormative, I want to claim that self-reflexivity should be developed and valued in qualitative research as part of the research process. Most important, it should involve being reflexive about one's developing theories, research dilemmas, biases and vulnerabilities, attempting to find a personal voice that is at once powerful, sensitive and also vulnerable. Furthermore, Audrey M. Kleinsasser (2000, 158) thinks of reflexivity in the context of writing-to-learn, making the familiar strange. She quotes Lynn Worsham to explain:

> Our emphasis should shift from the notion of writing as a mode of learning to that of writing as a strategy, without tactics or techniques, whose progress yields "unlearning." This result does not mean that writing produces ignorance; rather, it produces a sense of defamiliarization vis-à-vis unquestioned forms of knowledge. Writing would no longer function primarily as an agency in the articulation of knowledge and redistribution of power; instead, it would become an indispensable agency for making the world strange and infinitely various.
>
> —(1991, 101)

In light of this, unlearning my previous writing practices, always imagining otherwise, was a way for me to learn to make my biases and vulnerabilities, my thinking, visible. Unlearning became a way of learning. Yearning for a break, a rupture, a disruption, I offer my writing-story about my search for a PhD research topic as an example of how an unfinished collection of thoughts, inspirations, references and uncertainties can provide a way to open up creative thought and make room for a methodology that eventually emerges almost by itself, unplanned, uninvited, but very welcome.

NOTE

1. In this chapter, all the quotations in italics that mark different sections are from my research diary, which I wrote down in a notebook that includes drawings and quotations from Lewis Carroll's *Alice's Adventures in Wonderland* (1865) and *Through the Looking Glass and What Alice Found There* (1872).

REFERENCES

Amit, Vered. 2000. *Constructing the Field: Ethnographic Fieldwork in the Contemporary World*. London: Routledge.
Cahill, Caitlin. 2007. "The Personal Is Political: Developing New Subjectivities through Participatory Action Research." *Gender, Place and Culture* 14: 267–92.
Cruikshank, Barbara. 1994. "The Will to Empower: Technologies of Citizenship and the War on Poverty." *Socialist Review* 23: 29–55.
Ellis, Carolyn and Arthur Bochner. 2000. "Autoethnography, Personal Narrative, Reflexivity: Researcher as Subject." In *The Sage Handbook of Qualitative Research*, edited by Norman K. Denzin and Yvonna S. Lincoln, 733–68. Thousand Oaks: Sage.

Jones, Amelia. 2002. "The 'Eternal Return': Self-Portrait Photography as a Technology of Embodiment." *Signs* 27 (4): 947–78.
Jones, Stacy Holman. 2005. "Autoethnography: Making the Personal Political." In *The Sage Handbook of Qualitative Research* (3rd ed.), edited by Norman K. Denzin and Yvonna S. Lincoln, 763–91. Thousand Oaks: Sage.
Kleinsasser, Audrey M. 2000. "Researchers, Reflexivity, and Good Data: Writing to Unlearn." *Theory into Practice* 39 (3): 155–62.
Pérez de Mendiola, Marina. 2004. "Mexican Contemporary Photography: Staging Ethnicity and Citizenship." *Boundary 2* 31(3): 125–53.
Phelan, Peggy. 1993. *Unmarked: The Politics of Performance*. Florence, KY: Routledge.
Reed-Danahay, Deborah. 1997. *Auto/Ethnography: Rewriting the Self and the Social*. Oxford: Berg.
Richardson, Laurel. 1994. "Writing: A Method of Inquiry." In *The Handbook of Qualitative Research*, edited by Norman K. Denzin and Yvonna S. Lincoln, 516–29. Thousand Oaks: Sage.
Richardson, Laurel. 1995. "Writing-Stories: Co-authoring 'The Sea Monster', a Writing Story." *Qualitative Inquiry* 1: 189–203.
Richardson, Laurel. 1997. *Fields of Play: Constructing an Academic Life*. New Brunswick: Rutgers University Press.
Richardson, Laurel. 2000. "Writing: A Method of Inquiry." In *The Handbook of Qualitative Research* (2nd ed.), edited by Norman K. Denzin and Yvonna S. Lincoln, 923–49. Thousand Oaks: Sage.
Richardson, Laurel and Elizabeth Adams St. Pierre. 2005. "Writing: A Method of Inquiry." In *The Sage Handbook of Qualitative Research* (3rd ed.), edited by Norman K. Denzin and Yvonna S. Lincoln, 959–78. Thousand Oaks: Sage.
Rubinstein, Daniel and Katrina Sluis. 2008. "A Life More Photographic." *Photographies* 1 (1): 9–28.
Sontag, Susan. 1979. *On Photography*. London: Penguin Books.
St. Pierre, Elizabeth Adams. 2002. "Circling the Text: Nomadic Writing Practices." In *The Qualitative Inquiry Reader*, edited by Norman K. Denzin and Yvonna S. Lincoln, 51–70. Thousand Oaks: Sage.
Wolf, Diane L. 1996. "Situating Feminist Dilemmas in Fieldwork." In *Feminist Dilemmas in Fieldwork* (pp. 1–55), edited by Diane L. Wolf . Boulder, CO: Westview Press.
Worsham, Lynn. 1991. "Writing against Writing: The Predicament of *Écriture Feminine* in Composition Studies." In *Contending with Words: Composition and Rhetoric in the Postmodern Age*, edited by Patricia Harking and John Schilb, 82–104. New York: Modern Language Association of America.

7 The Infinite Resources for Writing

Sissel Lie

Serendipity, the effect by which one accidentally discovers something fortunate while looking for something else entirely, becomes a special form of chance in relation to the creative process. Derived from *Serendip*, the old Persian name for Sri Lanka, the word was coined by the English author and art historian Horace Walpole in 1754 in a letter he wrote to a friend. Walpole's original definition of "serendipity" emphasizes the "sagacity" of being able to link together apparently unimportant facts to reach an important conclusion. Serendipity is a major component of scientific discoveries and inventions, where a prepared and open mind can achieve what seem to be almost accidental breakthroughs in fields of scientific specialization.

For me, the word "serendipity" implies the use of the resources we have for thinking and writing. Ideas come from a combination of knowledge, information, availability, attention and readiness; they depend on situations and coincidences. They might come from totally unexpected inspirations. Perhaps the most striking example is what happened to me on a visit to a castle in France. At the time I was working on the memoirs of a French princess. We were invited to have a glass of champagne with the host and hostess of the castle. When I came into the room, I went straight towards a painting at the far end of the room, saying, "I know her," but I did not realize who she was. "Oh, do you know Mlle de Montpensier?" It was an unknown painting of my princess from her youth, and this sweet portrait explained a lot to me about her many-sided personality and helped me in my writing about her text. Thus an unknown painting can be the start of a writing process, be it in a castle or in a book, and totally unexpected.

This is also serendipity: you are available and attentive, and by strange coincidences you happen to meet people or find inspirations just when you need them to be able to go on with your writing project. You do not need to know everything about the subject you want to explore, but to reach this point of serendipity you have to start the thinking process, and a very effective way of starting this process is to begin writing.

Surprisingly, negative reactions and opposition to people, events, books or ideas can lead to interesting questions and insights. The capacity to explore negative reactions is an important part of creative thinking and writing. For years I had this strange preoccupation with Mlle de Montpensier, cousin of the Sun King. I wrote a short story about her and several academic articles, but she continued to haunt me. In the end I had to write a novel; this meant going on writing until I found out what she wanted to confront me with, something that I had used so much energy to repress. It worked, and all of a sudden, at the end of the novel, I started writing about the problems we had in common. Once that was done, the haunting ended, and she could leave me for good.

THE ALMOST INAUDIBLE VOICES

So what do I mean by the infinity of our resources? The French author and professor of English literature Hélène Cixous writes in *Coming to Writing* (1991) that we all have a treasure chest inside us. She is preoccupied with writing the body, and the body writing, and underlines the close relationship between her poetic kind of writing and the unconscious. The text, she says, is always a translation by the unconscious of your experiences and knowledge. I want to add that all our knowledge, experiences, feelings, senses, engagement, curiosity and stamina participate in the writing process. They constitute resources for our thinking. Let us be written, says Cixous, talking about literary texts, and she recommends a kind of active passivity while letting the text come forth from the unconscious. Is thinking not more than we think? Writing academic texts is different; we question our material and have results we want to transmit to our readers. To establish communication is important. Still, in order to think, we need to make contact with all our resources.

I once read in a guidebook for academic writing that "we" should be used only by kings and pregnant women. In the natural sciences "we" is often the consensual "we", which is not what I seek. In early Gender Studies, "we" wiped out all differences among women and between them and the writer (see also Lie, Chapter 8, this volume). What I want to do is to discover the resources of writing with you. So let us look at what enables us to write better texts. For one, we have to believe in our hunches, our *idées fixes* and the almost inaudible voices inside us; take the opportunity to explore them; and be confident that they are interesting to others. Cixous says to "dare what you don't dare" (1993, 40).

Do not all the choices we make, all the questions we ask in our material, have something to do with ourselves, even when we do not see this at once? This does not mean that we should fill our academic texts with everyday problems, but it does mean that we need all our mental resources to write. A text where the writer is too preoccupied with him or herself is a tiresome journey for the reader, but there are many ways to write oneself into a text. Engagement, making something important known to the reader, or wonder that springs from a personal concern with the questions we ask will give the text a voice and make it more interesting to read. They bring us into the text without introducing our private lives per se. If we take ourselves and the exploration of our questions seriously, this inspires our readers.

It may happen that reason controls us too much and hinders us in our thinking. We have infinite resources to help us think, not only our reason, and sometimes we have to "walk into the dark", as Cixous says in *Three Steps on the Ladder of Writing* (1993). So let chaos reign, and be confident that there is a way out. When I feel panicked and my head does not contain a single intelligent thought, it helps to write down any small idea and try to develop it, or to ask myself: Has anybody written something concerning my topic that I can develop? Even if the first ideas seem too simpleminded, they may develop into something more interesting, especially if I discuss what I have written with somebody else, a helpful colleague or friend.

My reason brings order to chaos, but before we can put anything in order, we have to have something to arrange. Famous researchers often discover their best ideas through intuitive leaps in the thinking process. They wake up one morning and know the solution to their problems, or they write poems to open themselves up to new thoughts. Research in the field of writing sometimes talks about BBB (bed, breakfast, bus) solutions—ideas that come up when we are not writing. The more we let ourselves be engaged by the writing, the more we activate our whole potential to think. And the thinking goes on in us, even when we are concentrating on jogging or singing or doing the dishes. Little by little we can open up to the almost inaudible voices in us and make contact with these resources to think. Dreams, impulses, slips of the tongue and *idées fixes*—do you have the tendency to forget them as soon as they appear? If we write them down, they can constitute banks of ideas for us. Free writing can be a way to hear these voices. You write randomly, spontaneously, whatever comes into your head, or try to develop, without censoring, a concept, a topic. And do not worry about punctuation and orthography or the choice of words when you free write. You will have time to worry about this later.

Free writing can help us use these myriad resources. It can help us sort out problems, get ideas when we are stuck. You cannot always use the sentences or keywords from your free writing in your final draft, however. The academic genre in your field might have very specific requirements, while in your free writing you are talking to yourself, and this is not always comprehensible to others. Free writing is used to help you think. Afterwards you can rewrite to be sure that your text communicates with your readers. But during the whole writing process you can use free writing to clarify or develop points you need to reflect on.

If free writing does not help your thinking, why not do something else for a while: listen to music, shoo out the crocodiles from under the bed, eat chocolate? To get the body in motion is a good idea. The only inconvenience is that when you are jogging or dancing you are unable to write down the ideas that pop up. I desperately repeat them until I get to pen and paper or my computer.

Are you also one of those who write with lipstick on a paper napkin to safeguard sudden ideas? If you do not write them down, you are sure to forget them. When you have an assignment, start at once while the ideas float by. To be able to do so, keep a notebook with you at all times.

CONSCIOUS USE OF TIME AND SPACE

Thinking is a long and slow process; most of us need lots of time. How do you organize your day to liberate time for writing? When do you think clearly: in the morning, in the evening? Some do not think until after 10:00 in the morning; some get up at 4:00 in the morning to write. Where do you think the best? Some like to write in cafés, others at the end of the world in absolute silence. The writers must create the best possible time and space for themselves, prioritize themselves and their writing during some periods and be in the writing-thinking process twenty-four hours a day. Lovers, partners and families then cope for themselves and step aside for the writer's need for concentration. I have periods when I write notes all the time but also periods when I keep my notebook far away. I become aloof when I am pregnant with a text; it is with me every moment, and I want to be absorbed by the text, not to be interrupted, not to meet the expectations of others who want me to care for them or solve everyday problems and practical questions. This is when the text grows and expands. I start to write freely about a concept, an idea, then become more focused on what I want to write about. If I have to cut the contact with the writing project too often, the project may become less and less important and in the end does not seem interesting any more.

THE FASCINATIONS OF THE MATERIAL

It is necessary to begin writing about the material as soon as possible. Where does this strong resistance to starting with the analysis of the material come from; are we afraid of not being able to use it adequately? That it will resist our efforts to explore it? The material contributes to our questions, as well as to the answers. We may ask: Which question is this material an answer to? I do not ask the same questions of a Renaissance poem comparing a young woman to a rose that will soon wither and of a short story focusing on the technical progress at the beginning of the twentieth century. The questions will also change with the readers I have in mind. Thus, we must not only begin thinking about the material but also ask ourselves if we started out with the right questions. Then we will discover if we have too much material, or too little, or just the amount we need.

Why did you choose to do research on this particular subject, with this material; what is so fascinating about it? Can you write to someone who is not a colleague about it, or explain it to your cat? Sometimes it is due

⸱ a lack of concentration when you have the feeling of gliding across the urface of your material with no grip on it. Describe it in detail or discuss with someone; write about it, again and again. When we are stuck, we an also remind ourselves that the text we are about to write is probably ɪot the last thing we will write on the subject, and that to write the ultimate ɛxt is not the aim when all we want is to engage in a dialogue with other ɔholars and texts.

The material you have and the knowledge you gain can be used in dif- ɛrent genres. The world outside of academia needs to know what you have ɔund out: write essays; write in newspapers. The exercise will spread the ɪessage and make your writing more fluent.

⸱HE GENRE AS A HELPING HAND

ɪs we know, chaos can be creative, even if it makes us panic. Sometimes, ᴠhen we are stuck in chaos while writing, it helps to check what the genre ⸱emands from us. A genre is not necessarily a straightjacket. If you have ɔ write in a very structured genre, this does not prevent you from writing ɪore freely in the margins or anywhere, but the genre can help us think at ɪe beginning when we are struggling to find out what we are going to write. ɪre experiments with the genre encouraged or possible in your field? Scien- ɪfic fields may be looking for new ideas, while they are very conservative ᴠhen it comes to genre. Do we need new forms for new thoughts? If you ɪhoose to change the genre, explain to yourself why you want to do so. Are ɔu sure to get your questions and answers across? Can you find a reader to ɪelp you write in a new way or model articles that inspire you?

If we are writing articles, the journals to which we will send them usually ⸱ffer a detailed description of what they want the article to look like. As ɪifferent academic cultures do not produce the same kinds of writing, it is ᴠorthwhile finding out what we must do to have our article or dissertation ɪccepted. We look for models, ponder on how they write. Can we copy their ᴠay of organizing the text? If we do not feel helped by the genre or models, ⸱ut obstructed, perhaps we should continue the free writing longer before ᴠe adapt to stricter rules.

The writing process is like a spiral; we write, read, revise and write again. ᴖhis way of writing is laborious as it demands a lot of rewriting, but who ɪaid it was easy to think new thoughts? What encourages your thinking? ᴵ write sketches on the computer, print them out, correct them and write ɪore in the margins and between the lines, add these revisions to my text, ⸱rint it out on paper again . . . and go on like this until I feel sorry for the ɔrests that give me the paper and have nothing more to add when I re-read ɪhe text. The important thing is not whether I write only on the computer or ⸱nly on paper, or use both, but the rhythm between different writing moods ɪnd modes.

Our text can be seen as a chest of drawers or a patchwork quilt. We begin writing where we like and structure the text on the way, but we do need an overview even at the beginning. When you start, avoid thinking about what you are writing as huge and insurmountable; start with smaller portions. The introduction is a guide for the reader, and it is wise to write the final version once you know what you have written—that is, at the end. It is clarifying, though, to think about the introduction, make notes for it and write preliminary versions during the whole writing process (see also Nina Lykke's reflections on introductions, Chapter 9, this volume). Similarly, it is useful to be preparing the conclusion during the course of the writing.

We can work everywhere on a quilt at the same time. What about starting to work on our text at once, even if we have only very vague ideas about what we will be doing, and write at least half an hour every day? Where do we have something to say just now? We go on from there and put all the bits and pieces of texts in the different drawers of a virtual chest, which might have the names of chapters or of main questions. And remember: the names on the drawers can always be changed!

THE STYLE AS YOUR SIGNATURE

It is not only free writing that helps us think. The style is our signature. Examples, images, comparisons and repetitions are ways of explaining to ourselves and the readers what it is all about. Good examples and images make the text more enjoyable for the reader and easier to assimilate. Sometimes it happens that an image sticks in our mind, and we forget what it was meant to illustrate. I remember a carousel which was an example in the explanation of a mathematical problem years ago, but I do not remember the problem.

There is a convention in academic writing that objective language will convey the truth; a researcher must avoid creative use of language and rhetorical devices. But often, without realizing it, we use literary devices in seemingly very "objective" texts—repetitions, oppositions, comparisons and metaphors. Repetition can help to create cohesion in the text and remind the reader of its key concepts. It can also be a rhetorical device to insist on something important or to give a rhythm to the text. We need comparisons and images when we use the known to understand the unknown, and the concrete to understand the abstract.

The metaphors used in academic texts may be clichés which have lost most of their power to create mental images in the reader. We write about "steps in a process", but no one sees a staircase with people going up and down. We may tell our readers that we are taking them on a voyage, but no one thinks of planes or ships. When we find well-known images in the text, they create complicity between the text and the reader, and without realizing it, we open up to what the text has to communicate. Thus we need these kinds of clichés in academic texts; researchers take us on journeys, and the research process may be described step by step. The clichés link the texts to the reality the images are pointing towards, in a way that makes the text richer and easier to understand even if we translate them without even realizing that they are images; thus we should not be afraid of being banal.

New images and comparisons create new rooms in our understanding, as in the French poet Paul Éluard's description "The earth is blue like an orange".[1] Sometimes, though, the writer does not really succeed in awakening the right associations, as in a newspaper headline such as "Frozen Salmon Opens Doors". We might fear that creative language in academic texts will make the reader stray off in surprising directions, with the text becoming too multifaceted and losing the ability to focus the reader's associations, but images can also be the starting point of a productive new language. Sigmund Freud's psychoanalytic theories are examples of the importance of images— just think about the richness of a concept like the Oedipus complex.

We use descriptions in academic texts, but being too expressive is risky. In *Three Cups of Tea*, a non-fiction story subtitled *One Man's Mission to Promote Peace . . . One School at a Time*, we find the following description: "Gasherbrum, Broad Peak, Mitre Peak, Muztagh Tower—these ice-sheathed giants, naked in the embrace of unfiltered sunlight, burned like bonfires" (Mortenson and Relin 2006, 18). Here we have mountains seen as ice-clad giants in an erotic embrace with burning sunlight, exploding like bonfires, all in the same sentence; too much is too much! There are even stricter limits to how creative the language of an academic text can be. We often have a feeling for what kinds of literary devices work in an academic text and where the limits to experimentation are. However, academic genres may allow more possibilities than we actually explore. This does not mean that we need complicated language, which does not make a text more serious or interesting, even if we all know colleagues who think complications are a sign of cleverness. New thoughts may be difficult to understand, but they can become part of our general culture once we have understood and integrated them.

Sometimes we might also consider whether a more succinct text is preferable. Where can we cut? What about the sentences—have they become breathing exercises, and is it a good idea to read the text aloud? Have you written in a way that felt natural to you? In around the year 1000, male Japanese authors wrote intricate literary texts copying ancient Chinese writings. Women at the court, who had the leisure to write less serious texts, like journals and novels, used a language close to how they spoke. Their books are still alive and read, like Murasaki Shikibu's novel *Tale of Genji*,[2] while their male colleagues' works are lost in oblivion.

THE DIALOGUE WITH OTHER TEXTS

Many of us have experienced the pleasure of coming upon a book that talks to us about what we need at exactly that moment. We find a text that resembles the texts we would like to write; it inspires or provokes. Does it invite us into a dialogue? Do we want to go on exploring its questions or our difficulties with them? Our own text is written into a network of texts in dialogue with each other. It is important to find the texts that help us think more and better. There we find methods, theories, concepts. They help us structure and reflect on our own text. Citations can be the starting point for our own thoughts, especially useful when we are stuck. But we also know that we can be invaded by a book, good or bad, unable to free ourselves from it. For many fiction writers this is one of the reasons they stop reading at a certain point in the writing process.

Other texts also contain useful references, and sometimes surprising ideas pop up. I wrote an article on Samuel Beckett's play *Happy Days* (Knowlson and Pilling 1979)[3] and read what other scholars had written about Winnie, the play's main character. One of these scholars compared Winnie to Robinson Crusoe, which I thought was hilarious. This made me think, however, of Mary Poppins, from an English children's book. To write the comparison was highly pleasurable and gave me insight into Winnie's predicament, but it had little to do with the scholarly book I was reading.

We know that other texts can also be used to avoid the confrontation with our own writing. Reading too extensively is often a major fault in young academic writers because they never get started on writing. My first encounter with scientific writing was the sight of busy people with boxes full of cards with handwritten quotations; at that point writing seemed a total mystery to me. I did not at that time understand that it was not sufficient to respectfully write down what others had said. So why not take notes on what we think when we read to be sure our appropriation of the knowledge is happening? It helps understanding and remembering and clarifies what we agree with and where we are critical. Sometimes it is enough to read the introduction and conclusion to see if a book is really interesting for our work. And as I have already mentioned, it is ideal to discuss any text with others!

Texts can also permit another kind of flight. Do we cleverly repeat what other scholars have said and forget the responsibility we have to think for ourselves? Are we simply parrots? I heard a story about a little boy and a parrot. The boy was very preoccupied by the bird, and his mother asked him why. The little boy said, "The bird talks. Everybody says that the bird talks. But the parrot doesn't talk." His mother asked him what he meant, and the little boy said, "He doesn't say I." The boy understood that there should be someone thinking and taking responsibility for the words. In a certain way the academic genres ask for repetition of information—we situate ourselves in relation to other researchers—but we also have to appropriate the knowledge, make it part of what we think.

THE READER AS MIDWIFE

To write academic texts means to expose ourselves, and readers can be a great support in developing our self-confidence: "This is interesting," they say when the writer has almost given up. "Go on, we want more!" So even on the brink of despair, the writer stumbles on, gives a new version to the readers and gets encouragement and advice.

It is good for a text to be confronted with readers before it is finished. Writers who do not show their text to anybody before they have finished it lose the possibility of changing the text and improving it through dialogue. They lose the possibility of integrating different ideas and thinking in new, perhaps original, directions. Readers will give very different kinds of responses. Some have new ideas; some look at the structure; and some react to the lack of commas. When our texts are too provocative, the reader may give bad advice; then rewriting might weaken the qualities of the first version. It is important to resist advice that we feel is not good for our text; the writer owns the text! But what in the text created the negative reaction? Perhaps we need to change something else?

We can consider it a gift to a reader to be permitted to look into the writing process of someone else. To read texts in the process of becoming also demands generosity. As readers we must not be censors but friends who remember the fragility of the writer. The motivation for writing can easily be destroyed. I got a very negative response to my first novel from the publisher after a very positive one from my reading friends. I was devastated for several months, looking out of the window instead of working, and then started thinking of revenge! But how could I get back at a publishing house? After three months I thought: What is it that my friends read between the lines but that I have not written? Then I could get on with the work, and the novel ended up as a success.

As readers, we help texts into the world. We then point out their possibilities and also their drawbacks and weaknesses. Readers need to be curious and demanding, wanting to know exactly what the writer has on her mind and to stimulate the writer's curiosity, the need to know more: dig harder, dig deeper! We encourage the writer and give concrete advice, where to add and develop; we say what is working and what is not. If a reader does not tell the writer what is good, there is a risk she or he will delete this in the next rewriting. Can the readers help with new perspectives, ask an opposing question or turn the argument upside down? The writer may have something she or he does not dare to write, does not want to know. Even then, we, the trusted readers, can help.

We sometimes think we have excellent suggestions for revisions, but the writer does not seem to understand. The text is a way of expressing oneself, often closely linked to the writer's identity, and the writer cannot always integrate the advice she or he gets from readers. At this point we, the readers, have to let go and accept that the writer is not listening.

THE SUPERVISOR AS A GUIDE

Supervision is a form of response normally limited to an exchange about academic texts between two or three persons. If we can choose our supervisor we should consider what kind of competence we need most (on the subject, on methods, on the writing process, on the research design?). Should we have more than one supervisor? If so, they should meet regularly, and if the supervisors do not agree, and this becomes a problem for the student, it is always possible to introduce a third reader. Most supervisors who collaborate on responses think this is an inspirational kind of dialogue and learn a lot about writing.

The student is the most important person in this particular kind of relationship, and the counselling must always meet the student's needs at different points in the process. The division of power is asymmetrical; the student is the most vulnerable in the relationship. The supervisor can involve students in her or his own projects by brainstorming ideas with them and having them read the text in "two-way counselling", even when their projects are not related. This is useful both for the senior and the junior and makes them equals for a brief moment.

I participated in a project where two seniors and three juniors read and discussed the papers we were writing as a part of the methodology. As a senior, I profited greatly from the ideas of the juniors and realized how important it is for seniors to be reminded of how vulnerable we are when we have submitted an unfinished text to other readers. When will the juniors discover our incompetence?

The student may be lucky and find a supervisor who becomes a guide, a coach and a friend. Even if this does not happen and it is impossible to change your supervisor, you can discuss the procedure you will follow with the supervisor and reach clear agreements on when she or he is to read your texts and what kind of text you can give her or him and at what moments. How important is it to respect the deadlines you have agreed on? Of course, feedback on written submissions will be given as quickly as possible, and the supervisors will be concrete and specific in their feedback. The effective supervisor asks questions that lead to new thoughts, ideas and perspectives. She or he will not make the student's text her or his own and will always try to understand what you want to do, even when you are not sure yourself.

Supervisor and student can exchange and develop ideas by email but can still need a meeting plan. Do we prefer to agree on meetings when we need them? It is important to discuss the expectations and limits of your writing process at the beginning of the collaboration. What is the aim of this process? What do you wish to find an answer to? This discussion is repeated during the counselling process. An important discussion touches on the definitions and theories the student uses: How appropriate are the vocabulary and the theories in relation to the subject matter? Do they help you think? Will the questioning of your material bring new insight rather than simply confirming what we already know?

A good supervisor has a constant overview of the counselling process. She or he will encourage the student to work on the areas of the thesis or essay where curiosity and desire are strongest and may recommend working on several sections of the thesis or essay simultaneously. A principle for a primary school teacher I know is to write three pluses in the margin for every minus. I even have a reader who writes "HURRAH" when she likes what she reads. It is a nice feeling for the child within me to get my texts back with pluses and "Hurrahs", even if I always take the minuses more seriously!

Supervision is not a private matter between the student and the supervisor. Of course, the research community is a potential resource for every one of its writers and has a collective responsibility towards us all. Who has forgotten that research is dialogue, even before the final version of the results is available in print? Scholars in the same research department have a special responsibility for new recruits and should know what each student is working on, and the department should support the supervisors so that they become as competent as possible. The whole milieu in a particular research field should, of course, have an ongoing discussion about supervision and criteria for good writing. This discussion goes on in seminars, at lunch breaks and in smaller group discussions and provides for the development of a creative academic milieu. The students must be tied to both the local research environment (institutes, projects and research groups) and the international research community through courses, conferences and networking. The supervisor can help when it comes to forming an international network.

WRITING WITH PEERS

Working on texts together is extremely important for students. How can we make this happen? We can, for instance, organize a seminar where two of the participants send out texts one week beforehand. All participants read and prepare comments, but at the same time two of them are appointed as discussants and prepare a more thorough commentary. The seminar starts with the writer introducing her or his text, and at the end she or he comments on the response. The senior who is responsible for the seminar must take care that the writer does not use too much time to defend the text. One solution is to let the writer answer after the comments of the discussants but before a general discussion. The senior can present papers on equal terms.

After a round of comments from the group, the writer and readers discuss the text and the comments. A rule for readers is to look for the potential of the text and give concrete advice as to how to change it for the better. Writers who comment on other writers' texts become better readers of their own texts. My experience with groups of PhD students is that they have different, and often far more, contributions compared to a single supervisor. Should we discuss the academic genres and the success criteria for a good text? To clarify genre, we might ask ourselves what makes this particular text academic.

Peer counselling is a valuable and effective tool in the developing of texts, especially when this is combined with the comments of a senior. Some of these readers will have already integrated the silent or generally accepted knowledge about academic genres that pervades the research community. Still, a general discussion of goals and criteria could be fruitful for all the writers, both students and seniors. When the quality of the comments on a text is discussed, we should not forget that the readers are vulnerable to criticism as well. Do set a date for the next seminar with new papers to explore!

THE POSSIBILITIES OF THE NET

The information revolution is gradually changing our way of thinking about writing. Once upon a time we wrote on typewriters and had to retype the whole page when we changed a comma, or we would cut sentences out and glue them onto a new page. So we hesitated before changing anything. With computers we have a tendency to rewrite a lot, and I do think it makes for better academic texts.

We can collaborate in new ways. We can all write texts together via email, sending them back and forth. It is surprising and highly motivating how many ideas an answer or a new version from our fellow writer via email can trigger. On Skype we can even see, talk and write to each other and work on the same text in a group! The social Web makes it possible to open up this kind of communication, and the users can comment on, add to and change the content of the pages. The text can have links to other addresses on the Net and use photos and samples from other people's texts. There is a very strong feeling of participation in this community of readers and writers, and lots of possibilities for exercising your writing. What if you think of your blog on the Net as a way of practising writing? Why not start with five sentences about your project?

We get used to simple, half-baked messages and quick communication. Snail mail is almost history; strategies and styles are undergoing major changes. We can put information about ourselves on Facebook; we can present our project on Twitter. We can put photos on Flickr or choose pages with multi-media potential like YouTube (see also Koobak, Chapter 6, this volume). It is easy to move between our texts and the texts of others, to sample and be inspired. We can put our questions on the Web and get answers, finding people who work in our field who are willing to discuss things with us. We can google keywords, names or expressions and find information quicker than we can blink. *Wikipedia* is not always serious enough, but sometimes it is very useful—you can check the references—and it is a unique, democratic undertaking where you can participate in the writing and make it more reliable. Of course, your mobile phone also has a multitude of possibilities. You can use it instead of your notebook to record ideas. It is more socially acceptable to walk and talk loudly into your phone than to stand still in the middle of a crowd and write in a notebook.

A WRITING HISTORY

My life with Mlle de Montpensier lasted more than twenty years. I analyzed her memoirs in academic articles but did not get any closer to the reason behind my obsession with her. She was called "la Grande Mademoiselle" because she was tall, the richest person in France and the highest in rank after the royal family. She has come across in history as completely ridiculous. Did I admire her strength in the face of the court who laughed at her, alone in the midst of unpredictable and mean friends? At forty-three she fell in love with a nobleman of lower rank than hers. The king said yes to the marriage and then changed his mind. One year later, her suitor was thrown in jail. No one knows exactly why. She made it her duty to weep profusely every time the king met her at court, until he forbade her to show her sorrow. After ten years, he finally agreed to accept a large part of her fortune and release her suitor. When he returned from prison, he was notoriously unfaithful and disagreeable, and she finally broke with him. I thought for a while that my fascination stemmed from her misfortunes in love, and I decided to write a play about her. My patient readers read and read again and ended by asking me, "Where are you in this text?"

I did have the end of the story: "When we are dead, we'll go together to a place where all of us shall dance through eternity." Was my fascination linked to the idea of death? I started out again on a novel by setting up a parallel between Mlle de Montpensier's story and my own. My own memories started emerging. The novel was almost finished. One day while listening to a lecture, my pen started running over the paper, my sorrow was intense, and I knew I had found what I was looking for. I wrote my relationship with my father into my novel as I had written the story of Mlle de Montpensier and her father. It seemed I had several pages, but afterwards I realized I had written only a paragraph. However, it was enough to finish my novel and say goodbye to my princess. Even in academic writing we can have an existential engagement with our project, the feeling of a mystery that has to be unravelled. Sometimes it is a matter of life and death.

THE JOY OF WRITING

Does academic writing have anything to do with joy? There are small pleasures such as using red and blue letters in the text or buying paperclips of different sizes and colours or a new notebook now and then, for instance, one with the Empire State Building in three dimensions or pink roses in different shades on the cover. Have you ever experienced writing as fun, when the words arrive without effort and one can just go on writing and writing? The memory of this pleasure must be cherished; it is proof that the joy of writing exists, even when we are completely blocked. It might come from the happiness of succeeding, mastering something; from the enthusiasm when we find a solution to enigmas, an explanation for mysteries. To develop a thought can create sensuousness and joy. There is the pleasure of surprising oneself—imagine, I did this! Another pleasure is to explain in writing what I am interested in, to someone who genuinely wants to know. Few things are more enjoyable than to explore and share with someone else who wants to think together with me.

To write is a physical as well as mental process; I strain and stress, my back hurts, my eyes are dry, and my stomach protests. All of a sudden I find a solution, something that has to do with what I am, with all my experiences, memories, thoughts, feelings. Everything is in tune—it is like a fairy tale. The body explodes with pleasure and relief. I will never be the same again. I play with words, and I write as if I know how—which does not mean, at all, that everything I write can be used afterwards.

In this pleasure there is also pain, and doubt, and before I know it, I am stuck again. There are many places to get stuck and a long way to go to reach the flow of writing, but it does exist—along with the joy of being on the way!

EXERCISE 11: SUGGESTIONS AND QUESTIONS

1. *Consider yourself a well of ideas.*
2. *Do you know something that you do not know yet?*
3. *Meet the stranger in yourself to find answers to your questions.*
4. *Dare what you do not dare.*
5. *To think can be less rational than we believe.*
6. *Listen to your almost inaudible voices.*
7. *Do you write down your ideas at once?*
8. *Show your ignorance and ask. Other people are not that much more clever than you.*
9. *If you are stuck, describe your material and your questions over and over again, and try to use different words every time.*
10. *Personal engagement does not make an academic text any poorer.*
11. *Find readers you trust. You need a lot of encouragement to get going.*
12. *"Dry" is not necessarily synonymous with "objective".*
13. *Communicate the knowledge you have gained by using different genres.*
14. *If you need to conform to a strict academic genre, you can hide your playful self in the final draft.*
15. *Any writing is good exercise—except for labels and car registration numbers.*
16. *Unlike in cooking, many cooks are better than one.*

NOTES

1. Paul Éluard, French poet, 1895–1952. His poem "La terre est bleu comme an orange" (The earth is blue as an orange) can be found at www.fr/poeme-868/paul (accessed April 20, 2014).
2. Murasaki Shikibu, a Japanese noblewoman, wrote *The Tale of Genji* in the eleventh century. The novel is a classic work of Japanese literature. It has been translated into English several times. A recent translation is by Royall Tyler (Murasaki 2002).
3. The Irish playwright Samuel Beckett's theatre play *Happy Days* (Knowlson and Pilling 1979), first performed in 1961, belongs to the theatre of the absurd and portrays the absurd and lonely life conditions of Winnie, the main character, who from the beginning is buried in sand, first up to the waist and later in the play up to the neck.

REFERENCES

Cixous, Hélène. 1991. "Coming to Writing" and Other Essays. Edited by Deborah Jenson. Translated by Sarah Cornell, Deborah Jenson, Ann Liddle and Susan Sellers. Cambridge, MA: Harvard University Press. Originally published in La venue à l'écriture by Hélène Cixous, Madeleine Gagnon and Aie Leclerc. 1977. Paris: Union Générale d'Editions.

Cixous, Hélène. 1993. Three Steps on the Ladder of Writing. Translated by Sarah Cornell and Susan Sellers. New York: Columbia University Press.

Knowlson, James and John Pilling. 1979. Frescoes of the Scull: The Later Prose and Dramas of Samuel Beckett. London: John Calder.

Mortenson, Greg and David Oliver Relin. 2006. Three Cups of Tea: One Man's Mission to Promote Peace . . . One School at a Time. New York: Penguin Paperback.

Murasaki Shikibu. 2002. Tale of Genji. Translated from Japanese by Royall Tyler. New York: Penguin Paperback.

8 From an Empty Head to a Finished Text

The Writing Process

Sissel Lie

Some friends and I formed a consciousness-raising group in the 1970s. For a while we read feminist novels, and when we tired of them, one of us suggested that we write fiction ourselves. I thought this was ridiculous; how could we compete with Shakespeare and Racine? In the end I became a writer of fiction and discovered that academic writing and the writing of novels had some important characteristics in common, especially concerning the brainstorming of ideas. We read and commented on each other's texts and intuitively understood the vulnerability of the writer and the need to look through the mess of an unfinished text for its possibilities. Thus, my point of departure is one of partaking and communicating, and ever since then I have needed challenge and discussion to get on with both my fiction and my academic texts.

Ten years later, after I had published my first book of fiction, I met French professor of literature Hélène Cixous, whose theories of writing and sexual difference have had a big impact on feminist theorizing. I read her book *La venue à l'écriture/Coming to Writing* (Cixous 1991). She urged me and other women to write ourselves into History. I was fascinated by the way she used herself as an example for all women. I have an opera of voices inside me, she said. To write we must make contact with our body and our unconscious. Go to the School of Dreams (Cixous 1993), she advises us. The body thinks for us. She advocates an active passivity, making the writer a medium for what must come from inner sources. At this point, I was working on the surrealists and saw the resemblances between what came to be called Cixous' "écriture féminine" (feminine writing) and later "poetic writing", and the automatic writing of the surrealists (Breton 1988), where the writer is also a medium for what comes from inner sources and should write without the control of the intellect.

Cixous writes about fiction, but, inspired by her words and my own experience of writing, I concluded that we can let go of some of our intellectual control to get in contact with other layers of our consciousness even while writing academic texts. Some years after this meeting with Cixous, I discovered the process-oriented method of writing. This method, which originated in the US, was spreading fast in Norwegian schools at the end of the 1980s.

t looks at writing as a way of thinking and emphasizes the importance of collaboration between writers and readers during the writing process.

The following exercises, questions and reflexions are based on my method of departure, which is to stay in the richness of exchanging experiences of writing and of texts. They are meant to contribute to an understanding of writing as a process and to give my readers the opportunity of doing the same types of exercises that I use in my writing courses. I start with the conceiving of ideas through free writing and finish with the academic text; I have separated the process into five phases.

FIVE PHASES OF WRITING

1. *The first is the "thinking about writing" phase, during which participants get to know each other and discuss how they look at writing.*
2. *Then we have the "writing to think" phase, where the writing is mainly addressed to the writers themselves.*
3. *The third phase is concerned with writing to communicate.*
4. *The fourth phase is about revision and rewriting of the text.*
5. *The fifth phase is when the participants evaluate the exercises.*

The following exercises are meant for a group with a moderator but can also be used by a small group without a moderator, or two persons who read for each other.

Most of the exercises are done in a very short time, to encourage spontaneous expression and prevent the writers from censoring their texts. At the end of each exercise it is useful to have a plenary discussion or a round where everybody has their say. The moderator should keep an eye on the clock to be able to get through the series of exercises in the time allocated. She or he can decide to give the writers more or less time to do the exercises and the plenary discussions, planning in advance how long each session should last. The longer exercises can be more flexible and adapted to the time available.

You are free to choose only one or a few of the exercises, but I recommend that if you do not have much time you keep to the exercises and leave out the revision part. Reading and commenting on texts written by the participants are just as important as the writing exercises. A moderator is free to use her or his own writing and reading experiences and to call on the experiences of the participants at any time.

Creating a group that works well together also depends on how the participants are situated in the room. A horseshoe with the opening towards the moderator is one solution; a circle is another. During the seminar some of the participants may become heated. The moderator should seat those who disagree on the same side of the room, so that they cannot see each other and the group does not lose time in futile arguments. Participants who have a tendency to speak too much can be reined in by the moderator, who gives everyone a time limit and asks all to speak. And do remember to have breaks and small talk and to indulge in more private discussions.

THINKING ABOUT WRITING PHASE

EXERCISE 12: THINKING ABOUT WRITING

1. *The participants introduce themselves, and the moderator explains what kind of exercises the group will be undertaking.*
2. *She or he then asks the group to write and read aloud at least three reasons for looking forward to the seminar and three reasons to be sceptical about it. Usually something will come up about people's reluctance to do writing exercises and their anxiety about having to share unfinished texts with others. The moderator can return to this discussion at the end of the seminar when the participants have the exercises behind them.*
3. *The participants have written about pleasures and problems with their academic writing before they come to the seminar, sending their texts to the moderator by email.*
4. *The group discusses the problems and pleasures they experience when writing academic texts. The moderator will take care to show the group quotations from the emails of all participants and initiate a discussion where she or he lets everybody speak.*

The participants usually have different ways of coping with writer's block, with the pleasures and pains of writing, and can give useful advice to the others. In a group of seven to ten people, most of the questions that need to be addressed in the seminar will have been discussed in the emails sent beforehand.

This phase is meant to give participants the feeling of being seen and recognized for the valuable information they can give on their particular writing process.

WRITING TO THINK PHASE

The next cluster of exercises is meant to help you experience how you can generate new thoughts and ideas through writing.

EXERCISE 13: WRITING TO THINK

1. *The group embarks on an exercise in "writing to think". They choose a word themselves, or they can all use the same word proposed by the moderator, for instance, "sunglasses". This word must be concrete and not charged with complicated emotional or intellectual associations. Later on, this mode of "free writing" will be useful for developing concepts and ideas, but to develop skills in free writing we should start with words that do not risk blocking the writer's imagination. The group writes for 3 minutes. The writer should not lift the pen from the paper, or the fingers from the computer, and should write whatever comes to mind. It is important not to stop writing, so if the writer gets stuck, she can write LLLL or "I am stuck I am stuck . . ." until she or he gets back to her or his writing.*
2. *Then the writers in the group turn to the person next to them and read their texts in pairs. In the process-oriented method of writing this is called buzzing. Buzzing is a nice way to start reading aloud spontaneous texts in public, an exercise that may seem very difficult to some.*
3. *Sometimes things of a personal nature may come up while writing; the participants can put brackets around it and leave it out when the text is read.*
4. *Then there is a plenary discussion about what kind of text the participants wrote: keywords, poems, histories, or was it argumentative?*
5. *The group may also discuss different ways of thinking and writing: think first and then write, or write to think. Did they write anything they did not plan? Were they surprised by anything they wrote?*

Free writing means writing spontaneously, trying not to censor the text. The moderator explains that free writing is useful for brainstorming when you are starting work on a text, and also later on, when you are working on parts of the texts or concepts that need clarifying or developing. Free writing is an effective way of brainstorming ideas, but most writers need to work on this method for a while to be able to really profit from it.

This kind of writing can be used to sort out problems, to get ideas, to clarify our thoughts or to cope with writer's block. Once the process of writing has started, the fact that we are writing will help us think! The point of free writing is not psychoanalytic inquiry; it does not seek to make contact with the unconscious, like automatic writing, even if it is inspired by the associative techniques of psychoanalysis. But it does make you reflect in new ways. "Thinking is trying to think the unthinkable," says Cixous, and continues, "[T]hinking the thinkable is not worth the effort" (1993, 38).

This exercise is mostly meant to be fun and to free up creative energies. When using free writing at the beginning of an academic project, you will get ideas about what you want to discuss. These first drafts of a text can be much freer than later versions, especially if the academic genre seems restrictive. You can ask yourself if you should show the text to a friendly reader and discuss its possibilities. As a writer you take a risk when you show an unfinished text to somebody else; therefore, you must be careful when you choose these first readers.

EXERCISE 14: WRITING TO REMEMBER 1

1. *Writing is also remembering, and sometimes it is about becoming conscious of what has formed our way of seeing things. For instance, we may try to approach why we like or dislike writing. The participants start making a list of genres they might have tried out as children (journal, car registration numbers, poems, shopping lists, etc.); they should name a minimum of three genres. Again, the writing should not last more than 3 minutes.*
2. *The writers then choose one item on the list and communicate this to the others.*
3. *Then they choose the same word or another on their own list or from someone else's list to write about. Getting ideas from other participants is called "stealing" in the process-oriented method of writing, but it is considered a positive thing. Following the principles of free writing, they write for 5 minutes about a writing memory based on a particular genre they used as children.*
4. *The following plenary discussion starts with each participant reading one paragraph.*

This kind of memory writing can cause you to remember how your efforts at writing were destroyed by teachers with red pens. In one of my writing courses, a participant from the North of Norway who was plagued by writer's block remembered that when she got her papers back from her teacher, they were covered with red. She called the comments "Sunset over the Tana River". As an adult she had integrated this teacher as an internal censor, making it difficult for her to think that what she wrote was worthwhile; she was stopping herself before she had written anything.

The number of children who were proud and happy about what they had conceived, but were met by rejection from their teachers, is heartbreaking. Painful memories that you do not want to remember may come up.

There is always this risk of writing ourselves into a past that we would rather remained forgotten, and a writing course cannot take responsibility for healing old wounds; the moderator has to think this through beforehand and decide how she should cope with tears and aggression.

EXERCISE 15: WRITING TO REMEMBER 2

You can replace the above exercise with another which usually creates a happy moment for everybody. It is based on my version of a short text by the French writer Georges Perec. The participants have 5 minutes to try to remember "small" events or things that were important to them, and they start every memory with the sentence: "I remember . . ." Some of my examples are "I remember small siblings who had to be dragged along and were often left behind the door because they were too small," "I remember my grandmother who put her teeth in a glass of water at night . . .," "I remember the ugly words that were so awful that they had to be written in the sand before you and should never be spoken," "I remember the song 'She Was Too Young to Fall in Love'. . ." and "I remember the lessons in Norwegian where you had to be for and against and should always write a comma before 'but' . . ."

1. *The moderator has written examples which she or he reads aloud.*
2. *The participants write for 5 minutes. "I remember . . ."*
3. *Each participant reads one or two memories.*

EXERCISE 16: WRITING WITH THE SENSES

In the next exercise, the group tries to use sensual language in descriptions. The writers need some kind of fruit (grapes, for instance) and some dry bread.

1. *The exercise consists first of describing the fruit: "What size is it, what colour, length and breadth? What smell does it have; how does it feel to touch; what does it say to you?" They are not supposed to start tasting, smelling, looking and listening until they all have their grapes. The writers have 3–5 minutes to write a kind of free writing, but they must keep the moderator's questions in mind. When they have finished, everybody chooses one word or one sentence to read to the others.*
2. *Then the bread is distributed, and the writers do the same with this: describe its size, colour, length, breadth and smell; how it feels; what it says to you. Again, this exercise should take about*

> *3–5 minutes. Each group member chooses a word or a sentence to share with the others. (If the group is not too big, the participants can read a paragraph.)*
> 3. *Then they should all choose a word or a sentence from one of the two texts, describing the grapes or the bread, to characterize their own academic project.*
> 4. *At this point, many of the participants will be bewildered or surprised, so the moderator should guide them with questions. The answer could be "My dissertation is dry and full of holes" or "My article is sweet and pale like my grapes."*
> 5. *The participants read the characterization of their project to the others. Then the question from the moderator could be "What does this description do to your thinking about your academic project?" or "Did you find this exercise interesting? Why?"*

The participants will probably react very differently to this exercise: some of them will not understand why this is interesting; others may have had an illumination. This often leads to very interesting plenary discussions. The group can then discuss what a sensual description can do to an academic writing project. The group can also discuss what a sensual description can do to your thinking about your material.

WRITING TO COMMUNICATE PHASE

In one of the many writing courses that I have taught with a colleague of mine, Torlaug Løkensgard Hoel, she described the start of a writing process as chaos inside our heads and drew this on the blackboard as a cloud filled with letters, which then developed into a box with five compartments illustrating the finished text. I protested, "First there should be an empty white cloud, meaning nothingness. Then there is chaos!" Often when I want to write, my head feels completely empty; there are no competing ideas or unstructured thoughts. I look around, but no, there is not a single word in sight. (This also happens in discussions when I am deeply impressed by all the clever people around me.) What helps at this stage is to write about something I have read on my subject and to write down any idea that might float up.

As I have suggested with the first exercises, the steps from an empty head to text can pass through different kinds of free writing. The bits and pieces one writes while brainstorming for ideas in connection with an academic project will quickly need to be adapted to a genre and organized into some kind of structure. What about imagining a virtual chest of drawers for organizing the overall structure or the structure at a chapter level? Can chapter summaries or ideas be put into the different "drawers" or into different files on the Net?

There are different ways of making a text, but for most of us it is necessary to write any text more than once. I see the writing process as a spiral where the text is read and rewritten again—and again—on its way to the final version. New ideas might make some of the pages that we thought were finished obsolete, but even if we have to throw away whole sheaves of pages, they are not wasted. We have been thinking and developing our project while writing.

EXERCISE 17: WRITING TO COMMUNICATE

We have now reached an exercise where we are specifically addressing the others in the group and presenting something about our academic work that we want to discuss. The exercise is as follows:

1. *Write about something in your research/your writing that has recently interested you/irritated you/made you happy/enthusiastic. The participants have 10–15 minutes.*
2. *If the participants hesitate and do not know what to write, it is always possible to start with a round where everybody proposes a theme for a text, so they can steal ideas.*

Often the first draft of a text will be unreadable to others because it is written in a private language. It is the kind of writing we may use in diaries or notebooks. The next phase is the "writing to communicate" phase, which can be based on your first drafts. You will still use a free mode of writing, but one where you start taking into consideration, for instance, the genre and the style. Some writers may see themselves as writing from a lonely tower, like the Romantic geniuses, but we are all influenced by other texts and genre definitions, and by the language that was there before us. If your text is going to be an academic one, you must reflect on how you write in your particular field. You must also consider who your readers are and how to attract them and be understood by them.

This is a phase where you work with readers, if you have not shown your first drafts to anyone. If it is difficult to ask people to read, you can always offer to read their texts in return. An interesting effect of this kind of collaboration is that through such scrutiny, as the reader of others' writing, you actually become a better reader of your own texts. However, we all have our own personal, often quite unfriendly readers peeping over our shoulders when we write. These phantom readers can give us hope because we have already been able to write good texts, so it may happen again. Sometimes they can act as censors and give us an excuse not to write what we could have said and do not quite dare to take the responsibility for.

EXERCISE 18: SILENCE YOUR PRIVATE CENSOR

A way to silence your private censor is to move about!

1. *The group has a short discussion about everyone's projects.*
2. *The group takes a walk, bringing along pen and paper: Take ten steps, then stop and write whatever comes into your mind. Then take ten steps again, and stop and write. This should be repeated ten times.*
3. *Bring back what you have written.*
4. *Discussion: Did you write anything relevant to your project?*

As a writer you must take care to signal to your preliminary reader where you are in the writing process and what kind of response you need, but there are different readers for different stages of the process and different kinds of responses. The reader can help with developing ideas; sometimes she or he can explain what you are getting at. She or he can also help in organizing ideas. It is of no use, in a first draft, to correct orthography and punctuation, but this kind of comment can be very useful later on. Later the reader can also argue with you, disagree and contest your ideas.

At the beginning of the writing process we are vulnerable and need support because it is easy to lose motivation. In the end we need all the criticism we can get, the goal being to produce a better text. When we read a text for somebody, we need to take into account that most writers are fragile when it comes to negative criticism. Who wants to continue writing a text that has been torn apart by critical comments? So the question is: What can the writer take? In fact, readers are in an exposed position as well and can be hurt. What if your comments as a reader are inadequate, even ridiculous?

Challenge and constructive criticism from the reader can inspire and create a better text, and the reader must take care to signal what is good in the text. We all know how we can become blind to our own texts and perhaps leave out good points in the subsequent revisions. All writers face this dilemma. The text belongs to the writer, and the writer is the one who decides which comments will be useful for her text. If your reader's reaction is strong and negative, you must ask yourself whether this is the reader's problem rather than that of your text.

When starting on a text, you should consider ways of bringing along a group of readers. When you have a group, it is a good idea to send out the text beforehand with questions to your readers, and for the group to agree on the procedure at the first meeting. And a good idea for the readers is to never use red ink!

EXERCISE 19: GIVING RESPONSES

1. *As readers of an early draft of an academic text, the participants are supposed to follow the instructions for the first round of response giving in a group. In a group where people know each other well, they can discuss and decide the procedure themselves.*
2. *This time we start with a general excuse, said either by the moderator or by everyone simultaneously: "I have not had enough time, and this text could have been better, but I will read my text to you anyway!" After this we do not need to waste our time on excuses.*
3. *Everybody in a group of three will get the same amount of time: about 10 minutes for comments on their text from each of the two readers. The writer reads the text aloud twice, while the other two take notes. Once the commenting has started, the writers are not supposed to defend themselves or use too much of the allocated time to respond.*
4. *Then the group has 10 minutes or a little more at the end for a general discussion; the whole exercise takes about 40 minutes.*
5. *If you, as a reader, feel you have nothing to say—it is difficult to comment on a text someone has read to you—you take a deep breath and start talking about anything that might have interested you in the text. If you really have nothing to say, give a summary of the text.*
6. *When several groups work at the same time giving responses, it is a good idea to have a plenary discussion afterwards about how the groups worked and whether it is useful for the writer not to respond to comments.*

Writers who listen and take notes will profit more from the responses than those who are preoccupied with defending their text. But often new thoughts come up in a dialogue, so you have to find out what kind of comments you prefer.

This first time the focus is on the possibilities of the text. The comments will be mostly on ideas and about what kind of text this is, and what the important questions are. They can also be on successful phrasing, interesting expressions, eye-opening images, useful comparisons, etc. The reader should have one positive comment or a question and, eventually, suggestions for improving the text. Another kind of comment could be to ask: How does the text catch the reader's attention?

REVISING AND REWRITING PHASE

EXERCISE 20: REVISING AND REWRITING

1. *The participants now need time to reflect on and rewrite their texts.*
2. *The group of three will meet again to discuss the new version when it is convenient. This can be the next day or after an hour. When revising, there should be more focus on how the text is constructed, on the argument and the cohesion of the text. Are there any theories that might be useful for your thinking?*

For the research work to be taken seriously, it must show precision and accuracy. Take care to quote correctly. The reader will lose confidence in what you say if you cannot transcribe a quotation correctly. Tell the reader why you have chosen the quotation. The reader does not know why if we do not explain, and a reader like me will have a tendency to skip very long quotations, so quote only the part you really need. And for references be consistent; use the same system for all references and credit your sources.

This phase addresses the development of the text. Now it is important to check whether the questions asked at the beginning have been answered by the end. Other questions that arise in relation to an almost-finished text are the following.

EXERCISE 21: CHECK THE COHERENCE OF THE TEXT

1. *Has the writing process led to answers to new questions?*
2. *How do I situate myself in the text?*
3. *To whom do I address myself?*
4. *What is the focus of the text?*
5. *What are the main questions?*
6. *What do I mean?*
7. *How do I argue for this?*
8. *Do I show what is most important in my arguments?*

Sometimes it is necessary to move paragraphs and sentences to create a more coherent text. And there are many ways of creating coherence: by repetition, conjunctions, titles and subtitles. If you sum up every paragraph with a word or a sentence, it is easier to see if your argument is consistent, and it helps when you write the conclusion. And when you look at your paragraphs, you can ask yourself: Where is the topic sentence? No topic sentence should be in the middle of a paragraph. A paragraph should not be only one sentence, and, of course, neither should it cover whole pages. And remember that the paragraph is a unity of meaning; with the topic sentence come examples, comparisons, enumerations and argumentation. When at the end of the writing process the paragraphs have found their ultimate place, observe how they fit together. Can we do more to make a coherent text? What about stealing the cliffhanger principle from fiction when we write a dissertation or essay and end the chapter or sub-section with something that entices the reader to continue on to the next one?

We do not have to be frightened of metaphors in academic texts; even if they are clichés they contribute to giving life to the text and make the reader feel at ease, because these are well-known modes of writing. We do not risk, as with original metaphors, sending the reader off to wander in her or his own associations. However, original metaphors can be important in establishing fruitful relations between what we know and what we want to understand, and metaphors have been used as a way to briefly express important scientific discoveries (see also Lie, Chapter 7, this volume).

This can be the moment when we ask ourselves if there are ways to liven up the text or make it more experimental. We may then look to forms of essayistic writing to see how they treat examples, images and the like. I found, for instance, the following in a review by Hilary Mantel of Marilyn French's book *From Eve to Dawn: A History of Women*:

> French's examples from literature and art are equivocal; the gap between rhetoric and performance never opens wider than when we are told that Shelley is the " 'feminist' 'favorite poet' ". It's hard not to imagine the hand of his drowned first wife reaching out of the Serpentine, groping for a pen to tell her side of the story.
>
> —(2009, 20)

This is a polemical statement, but Mantel makes her point in a very effective way, and I feel elated and curious: What was the life of Shelley's first wife like? A question to consider is how pleasurable a text can be before it ceases to be thought of as academic. The answer is different in different fields of research, but even so, as academics, many of us have a tendency to shun "literary" writing; something prevents us from exploring the potentialities of language in the academic genres. Do we need new forms to think new thoughts? Readers sometimes have a tendency to be sceptical when faced with originality, and they want the text to resemble what they already know.

A solution is to look for a model text within our field that is both pleasurable and academic. Who writes texts that you want to read? Should your text be more personal? Can something be done to the examples to make them more interesting, more colourful? Perhaps you can break up traditional structures and narrate the story in another way. What about introducing texts or parts of the text with literary quotations? This last suggestion, though, may upset readers who do not want to lose the academic argument in bits and pieces of literature.

Save all your successive drafts. At a conference the French philosopher Jacques Derrida made fun of himself and told us that he had six computers in his house and would run from one to the other to make copies, terrified of losing his text. Sometimes we are happy to find early drafts containing thoughts we forgot about during revision. And beware of the moment when your text begins to seem banal and you want to start all over again. At that point you have read it so many times that nothing seems new any more—but it probably will to the readers.

Now, when the text is close to being finished, it is time to start the mourning process: What questions do you not have space to address this time? What do you have to let go? Can those questions be addressed another time, in the ongoing dialogue between the writer and other researchers? Feel free to say something about this in your conclusion!

EXERCISE 22: COLLABORATIVE REWORKING

1. *The group of three will work together on the new version of the texts. Now the participants know each other better and can be more critical, but always with the aim of writing better texts, not of destroying them. First of all they agree on how they will proceed.*
2. *Over the course of several days before the course, the participants can also send the moderator an academic text they have written.*
3. *The moderator will then take examples from these texts to discuss, for instance, how to introduce an article and how to end it, how to address the readers, what kind of style to use, how to address theory and method and how to describe the material. Do not use examples from the texts to show how you should not write, even if it is tempting.*

I want to suggest some more questions for readers relating to the texts: Are we manipulated by the text into agreeing with something we do not truly agree with? Does the text express enthusiasm and engagement, or is it scared of the reader? Look for reservations, like the overuse of "perhaps". When the writer seems unsure of what she or he is saying, the text may sound too defensive and make the reader doubt it. Too much self-censoring is not good for any text. If you believe in what you write, the text expresses that.

The following questions might also be asked of any text by a reader: Between the text and the reader, what kind of underlying agreement is there (genre, style, conventions, attitudes)? Are there established orthodoxies the reader can help to kill? The text may be using different kinds of rhetorical devices to obtain authority: Do the repetitions, exaggerations and emphases work? The style is the writer's signature; how do we use images, comparisons, adjectives, quotations?

Does the text invite a dialogue when the pronoun "we" seems to include the reader? Or does it address itself directly to a "you"? I have used "we" in this article, and I have also addressed myself directly to "you". When I address my readers directly, I assume that they agree with me and that they are like me, which can be highly controversial in academic texts. I may also feel provoked by "you" when I, as the reader, may not necessarily share your point of view or do not want to be part of a dialogue. It is annoying, for example, when the writer addresses too many questions to me as a reader that I cannot respond to. The pronoun "I" is banned from some academic writing, while others recommend the use of "I", which shows that the writer is taking responsibility for her or his text. Either way the text will always have traces of its writer, even if you have tried to conceal yourself. "As mentioned before" or "which will be discussed later"—who mentioned it, and who discusses it?

When we are working on a text as writers or readers, it can be improved in different ways, for example, by addition: What more is needed in the argument or in the descriptions? It might be necessary to delete the superfluous, or to replace or change something. The text might also need clarification of obscure points or concepts, or something may need to be added where the text seems too laconic or where the argumentation is not sufficient; or, indeed, it is necessary to make corrections when there are mistakes. The question mark is a good alternative to affirmation if you want to invite the reader into the text, and the reader who writes comments in the margin invites the writer into a dialogue with the question mark. It is also more interesting if you are positive towards the contributions of other researchers than if you want to show where everybody else went wrong, to make room for yourself.

A group of readers can be of great help to stop a writer like me who hopes that a text is finished after the first draft. They can also help when you feel it is problematic to go any further: Does the text avoid difficult questions? Perhaps those are the very questions that the reader wants to read about. What about the joy of writing and thinking, if we are censoring our text all the time? If you know that you can share with others what seems too chaotic or too personal, they can help decide what you should not write. Let these readers mobilize all their generosity and curiosity and push you to the limits of your capabilities and of what you dare to write. Hélène Cixous insists on thinking "the worst" (1993, 40). She refers to the production of the literary text, and to the danger of approaching your own taboos, but I think we can also apply this advice to an academic text. Ideas might come up that question what you thought was right and wrong. You may come to conclusions or get results that are not at all popular. Have we gone to the limits of what we can think and write? If we write in such a way, the process will change the writer, the text and the reader.

EVALUATION PHASE

EXERCISE 23: EVALUATION OF EXPERIENCES WITH THE EXERCISES

The last exercise is to answer the question "What did I think was most interesting for me in these exercises?" The participants have 10–15 minutes to respond in writing, and they are supposed to give their written answers to the moderator.

The plenary discussion afterwards is important to allow the participants to reflect on what will be useful in their subsequent writing of academic texts. The moderator can launch a discussion about what in the series of exercises can be improved.

I never grade this kind of writing course, but when it lasts more than one day, I do this exercise at the end of the first day and comment on the answers from the participants when I give them back the next morning.

This series of exercises and reflections has touched on various elements of the writing process, from brainstorming ideas to finishing the text. Some of these exercises might have worked well, while others did not. As a participant you might have been upset by the orders from the moderator, or by the short time that you had to finish the exercises, or you may feel elated by some of the texts you have written and the discussions with the other participants. Of course, you may replace these activities with any exercise that can contribute to generating and freeing up ideas, increasing your thinking capacity through writing.

The moderator now has the opportunity to stress the importance of writing for at least half an hour a day, for anyone who has a text to write, and also of trying to use free writing regularly. For free writing to function well, it has to be practised, but it will end up being a useful mode of thinking.

SUGGESTIONS, QUESTIONS, REFLECTIONS

1. *Make a list of all your excuses for not writing, and have a hearty laugh.*
2. *Do you start writing at once when you have a project and write for at least half an hour a day?*
3. *Why not write a little bit if you cannot write much?*
4. *Write about something you want to explore.*
5. *Do you write in a way that seems natural to you?*
6. *Do you surprise yourself when you write?*
7. *Try not to censor yourself when you are writing; let your readers do this later.*
8. *Do you focus on what is most interesting?*
9. *Can you appropriate theory to help you think?*
10. *Is the academic genre less or more of a straightjacket than you imagined?*
11. *Patience is important; thinking is a slow process.*
12. *To discuss is a mode of thinking, just like writing.*
13. *Do you have a writing group that is waiting for your text?*
14. *Sometimes you have to write a lot of foolish things in order to write something worthwhile.*
15. *Think of three risks you have taken in your writing.*

REFERENCES

Breton, André. 1988. *Second Manifeste du Surréalisme. Oevres Completes I.* Edited by Marguerite Bonnet, 775–828. Paris: Gallimard.

Cixous, Hélène. 1991. "Coming to Writing" and Other Essays. Edited by Deborah Jenson. Translated by Sarah Cornell, Deborah Jenson, Ann Liddle and Susan Sellers. Cambridge, MA: Harvard University Press. Originally published in La venue à l'ècriture by Hélène Cixous, Madeleine Gagnon and Annie Leclerc. 1977. Paris: Union Générale d'Editions.

Cixous, Hélène. 1993. Three Steps on the Ladder of Writing. Translated by Sarah Cornell and Susan Sellers. New York: Columbia University Press.

Mantel, Hilary. 2009. "Review of Marilyn French's book *From Eve to Dawn: A History of Women.*" *New York Review of Books*, 30 April.

9 The Choreography of Writing an Introduction

Nina Lykke

How does one write the opening section of an academic publication? How do you make the transition from choosing a topic, collecting materials, mobilizing your resources and writing up bits and pieces to actually starting to introduce and shape the text you eventually want to publish? It is my experience from many years of supervision that students often have problems with opening sections of both papers and longer texts (dissertations, etc.). People sometimes postpone these sections until the end of the writing process, and sometimes they appear to be even more troubling than the analytical parts. In the opening sections everything needs to come together in a condensed, concise but also catchy manner, and this can cause trouble. To avoid being overwhelmed by this problem at the end of your research, it is advisable to work with your introduction and its rhetorical strategy or "narrative" (the condensed, concise and catchy introductory short version of your paper, dissertation, book, etc.) from the beginning. You can change the introduction along the road; the last version does not need to correspond to the first version. But it is a good idea to have some version ready to hand at all times and to use it as a guiding tool for your work. This will spare you the trouble of having to conjure the introductory narrative out of thin air at the end.

The aim of this chapter is to help and inspire you in the process of writing introductions and giving them a publishable shape. In so doing, I will draw on experiences from both academic and creative writing. I like to consider the process of writing an introduction as a choreographed dance where academically structured and planned moves work together with creatively improvised and intuitive moments in an embodied synergy. Academic traditions prescribe that you think a lot about the logic, coherence and structure of your writing and forget about the pleasure of creative moments. To the authors of this volume, both are crucial.

In this chapter, I shall present a sequence of writing exercises which, taken as a whole, can lead you step by step through the various stages of writing the introductory section of an academic text (paper, article, dissertation, etc.). The sequence of exercises has been developed through my teaching of academic and creative writing at the undergraduate, graduate and postgraduate levels as part of courses and programmes in Feminist and Intersectional Gender Studies.

The exercise sequence is based on a *choreography of six moves*, which I have adapted and reworked under inspiration from a study of opening sections of scholarly articles (Swales 1983). I have reworked, revised and from a feminist perspective twisted the model for writing academic introductions that was developed in this study. In so doing, I took as a point of departure my teaching of academic and creative writing as well as my own research on links between epistemologies, methodologies and writing processes in Feminist Studies (Lykke 2010). My work was also inspired by feminist sociologist Laurel Richardson's (2000) ideas about "writing as a method of inquiry".

In this chapter, I shall first present the mentioned sequence of six moves. Second, I shall illustrate how this sequence can be usefully applied to understand the rhetorical strategies of feminist academic texts. I will use the sequence as an analytical tool to do a reading of a textual example: the introduction to US law professor and critical race theorist Kimberlé Crenshaw's famous article "Mapping the Margins: Intersectionality, Identity Politics, and Violence against Women of Color" (1991)—a key text on intersectionality. Third, I shall present different clusters of writing exercises specifically designed to give readers the opportunity to try out how to produce an opening section to a text of their own which includes all six moves.

THE SEQUENCE OF EXERCISES AND ITS CHOREOGRAPHED LOGIC

Four of the six moves on which my choreography of writing an introduction is based were first developed to help students meet standard requirements of conventional science reporting. As head of the English as a Foreign Language section of the Language Studies Unit at the University of Aston, UK, John Swales (1983) undertook a study on the writing of scholarly introductions. He investigated how the opening paragraphs of academic articles from both the natural and the social/human sciences were structured. He identified four moves that were typically found in the majority of his sample of forty-eight scholarly articles.

TO WRITE AN INTRODUCTION—FOUR BASIC MOVES

(cf. Swales 1983, 192–93)

1) *Establishing the field (by asserting significance and/or current knowledge)*
2) *Summarizing previous research (by referring to authors and/or a thematic approach)*

> 3) *Preparing for present research (by indicating a gap and/or raising questions about previous research)*
> 4) *Introducing the present research (by stating its purpose and/or presenting an outline).*

My use of the moves is inspired by Swales' study. I find it useful, even though it is based on conventional research articles written in traditional academic styles (depersonalized third-person narration, focus on denotative[1] language, etc.) which predate the linguistic turn and the postmodern breaking up of academic conventions. But as will become clear from my analysis of the Crenshaw text (1991), I also use the moves in somewhat twisted feminist ways. I want to make them relevant in the context of Feminist Studies, which engages with critical and innovative processes of troubling canons, epistemologies, methodologies and genres of conventional science—processes which, as I see it, must have repercussions for the manner and style of writing. I also want to adapt the moves so that they can work in the present-day era of critical post-representationalist scholarship, built on the assumption of language as an active agent, and not just a mimetic and transparent representation of the world "out there".

In addition to twisting Swales' four moves, when I use them as tools for the analysis of feminist texts, I have also, as the very first act of twisting, added two more moves.

TO WRITE AN INTRODUCTION WITH A FEMINIST TWIST— TWO ADDED MOVES

> 5) *Situating the researcher-subject-narrator (by reflecting on the position of the researcher-subject-narrator of the text and her/his impact on the research/text)*
> 6) *Capturing the audience (for example, by introducing a "juicy" or significant title, story, example or quote and/or by writing passionately and in an embodied manner, etc.).*

Move 5 emerges directly out of the epistemologies of Feminist Studies, where situated knowledges (Haraway 1991) and the politics of location (Rich 1986) make up key points. According to many feminists, all researchers need to make themselves accountable for their research results, and this implies making visible the location of the researcher-subject and the position from which the research is carried out.

Move 6 is inspired by journalism and creative writing. It is motivated by a wish to develop a space to reflect on ways to work with "catching-the-audience" strategies which take into account the fact that, for political reasons, many texts written in the context of Feminist Studies make a point of addressing broader audiences than merely a narrow circle of colleagues located, for example, within a specific discipline.

PUTTING THE SIX MOVES TO WORK: THE CASE OF CRENSHAW

Together with students, I have tried to apply the moves to many different introductions to scholarly feminist texts, even stylistically very experimental ones. Most often we ended up concluding that Swales' four-move sequence could be reasonably applied as a key tool to understand what is happening rhetorically in the opening parts of these texts even though the moves originally were developed against the background of Swales' sample of more conventional articles. However, it is noticeable that the sequence often appeared in twisted versions in the feminist texts and that the two last moves (5–6) could often be used as relevant analytical tools in addition to the four-move model. Nevertheless, it seems that Swales' sequence of moves, with certain twists and additions, can work for many feminist scholars as well.

To illustrate how the sequence—with some twists—can be used as an analytical tool to better understand the rhetorical strategies of feminist texts, I shall try to analyze an example: the introduction to a key feminist text on intersectionality (Crenshaw 1991).

Before I start the analysis of the rhetorical and narrative strategies of Crenshaw's opening section, I shall, however, underline once more that this analysis is meant as a case study. It is an example of how the six-move sequence *could* materialize, not a normative recipe for how it *should* materialize. Feminist research texts are diverse, and it is important that readers keep in mind that analyses of opening sections of different feminist articles will illustrate the moves in rather different ways, even though it is also my claim that the six-move sequence as such can be applied usefully to many different kinds of scholarly feminist texts. My presentation of the sequence of six moves, as well as the illustration through the Crenshaw case, is meant as an aid for readers when constructing their own introductions, but it should not be used as a normative straightjacket.

I will go through the introduction to the article to see how the six-move sequence can be reasonably applied.[2]

Move 1: Establishing the Field

The first move, *establishing the field*, corresponds to paragraph 1 in Crenshaw's introduction. Here she establishes the field: violence against women of colour understood as a product of social systems of domination and not as isolated incidents. She asserts current knowledge about violence against women, referring to the paradigm shift *from* a psychological understanding of violence as individual aberration *to* a systemic and social one (violence as a product of systems of social domination and inequality). She emphasizes that the latter—systemic and social—understanding has been generated by the collective identity politics of women's movements, and she also draws attention to parallel developments of identity political recognitions of systems of domination by feminist and anti-racist movements.

Seen against the background of Swales' move 1, what is happening in the first paragraph of Crenshaw's text is not only an assertion of an *academic* field of knowledge. The move is twisted in the sense that what Crenshaw interpellates is a highly *political* field of knowledge. According to Crenshaw's opening, the interpellated knowledges about the entanglement of violence and systemic social dominations are primarily generated by social movements. This is in contrast to Swales' more conventional examples of opening paragraphs, where a disciplinary field or sub-field of academic knowledge is established. This does not mean that such a conventional opening could not be found in a scholarly feminist text. But Crenshaw's opening paragraph and the way in which it both reproduces and twists Swales' move 1 are nevertheless very much in line with the deconstruction of dichotomies between scholarly work and politics for which many feminists have argued. What Crenshaw does here, namely, to establish the field through the interpellation of a piece of politically generated scholarly knowledge, represents a twist of move 1 which it is reasonable to expect in many kinds of research texts inspired by Feminist Studies.

Move 2: Summarizing Previous Research

Move 2 in Swales' model is an outline of *relevant previous research* with academic references to key texts, key authors and/or key themes. This move implies the inclusion of a number of references. To some feminists the academic tradition of inserting many references has appeared to be somewhat at odds with a wish to produce texts that are accessible to broader publics. This may be why Crenshaw has clustered her many references to previous research on violence against women and critical race theory in the notes to her text, and why her article generally is endowed with rather long and elaborate notes. Against the background of Swales' sequence of moves, I interpret Crenshaw's notes 1, 2 and 3 as her way of including relevant previous research, i.e. her way of doing move 2. In these notes, Crenshaw refers to and briefly summarizes a range of key feminist texts on violence against women (notes 1 and 2) and on critical race theory and theories of race and gender (note 3). Thus, she underpins the claims of paragraph 1 by demonstrating that the movement-produced knowledges about systemic dominations linked to gender and race are strongly sustained by two strands of scholarly research: feminist research, on the one hand, and critical race theory, on the other.

Move 3: Preparing for Present Research

Move 3 in Swales' model, *preparing for present research* by indicating a significant *gap or lack in previous research*, can be seen in Crenshaw's opening in paragraphs 2 and 3. In two steps, she points out a major gap in previous knowledge produced by feminist and anti-racist identity politics. The first step (paragraph 2) engages with liberal discourses and a mainstream liberal response to identity politics, which criticizes the fact that identity politics does not transcend, but rather confirms, difference. This first step is for Crenshaw a launching pad for a second step (paragraph 3): her own key argument against the status quo of knowledge generated through identity politics—an argument which is very different from the liberal critique. According to Crenshaw, the horizon of the liberal discourses, introduced in paragraph 2 to be dismissed again in paragraph 3, is limited: they do not leave space for an understanding of the social empowerment that may grow out of identity politics. The problem, Crenshaw states, is *not*, as liberal discourses claim, that identity politics does not "transcend difference" but, *conversely*, that "it frequently conflates or ignores intragroup differences" (1991, 1242). The gap that Crenshaw points out is that feminist and anti-racist identity politics, as well as the knowledges and political practices built on it, has missed out on intragroup differences and, more specifically, has totally overlooked the situation of women of colour:

> Although racism and sexism readily intersect in the lives of real people, they seldom do in feminist and antiracist practices. Thus, when the practices expound identity as "woman" *or* "person of color" as an either/or proposition, they relegate the identity of women of color to a location that resists telling.
>
> —(1242)

Or, in other words, Crenshaw's text follows Swales' model sequence: she points out a major gap in current knowledge that she wants to fill. However, this is again Swales with a twist. Once more, Crenshaw blurs the boundaries between scholarly knowledge production, politics and practice. The gap pointed out by Crenshaw is not only a matter of *scholarly shortcomings*; it is also and much more importantly a question of a *political* knowledge production and *practice* which *lack* crucial insights and conceptual tools.

Move 4: Introducing the Present Research

In Swales' model sequence, the indication of gaps (move 3) paves the way for *move 4*, *introducing the present research* by *stating its purpose and outlining the structure and contents of the article/chapter/thesis*. Move 4 is the textual space in which the researcher-subject-narrator is supposed to appear as the one who holds a key to filling the gap through her or his own new and innovative research contribution. At this point, it becomes very clear that the moves are rhetorically dependent on each other. The stronger the indication of a gap or lack in move 3, the more clearly the present research of the researcher-subject-narrator will be rhetorically enabled to stand out as innovative and original. In Crenshaw's text, the transition from move 3 to move 4 to a large extent very precisely follows Swales' model in this sense, but again with a twist.

Move 4 begins in paragraph 4 with a *statement of purpose*. Crenshaw's purpose in the article is to fill the gap outlined in paragraphs 2–3—that the mono-dimensional identity politics of previous feminist and anti-racist movements has kept the identities of women of colour in an unspeakable position:

> My objective in this article is to advance the telling of that location [the previously unspeakable location of women of colour] by exploring the race and gender dimensions of violence against women of color.
>
> —(1991, 1242)

In terms of rhetorical strategy, this is a filling of gaps, following Swales' model, but with a twist parallel to the one I pointed out in move 3. As with her indication of the gap, Crenshaw's analytical strategy to overcome it targets not only *scholarly discussions* but also *political and practical outcomes*. Crenshaw claims that she wants to demonstrate how the experiences of women of colour, produced by "intersecting patterns of racism and sexism" (1243), are represented neither in feminist nor in anti-racist knowledge production. But in addition to pointing out this kind of theoretical shortcoming of current feminist and anti-racist discourses, she has set a second—political—goal for herself: she will change feminist and anti-racist resistance politics and practices to include intersectional perspectives:

> Although there are significant political and conceptual obstacles to moving against structures of domination with an intersectional sensibility, my point is that the effort to do so should be a central theoretical and political objective of both antiracism and feminism.
>
> —(1243, note 4)

Crenshaw's statement of purpose is followed by a presentation of the methodological tool she will use to fill the gap in previous feminist and anti-racist theorizing, politics and practice. This tool, the concept of intersectionality, is presented in paragraphs 5–6, which form the background for the second part of move 4: paragraph 7's outline of the "narrative" or rhetorical structure of the article. Here again, the text follows Swales' model—that move 4 is supposed to include an *outline of the structure and contents of the text*. The narrative of the article is very clearly rhetorically structured with the concept of intersectionality as its pivot. Paragraph 7 outlines how the different parts of the article deal with different dimensions of the concept: first, "structural intersectionality" (how the experiences of women of colour are formed structurally by the intra-acting power differentials of gender and race); second, "political intersectionality" (how feminist and anti-racist politics and practices have paradoxically contributed to the marginalization of the issue of violence against women of colour due to their lack of attention to intersectionality); and, third, how an intersectional approach can be useful from a wider political perspective.

Move 5: Situating the Researcher-Subject-Narrator

In addition to the four moves which, as described above, follow Swales' model, although in somewhat twisted versions, what I earlier introduced as *move 5 (situating the researcher-subject-narrator and her or his impact on the research/text)* can also be reasonably applied to Crenshaw's text. The text's researcher-subject-narrator appears visible in the first person (e.g. "My objective in this article . . ."; Crenshaw 1991, 1242), whereas conventional academic texts, including Swales' examples, are normally told in the third person with an invisible omniscient narrator, aptly characterized by feminist scholar Donna Haraway as a narrator who speaks from the position where you can play god, do "the god-trick" (1991, 191). The first-person narration characteristic of many feminist texts, including Crenshaw's, as previously mentioned, is related to discussions of feminist epistemology, self-reflexivity and the requirements of moral accountability for the position from which the text is told and the research done (Lykke 2010). The first-person narration of many feminist texts is often accompanied by a reflection on the position of the researcher-subject-narrator and her or his impact on the research/text. In Crenshaw's text, this reflection is to be found in note 8. Here she makes it clear that the article is written from "a black feminist stance" but also from a stance which implies that it is important to include intersections other than gender and race; she mentions "class, sexuality and age". She also argues more generally for the importance of the inclusion of a move 5: "It is important to name the perspective from which one constructs her analysis" (1244, note 8).

Move 6: Capturing the Audience

I have now commented on the ways in which all of Swales' four moves and one of my two added moves work in Crenshaw's text. Only *move 6, related to catching the attention of the audience*, is left to discuss. How does Crenshaw attract her audience in the opening paragraphs?

The article has become a very frequently quoted key text in Feminist Studies, so it evidently did make it in terms of catching readers' attention. It is, of course, difficult to assess what makes the success of an academic article. In addition to the qualities of the article and the author's research, success is also very much a question of timing and the ways in which certain theoretical approaches take off among broader groups of recipients at certain times as part of processes that are unforeseeable and uncontrollable by individual authors. So it is important to keep in mind that writing a good opening section with a lot of "catch-the-audience" potential is not a guarantee of automatic success with an audience. That said, as an author you can, indeed, improve your catch-the-audience potential in many different ways, and since Crenshaw's text made it, it is worth asking: What did she do?

The first thing I notice when I look at Crenshaw's opening section is that there is no specific "catch-the-audience" move included. She does not, for example, start with a juicy story, and the title is, at least for my taste, not particularly catchy. But still I was—as evidently many others were— "caught" by the text when I first came across it many years ago. Judging from my own reading of the text, I think that perhaps the most important rhetorical catch-the-audience strategy is the political passion with which Crenshaw speaks, combined with the very outspoken, emphatic, theoretically and pedagogically precise way in which she presents the gap in feminist and anti-racist discourses and suggests intersectionality as a conceptual tool for solving the problem.

Crenshaw's text has been criticized for doing the latter too effectively—in terms of contributing to the cementing of a concept that has its own problems. The crossroads metaphor on which the concept of intersectionality is based has been problematized. The metaphor of roads crossing each other and then departing each in their own direction may lead people to think of intersecting categories of race and gender as entities that just clash and depart like billiard balls but do not mutually transform each other (e.g. Lykke 2010; Staunæs and Søndergaard 2011). Against the background of this criticism, to which I have contributed myself, I would like to end this section of the chapter by emphasizing that Crenshaw, in her introductory section, in fact herself makes the point that intersectionality is not a once-and-for-all-time conceptual solution:

> I should say at the outset that intersectionality is not being offered here as some new totalizing theory of identity.
>
> —(1991, 1244)

Let me underline that I like this deuniversalizing move on Crenshaw's part, and I think it should be noted that this modest move did not prevent the strategies that she mobilized to catch her readers' attention from working extremely well!

HOW TO EXPERIMENT WITH YOUR OWN INTRODUCTIONS

In order to give readers some tools to experiment with different kinds of introductory narratives themselves, I shall now go through the six moves once more, but this time with a focus on clusters of writing exercises—one cluster for each move. I have developed the clusters of exercises alongside my teaching of creative and academic writing. Each cluster is specifically designed to produce a text that fulfils the requirements and goals of the particular move. You can choose other writing exercises to reach the same goals. Writing exercises are flexible and can be used for many purposes. The exercises that I have clustered under each move are intended as inspirations and suggestions, not as fixed recipes. You can, of course, also combine them with exercises introduced in other chapters of this volume.

Exercises that aim to open up creative processes will alternate with exercises and strategies for structuring and systematizing one's writing for academic purposes. Following up on Sissel Lie's discussion on the importance of recruiting trusted early-draft readers (see Chapter 8, this volume), the potential for shifting between individual work and collaboration with critical *and* generous partners is also explored. It should also be noted that these exercises, which are presented here in a sequence, can also be used separately or combined in other ways and for other purposes than the writing of introductions.

If you want to use the exercises in a classroom situation where you act as the teacher, you should start out by

- Indicating the purpose of the exercise (writing an introduction);
- Presenting the sequence (the six moves); and
- Suggesting that the sequence is to be considered as a game which the students play, with you as game leader and with a set of simple rules to which they must commit themselves, if they want to participate, but that they are free to decline to participate.

The rules are that you keep the time and tell students when to write and when to stop writing, when to talk to each other and when to stop talking to each other. Your role of leader and time-keeper means that you ruthlessly stop people's writing processes and conversations, even though they do not always feel that they have come to an end. You should tell the students at the outset that the rationale behind these somewhat strict rules is that it is very important for their learning experience that they work through all the moves you have planned in order to get the full picture of how to write an introduction. The moves and clusters of exercises are to be considered as a whole. If you have little time, you can leave out elements or clusters. But it is important that you plan your particular version of the sequence so that students get the opportunity to write key parts of an introduction within the given timeframe and that, in your planning of the writing session, you make sure that you have enough time to work through everything you planned. The exercise as a whole should also be experienced collectively by the group. There are moments where the whole group should share bits of writing with each other, and a basic dimension is that people should work in pairs.

To make all of this work, people need to go through the moves within the same timeframe, and it is important that the students know that this is why you appear to be a strict leader and time-keeper. It is my experience that people are normally very enthusiastic about the sequence and the exercises, but a prerequisite for this is that they know that when they are being interrupted in their writing and talking, it is for the sake of their experience of the whole game.

On the following pages, I shall present the sequence of exercises as I would do it in a classroom situation, i.e. with moments of sharing texts with other participants included. During all the moves, participants will thus shift between individual work and work with a partner. It is important that participants work with the same partner throughout the sequence of exercises, so you should ask them at the beginning to team up two by two.

When the moments of sharing are due in the exercise, you instruct the pairs to focus first on person 1 and afterwards on person 2, and you tell people when to change from person 1 to person 2 to make sure that everybody gets an equal amount of attention. Person 1 should first read her or his text, while person 2 concentrates on listening carefully, asking questions and commenting empathically with the purpose of helping person 1 to bring out the best possible phrasings. After a while you ask people to switch so that person 2 is now the focus. When both partners in the pair have presented their texts and received a response from the other, you should leave space for an individual reworking of the text in light of the comments from the partner. If time allows, you can insert another round of reading texts aloud, getting feedback in pairs and reworking the text individually. This element is part of all the exercises. To avoid repetition I will, therefore, on the following pages just indicate "reading and feedback in pairs".

I would like to underline that you can do the sequence of exercises on your own. Having a partner at hand is not an absolute must. If you do the exercises alone, you can just leave out the sections of work with a partner/partners. You can substitute these activities with self-reflexive moments where, for example, you read your text aloud to yourself and reflect on it.

You should also notice that I consciously chose not to go through the sequence following the order of moves from 1 to 6. It is important to notice that the moves should not be understood in a hierarchical, linear sense, to be done mechanically in a specific chronological order. Following the earlier metaphor, they should rather be perceived as moments in a choreographed dance, which need to be followed according to certain patterns and musical rhythms, but which also leave space for improvisations. The sequence can thus be done in different ways, and there is no one "right" order of things.

My favourite sequence, which I will follow below, is 6-5-1-2-3-4 in order to mobilize the personal commitment of the author and launch her or him into embodied ways of writing right at the beginning of the process.

TO CHOREOGRAPH AN INTRODUCTION

In terms of time, the writing-an-introduction exercise can be organized in very different ways. If, for example, you have a one-day workshop to do it in, you can let the group go in-depth with the text development, giving ample space for discussion, writing, rewriting and response and going through all the suggested steps in the exercises, lined up for each of the six moves. Conversely, if you have only very limited time, you can skip some of the steps under each move and, for example, give only 3–4 minutes per step and 3–4 minutes per person in the pair sessions. In this case you can do the whole exercise within one-and-a-half to two hours. It can work well both ways. If you are a teacher and do the exercise with a class, the important thing in terms of time is that you plan carefully beforehand how much time you will allow for the whole exercise and which steps within each move you want to use. You should take care to divide the time up between the number of planned steps so that you have enough time to guide the group through all six moves—and also allow at least 10–15 minutes for an evaluation at the end.

EXERCISE 24: DO SOMETHING FOR YOUR BODY

Purpose:

To underscore that writing is an embodied practice and that you write better if you feel good in your body.

Exercise:

Stand up against a wall. Feel the wall against the whole of your body. Stretch your arms towards the ceiling, palms turning towards your face: stretch, stretch, stretch as much as you can. Remember to relax your shoulders all the time. Pretend that you are flying—keep contact with the wall with your arms/wings, while you draw them slowly down, so that in the end they are hanging alongside your body. While you are doing this, feel the small muscles between your shoulder blades "talk to each other". Repeat the exercise several times—as long as you feel like it . . . The more the better if you want to make the stiffness in your shoulders go away . . .

EXERCISE 25: TOPIC ASSOCIATION

Purpose:

To call forth your associations with, passions for and ideas about your topic/theme.

Exercise:

Before you start this exercise, you must decide on a topic or theme for the text that you want to write an introduction for. If you do not have a topic already, you can, for example, make a list of what you consider to be burning issues—politically, theoretically, professionally, thematically. If you do the exercise in a group, it may be inspiring if all group members write a list of keywords for what each considers to be "burning issues" and then read their lists to each other, giving other group members time for a round of short comments. After this, you choose an issue from the list to be your topic for the rest of the exercise.

When you have picked a topic, you should do a meditation on it for 5 minutes, or longer if you have time. Sit down so that you are comfortable and relaxed, close your eyes, and let all the associations, images, ideas, concepts, etc. that your topic calls forward flow through your mind.

EXERCISE 26: MOVE 6—CAPTURING THE AUDIENCE

Purpose:

To establish an embodied, lively and engaging way of writing.

Exercise:

(developed through inspiration from Sissel Lie; see Chapter 8, this volume)

a) *1) Sit down comfortably with your eyes closed. Meditate on a fruit or sweet that you really like. Try to grasp it with all your senses. How does it taste? How does it smell? How does it feel? How does it look? Which sounds do you relate to your fruit/sweet? 2) Write a text on your fruit/sweet: "My fruit/sweet tastes like . . .", "My fruit/ sweet smells like . . .", etc. 3) Read your text to yourself, and circle the phrases about your fruit/sweet that you find most pleasurable and stylistically interesting. 4) Try to write a poetic, dramatic or narrative text about your fruit/sweet using at least some of the bits and pieces you have circled. 5) Reading and feedback in pairs.*

b) 1) *Go back to the poetic, dramatic or narrative text that you wrote and substitute your topic/theme for your fruit/sweet.* 2) *Reading and feedback in pairs. Discuss whether any of the substitutions produce new ideas about your topic. Some of the substitutions will probably just produce odd bits of text, but some might generate unexpected phrases that may actually work in the context of your topic.*
c) 1) *Do a new meditation. Sit down comfortably with your eyes closed. Try to imagine a scene that catches your topic/theme in a nutshell; you can try to imagine that your topic/theme is being presented as a film or theatre play and construct a scene that presents crucial aspects of it. Or you can try to think of a scene as part of a personal memory where you felt that crucial issues concerning your topic were at stake. Remember that even a purely theoretical topic/theme can be articulated in a scene. Try to mobilize all your senses when you imagine the scene. If possible, let your mind flow back to the work you did with the fruit/sweet and with the subsequent substitution of your topic/theme.* 2) *Write down a description of the scene. Try to make the description as sensuous, lively and engaging as possible.* 3) *Reading and feedback in pairs.*

EXERCISE 27: MOVE 5—SITUATING THE RESEARCHER-SUBJECT-NARRATOR

Purpose:

To spell out how you as researcher-subject-narrator are positioned in relation to your topic/theme.

Exercise:

a) Write a personal letter to your partner or to a good colleague/friend to tell her or him why this topic/theme is important. Start and end with a personal greeting: "Dear/Hi xxx, I have chosen to write about xxx topic/theme. This topic/theme means a lot to me because . . . — with love from/best wishes from xxx." Try to explain your (political, personal, theoretical, ethical, etc.) motivations and relations to the topic/theme. b) Reading and feedback in pairs.

EXERCISE 28: MOVE 1—ESTABLISHING THE FIELD

Purpose:

To establish in writing why and in what ways your topic is important and relevant to write about.

Exercise:

a) Write down all the brainstorm keywords you can think of regarding the importance and relevance of your topic. Do not censor yourself. Write down all the words that come into your mind. b) Read your keywords to yourself and circle those which you think are most to the point. c) Write a coherent text based on the keywords you circled. d) Reading and feedback in pairs.

EXERCISE 29: MOVE 2—SUMMARIZING PREVIOUS RESEARCH

Purpose:

To give a genealogical[3] account of key themes and key works which in hindsight have been important for the articulation of your topic—your "intellectual autobiography" (see Kathy Davis, Chapter 11, p. 173 and note 3, this volume) with respect to your topic.

Exercise:

a) Write a one-liner in answer to the question: What is your topic/ theme? Put a ring around the one-liner. b) Write down keywords for all the theoretical, methodological etc. inspirations from previous research you can think of that relate to your topic/theme. Draw a rhizomatic map of relations between the keywords. ('Rhizomatic' refers to 'rhizome', a term which French philosophers Gilles Deleuze and Felix Guattari (1992) borrowed from its botanical context where it refers to the ways in which some plants (e.g. grass and strawberries) spread by sticking out new shoots in all directions, to signify the non-linearity of thought processes. Think of this process when you draw your map, putting criss-cross lines between your keywords.) c) Take a careful look at your rhizomatic drawing of keywords and reflect on which are the most important inspirations, seen from your present retrospective perspective. Circle the most important keywords. d) Write a coherent text on the genealogies of your one-line articulation of your topic, based on the keywords you circled. e) Reading and feedback in pairs.

EXERCISE 30: MOVE 3—PREPARING FOR PRESENT RESEARCH

Purpose:

To come to terms with what is new and original in your text and to enable yourself to articulate, in a condensed and concise form, what your research contribution is.

Exercise:

a) *Introductory comment: This part of the sequence of exercises is a bit different from the previous ones. Now you will begin by concentrating on your partner's work instead of your own, while your partner in return focuses on your work. In the classroom version of the exercise, this should work without problems because the pairs who have been working together from the start of the game will now have insight into each other's work based on the conversations they have had so far. In the version where you do the exercise with a present friend/colleague, the same applies. But this part of the exercise becomes a bit more difficult to carry out if you are doing the sequence on your own without any kind of partner involved. However, the exercise can still be done. In the latter case, I suggest that you take a walk before doing this exercise and that during the walk you try to call forward a good friend/colleague in your imagination. Remember talks you have had with this person, experiences you have shared with her or him, etc. You should do the exercise when you get back and make some effort to try to act as a "stand-in" for your friend/colleague in the parts of the exercise where the partner plays a leading role.*

b) *Exercise: 1) Against the background of your knowledge of your partner's research, you should prepare some interview questions for her or him. Pretend that you are a journalist who wants to write a popular science article about your partner's research contribution. 2) Interview your partner—try to frame your questions so that your partner really gets a good chance to spell out what is new, original and interesting in her or his research. 3) In your role as interviewee, you should, after the interview, write down brainstorm keywords in order to memorize and remember what happened in the interview. Did you as the interviewee feel that your partner's questions were relevant? If yes, in what ways? If not, why not? Did you feel that something was missing in your partner's approach to your work? If yes, what did your partner miss? If no, how did it feel to be asked these questions that really went to the core of your work? Did you discover things about your work that you had not thought of before? 4) In your role as interviewee you should then take some time to read and reflect on the keywords and circle the most important ones. 5) In your role as interviewee you should end by writing a coherent text on your research contribution. What's new and original in your research? How does it go beyond previous research? Use the text you wrote as part of move 2 as inspiration when answering the latter question. e) Reading and feedback in pairs.*

EXERCISE 31: MOVE 4—INTRODUCING THE PRESENT RESEARCH

Purpose:

To outline the purpose and construct the "narrative" of the full text (article, dissertation, book) for which you are preparing the introduction and to give a written account of both.

Exercise:

Purpose Exercise: a) Re-read the textual results of all the previous moves, and write an overall reflection on them. b) Try to articulate a limited number of significant research questions that correspond to the text on your research contribution (move 3). c) Write a text about the purpose of the full text (article, dissertation, book) for which you are preparing the introduction—related to the research questions posed under b. d) Reading and feedback in pairs.
    Narrative Exercise: a) Write a non-stop text with a point of departure in each of your research questions. A non-stop text means that you are not allowed to stop writing. If your head suddenly feels totally empty, you just continue blahblahblah . . . until something else occurs (see also Sissel Lie's discussion of automatic writing, Chapter 8, this volume). b) Read your non-stop texts and circle the phrases which best "cover" what you want to answer in your research questions. c) Write up the answers in coherent sentences, using these phrases. d) Re-read the scene you constructed at the beginning of the exercise under move 6. Try to write a synopsis for a "literary" text in a genre of your own choice (e.g. a comedy, a crime story, a fairy tale, an action film, a lyric poem) where this scene is included. Reflect on the position of the text's narrator as well as its characters and plot. e) Try to integrate your research questions and the answers (cf. c above) in the synopsis of your "literary" text (cf. d above). You may need to revise the synopsis somewhat in order to integrate the questions and answers into it. f) Reading and feedback in pairs.

EXERCISE 32: WRAPPING UP

You have now gone through all six moves. As the last part of the exercise you should gather together all the textual results and write a fully coherent text with the relevant exercises from each move included. Perhaps you will have to revise certain text elements or leave out others that do not fit in the final product. You should remember that the exercise is not a recipe to be followed mechanically. If possible, you may also use your partner as a reader and critical discussant for the final piece. If you do the exercise in a classroom, it is a good idea to end the exercise with a reading session where everybody shares the results of parts of the exercise with the whole class (or with a smaller group, if it takes too much time to let everybody read to everybody).

CONCLUSION

In this chapter I have focused on ways to combine creative and academically structured ways of working when writing introductions to academic texts. I have used the metaphor of a choreographed dance as my pivot. To learn the traditional academic skills of establishing the field, outlining previous research, defining how your research goes beyond it, articulating your research questions, stating your aims and outlining the structure of your paper, dissertation, etc. is certainly important. Mastering these skills is crucial for your success as an academic writer—in much the same way as a tango dancer, for example, cannot succeed without knowledge of the patterns of steps and bodily moves that make up the dance she or he is going to perform. For people taking tango lessons, however, this is basic knowledge, and there is still a lot to learn when you have just mechanically understood the basic geometry of the tango steps and moves. Before you can perform a tango, you must be able to make the rhythms, the drama, the poetics and passions of the music resonate in your body, to feel the bodily pleasure of moving along with your partner and to make all this work in synergy with your knowledge of the choreographed patterns of steps and moves. What is evident to the tango learner, however, is not always as evident to research students and other academic writers, because academic writing traditions are so heavily burdened with an exclusive focus on logic and coherence, leaving passions, embodied intuitions, poetics, etc. aside. The point I wanted to make in this chapter is that it is a requirement, if you want to master the sophisticated art of writing academic introductions, that you learn the lesson of the tango dancer: you need to be open to the emerging synergies of carefully planned choreographies and embodied intuitions.

ACKNOWLEDGEMENTS

I want to thank Sissel Lie for very inspiring comments on this chapter.

NOTES

1. "Denotation" refers to the lexical meaning of a word; it is opposed to "connotation", i.e. the individual associations related to a word.

2. Crenshaw's introduction is seven paragraphs long, including ten notes. To follow my analysis, I suggest that you have Crenshaw's text to hand. It can be downloaded, for example, from www.jstor.org/discover/10.2307/1229039? uid=3737880&uid=2134&uid=2&uid=70&uid=4&sid=21101097833261 (accessed April 20, 2014). Please note that the article has been reprinted many times and that some versions of it to be found on the Net do not include all ten notes. The following references to notes in the texts refer to the *Stanford Law Review* version of the article from 1991 (Crenshaw 1991).

3. The concept of genealogy is taken from Michel Foucault (1984). A genealogical analysis takes as its starting point a here-and-now perspective and constructs, via a retrospective analysis, a kind of "family tree" for a certain strand of theory, conceptual framework, terminology, theme, etc. A genealogical analysis disrupts the idea that the history of concepts and theory develops as a linear, rational sequence of events. On the contrary, it is based on the assumption that conceptual links and mutual impacts between different strands of theory are best understood in hindsight.

REFERENCES

Crenshaw, Kimberlé. 1991. "Mapping the Margins: Intersectionality, Identity Politics, and Violence against Women of Color." *Stanford Law Review* 43 (6): 1241–99.

Deleuze, Gilles and Félix Guattari. 1992. *A Thousand Plateaus: Capitalism and Schizophrenia*. London: Continuum. Translated by Brian Massumi from *Mille Plateaux. Capitalisme et schizophrénie*. Vol. 2, Paris: Minuit, 1980.

Foucault, Michel. 1984. "Nietzsche, Genealogy, History." In *The Foucault Reader: An Introduction to Foucault's Thought*, edited by Paul Rabinow, 76–100. London: Penguin Books.

Haraway, Donna. 1991. "Situated Knowledges: The Science Question in Feminism and the Privilege of Partial Perspective." In *Simians, Cyborgs and Women: The Reinvention of Nature*, 183–201. London: Free Association Books.

Lykke, Nina. 2010. *Feminist Studies: A Guide to Intersectional Theories, Methodologies and Writing*. New York: Routledge.

Rich, Adrienne. 1986. "Notes toward a Politics of Location." In *Blood, Bread and Poetry: Selected Prose 1979–1985*, 201–31. London and New York: Norton.

Richardson, Laurel. 2000. "Writing as a Method of Inquiry." In *Handbook of Qualitative Research*, 2nd ed., edited by Norman K. Denzin and Yvonna S. Lincoln, 923–48. London: Sage.

Staunæs, Dorthe and Dorte Marie Søndergaard. 2011. "Intersectionality: A Theoretical Adjustment." In *Theories and Methodologies in Postgraduate Feminist Research: Researching Differently*, edited by Rosemarie Buikema, Gabriele Griffin and Nina Lykke, 45–60. London: Routledge.

Swales, John. 1983. "Developing Materials for Writing Scholarly Introductions." In *Case Studies in ELT*, edited by R.R. Jordan, 188–202. London: Collins ELT.

10 Politics of Gendered Remembering
Feminist Narratives of "Meaningful Objects"

Andrea Pető

Teaching in Gender Studies classrooms poses particular challenges. Often students come from disciplines other than Gender Studies, and some of them have other principal disciplinary interests. To address this situation, and considering that "our past is too important to be entrusted to historians alone",[1] I have developed a history course which includes a sequence of exercises that not only "transmit" historical facts and canonized narratives to Gender Studies students but also promote an understanding of how gendered narratives dealing with the past are formed in different genres of writing.[2]

Students working through these exercises are requested to think about which narratives they are using when they write about past events and objects and how their choice of narrative was made, while also considering the advantages and disadvantages of identification with the narrative (Heilbrun 1988, 11–31; Smith 1991). They are also required to ask themselves whose problems are being addressed in the historical articles that make up course readings, and who may profit from the knowledge and insights provided by the historical narrations of different authors.

In this chapter I present two writing exercises[3] that explore different sites of remembering; the exercises make the rules of remembering more identifiable and open up space for rethinking the past. I conclude with an exploration of how and what students can learn from this kind of feminist writing exercises.

HOW TO FRAME WOMEN IN HISTORY

The first exercise challenges the accepted frames of remembering. It is an attempt to promote an understanding of privileged narratives and the ways in which they remove the personal from History. In contrast to privileged narratives, the exercise reintegrates the personal into historical narrative.

The exercise begins with an object relating to the life of a foremother of each student. The figure of the foremother is not necessarily a relative; it is, rather, a woman whom the student thinks of as an example or identifies with in one way or another. The life and the narrated life story of the foremother also serve as a "site of remembering", as defined by Pierre Nora, and at the same time as a method and practice of teaching creative writing

(1989, 7–24). In the act of doing this exercise, students are transgressing the canon of academic writing and blurring the boundaries with creative writing as they are encouraged to position the narrator at the centre of the narrative. More generally, the exercise can also be used to raise theoretical and methodological questions relating to history writing and to our conceptions of the past (Pető 2006; Pető and Waaldijk 2006).

EXERCISE 33: YOUR FOREMOTHER[4]

Find out as much as possible about the life of a woman who was alive and more or less adult in a year with symbolic "weight" in your country's history.[5] This may be a relative (grandmother, aunt), a friend or somebody who was a public figure in your country. A criterion for the selected woman, the foremother, is that she is no longer alive at the time of writing. You are advised to find someone who matters to you personally; this may be either as a political or intellectual inspiration or as a person you know or are related to. This woman will be referred to as the "foremother", but please note that she is not necessarily a family relation. You will have to write a description of this woman and bring it to class. The paper should be structured as follows:

1. *Begin by writing down the name and the place and date of birth and death of the foremother.*
2. *Try to describe her in terms of nationality, class, ethnicity, religion and sexuality. Did she receive an education? (Use a maximum of 100 words.)*
3. *Then try to write something about her experience with locatedness (reflect on what you know about it and try, if possible, to gain more knowledge): Did she live in the same place during her whole life? Did she meet people from other regions of her country, from other parts of Europe, from other parts of the world? Did she lose family or friends through migration? (Use a maximum of 150 words.)*
4. *Finally, describe her life in relation to a year with symbolic weight in your country's history: family relations, job, sexuality. Where and how did she live? (Use a maximum of 250 words.)*

Tip 1: To gather information you may use both informal sources (memories and recollections, stories and anecdotes, conversations with friends and relatives) and more formal sources (history books, archival materials, newspaper clippings). Include references to your information sources.

Tip 2: Be prepared to reflect on your position as a narrator of the foremother's life story in the class discussion of your description.

hrough this exercise, students gain an understanding of how, by means
f various mediating channels, history as a personal past is constructed
nd established. Examples of such mediating channels are family histo-
es, discussions and debates within families, personal experiences and
isual sources, as well as—most important in terms of the current subject
natter—objects (and stories relating to objects). Stories told by older
emale members of families—stories that I suggest students explore in these
lasses and seminars—represent an emotional opportunity for participants
o think about themselves in different historical terms. These stories make
isible how the national and canonized history taught in textbooks is linked
vith personal histories. The students are also asked to bring an object, or
photo of an object, that belonged to their foremother. This opens up the
pportunity to construct narratives around this object but also to install an
xhibition in the classroom where students can act as guides to their own
bjects.

The purpose of this exercise is to deconstruct the universalism of narra-
on about the "past" and to avoid what is sometimes called the "god-trick"
a decontextualized and detached way of narrating historical "facts") when
peaking about an object attached to a person (Haraway 1991).

This exercise addresses the ways in which one can understand and give
neaning to collected historical "facts". It is important to acknowledge
hat, for example, writing "women's history" is never only a collection
f facts and figures about women in the past. To understand and give
neaning to those lives we need concepts, stories, narratives and systems of
neaning. We also need to reconceptualize the historian as a writer, and in
his process the tools of creative writing can be very useful (see also Petö,
Chapter 5, this volume). Moreover, in order to make feminist readings
f gender in a historical context, it is necessary to address questions of
ntersections with race, ethnicity, class, sexuality and other power differ-
ntials and to be critical of traditional historical narratives about national,
conomic, political and cultural developments. In this way the exercise
an widen students' "horizon of expectations", as Koselleck puts it (1985,
26–88).

Students are also asked to comment on whether the objects they col-
ected have an inspiring or depressing impact. They are asked to analyze
he construction of emotions as emotional discourses and "as a form of
ocial action that creates effects in the world, effects that are read in a cul-
urally informed way by the audience for emotional talk" (Abu-Lughod
nd Lutz 1990, 12). If students learn that emotions are not "given"
ut are constructions, and that talking about emotions influences those
ame emotions, then they are equipped with the means to influence that
iscourse.

This exercise can also be an academic writing course in itself, and it can
e used as a module in different teaching settings: as a one-day workshop,
s a full course at a university or as a summer school course.[6]

OBJECT WRITING

In the second exercise, students discuss the experience of writing about the past in relation to an object of their choice. In this writing exercise, the object is related to the student-author rather than to a foremother. The shift in focus encourages students to take more responsibility and to dare to scrutinize their own language and choices. In this exercise, the focus is the students' narratives.

The object-writing exercise also includes reading and taking notes from a list of recommended academic texts, critical thinking, group discussions and academic writing in class and at home. The texts should be analyzed in terms of their authenticity. Against the background of the object-writing exercise, these texts are to be scrutinized through the question: How is the authenticity of memory connected to the source? How do we know what "true stories" are? In this manner, the knowledge that the texts provide receives new validation from the class. The students also gain an opportunity to experience the differences between first-hand and distanced narration. Exposure to a plurality of narrations creates room to discuss the positioning of authors and to identify privileged interpretations and compare them with other kinds of interpretations which they potentially silence.

This exercise also further strengthens the creative writing component of the first exercise. Students are asked to bring to class at least one object (or digital photo) that has historical meaning to them, as well as an image of the object (photo, artefact, "thing", etc.). Analyses of "meaning", constructed from different viewpoints and narrative traditions, are the focus of the exercise. The image of the object is copied and distributed among the group participants beforehand in order to facilitate discussion and serve as a basis for the object-writing exercise. The texts produced by the students could also be distributed and discussed in groups.

EXERCISE 34: OBJECT WRITING

Instructions to Students:

Bring with you to the course at least one object (artefact, "thing", text, etc.) and/or a digital photo which has a historical meaning for you; include also an image of the object, photo, etc.

Tip: To gather background information about your object, you may use both informal sources (memories and recollections, stories and anecdotes, conversations with friends and relatives) and more formal sources (history books, archival materials, newspaper clippings, etc.). Include references to your information sources separately. Try to think about how this material object, in different aspects of life, illustrates memory and narratives about different pasts. Be creative and ambitious in positioning yourself in texts related to the object!

Instructions to the Teacher:

Print-outs of students' papers should be copied and distributed among the group participants to facilitate discussion. If you do the exercise in a large class, you can divide the students by assigning each of them a genre (i.e. ethnographic note, letter, textbook entry, academic essay, museum catalogue entry). It is also essential to draw up a list of reference literature which can be discussed by the group and which is appropriate for establishing links to existing feminist scholarship. This is particularly important when teaching interdisciplinary groups with students from various academic and national backgrounds.

Instructions to the Group about the Assignment:

(max. 500 words each about the following five separate assignments)

1. *Write an ethnographic note for the object as if it were an artefact in a museum or a virtual museum with references.*
2. *Write a letter explaining your choice of object to a friend.*
3. *Write a text about your object as an illustration in a history textbook for secondary schools.*
4. *Try to write an academic essay about the owner or producer of the object and her or his experience with locatedness: For example, did the person live in the same place during her or his whole life?*
5. *Address the issues of visibility and forgetting in relation to the object as academic essay.*

Students should also be asked to gather background information about their object. This information may, as mentioned above, come from both informal and formal sources. References to the information sources are made separately and can be analyzed in a different part of the exercise, for example, during class discussion. In their analyses, students can be asked to try to consider how the material object illustrates memories and narratives about different pasts.

In class, students initially talk about their chosen objects, having already written about them in the five different genres (ethnographic note, letter, textbook entry, academic essay, museum catalogue). Usually they immediately recognize differences in power relations and positioning relating to the narrative structures. In this way they have to face their own value system and may discover, for example, that they have uncritically been ranking personal information as less "authentic" (i.e. important) than a museological narrative written in the third person.

After each student has introduced her or his object, photographs or other kinds of representations of all the objects are redistributed among participants. Students are asked to identify whose object they have received and why it mattered to the person who chose it. In this round, students are introduced to relational and narrative practices relating to the past as well as to the present.

HOW DO STUDENTS LEARN?

The innovative potential of the object-writing exercise is linked to the move away from traditional authoritarian ways of teaching canonized history. In history teaching, a task that is frequently required is the gathering and processing of sources that, in a positivist mode, are evaluated in terms of their ability to give "objective" information about the past. The exercise I present here takes students beyond the positivist notion of an "objectively" given history about the past. When students, for example, analyze their own written texts or those of their fellow students, the exercise opens up a subversive perspective. It places students in the role of privileged narrator, through which they consciously determine the turning points, topoi and narrative frames that are expected by the particular genre in which they are writing. Initially the exercise can be undertaken by the whole class collectively—until students have learned the methods of text analysis. But it can also be performed effectively with the class divided up into smaller groups, with each group processing one type of text and/or genre and afterwards gathering to compare and contrast their different results. The groups can then evaluate the texts/genres through each other's understanding of them.

Longer reference texts may also be distributed among the groups. In this case, however, it is important that there is a collective evaluation at the end. The diversity of sources can be used to show that so-called History consists of many individual stories and that differing views and interests always exist side by side.

When writing stories about the objects, information may be gathered by visiting libraries, by doing research on the Internet or simply by systematizing existing knowledge. Collective or group analysis of "what we know" and "how we know it" is always important, as this also provides the basis for answering the questions: How do we know what we think we know, and how do power relations influence the system of knowledge?

Individual research will tend to relate to the immediate environment—to family members and friends. Students examine the pasts of their own families and those of their friends, thereby becoming acquainted with the lives of family members and others. In the course of the research, they confront the historical experiences of their families and acquaintances while gaining a direct understanding of what it means to live as a woman or a man under various historical circumstances and how privileged positions arise in various situations. This exercise also strengthens the relationship between education and the broader educational community (the social network of students), enabling students to learn management and coping skills in the field of social and cultural relations.

Using their own text as a source of knowledge is also empowering for participants. Writing serves as a way of learning about and getting to know one's past and the feelings linked to it. It also helps the student authors to theorize based on individual experiences and feelings while contributing to a paradigm shift as far as power relations in the teaching of history are concerned.

In the course of learning, it is also important to determine which arguments are used and by whom within a given genre. This helps to promote the development of a critical approach and a culture of debate as well as the formation of a new site for remembering and empathic thinking. The discussion also raises the question of how a feminist author should read clues about the past and how the student authors should define their role in the research and writing process (Fulbrook 2002; see also Petö, Chapter 5, this volume).

WHAT DO STUDENTS LEARN?

The first learning objective addressed in the object-writing exercise relates to feminist history writing and its relation to objects and stories (Waaldijk 1995). Students are provided with a reading list, and one of the first questions they should answer in class is how these readings influence the way in which they view "their" object. By this point, there should also have been a discussion of how feminist scholarship and mainstream academia address the issue of women's experiences (Fleishman 1998). Participants also learn to differentiate between first-hand narratives and mediated experience, and they learn to consider how different distances (in time and space) impose different meanings. Meanwhile, the "woman" as an object of symbolic politics and as a narrator is differentiated—which helps to avoid falling into the essentializing trap of seeing "true memories" as the only legitimate sources of "truth".

This learning objective is related to the concept of agency, which, as feminist theorist Seyla Benhabib (1992) points out, has given rise to a clash of paradigms within women's historiography. As feminist scholar Lois McNay claims:

A more rounded conception of agency is crucial to explaining both how women have acted autonomously in the past despite constricting social sanctions and also how they may act now in the context of complex processes of gender reconstructing.

—(2003, 141)

Inspired by feminist scholar Saba Mahmood (2005), I shall also claim that students learn to see agency as a capacity to question the world order while writing various narratives about the past and analyzing their modes of writing.

As the students listen to the narratives that have been constructed around their objects, they learn to differentiate between the narrative positions of "speaking as" and "speaking about". They also learn that personalization of the object means particularization, if its owner is not a privileged subject. Just think of the difference between a sewing box owned by somebody's grandmother or by the wife of a national politician. Connecting their experiences of these objects, students deal with the personal as something that is theoretical—and following Benhabib I shall claim that their commitment produces agency:

The feminist commitment to women's agency and sense of selfhood, to the re-appropriation of women's own history in the name of an emancipated future, and to the exercise of radical social criticism which uncovers gender in all its endless variety and monotonous similarity.

—(Benhabib 1992, 229)

The second learning objective is about understanding a major distinction in feminist theory: the difference between public and private, and the way it generates gendered spaces.

The third learning objective is to problematize the allegedly objective narrative of traditional academic language through the personalization of scholarship. Writing as a performed rite changes in accordance with the audience and power relations. A certain rhetoric crafts an expository space for past events. In the classroom it is worthwhile doing an exercise about the way in which privilege and power are transformed and constructed by academic writing.

Last, the fourth objective is to inspire a different relationship to time. The students are asked to reflect on the same material from different positions and in different circumstances. The "publish or perish" principle is transforming academic life and leading it to focus more on the end product while not valuing the thinking process. In opposition to such a stance, this exercise brings forward the process of thinking and reflecting while shaping the intellectual "habitus" of the students.

EVALUATION

Evaluating and grading these two exercises pose a challenge to the instructor. While writing about "their" objects, students may reveal details of their ersonal life, which can place the instructor in a difficult position. For this eason it is important that the evaluation of a student's work is made at different levels, thereby requiring the investment of time, thoughtfulness and notional openness.

The focus of these writing exercises is the approach and way of thinking rather than historical facts. Even so, it is important that the group sets ut from the same theoretical basis; everyone should have read the recommended works and discussed the extent to which they dis/agree with their authors.

Since personal experiences tend to have a deep impact on our ability) learn, it is crucial to provide tasks that students undertake in groups r independently. In order for students to experience the clash of differing viewpoints, the unfolding of various techniques of persuasion, and the rocess of opinion formation, it is also useful to initiate class discussions fter a while, the students themselves will probably do so on their own). Of ourse, explanations and summaries given by the teacher are also necessary. irection in relation to the learning objectives is imperative. Indeed, discussions should not be allowed to drift; instead, they should address what is eally important. The development of a teacher-student relationship based n personality and trust is vital.

By their very nature, these exercises necessitate an evaluation that differs om customary approaches. Differing opinions and views are often heard class; prejudices may be voiced, and personal fates mentioned. If these ssignments are rewarded "only" with marks, then the effect may be a negtive one, holding students back. In addition, individual written assessments elp to motivate and develop students. Evidently, such evaluations must e treated in confidence. In relation to the collective exercises, there is also n opportunity for the teacher to review the value system of teaching. As ducators, we should critically reflect on the ways in which our own habits f questioning have an effect on the class, and we should also take into ccount the relation between female and male students. The teacher could lso bring her own "important" objects to class—either the object itself or photograph of it. In this way, we can mitigate the hierarchies that necesarily arise in the course of teaching, and as instructors we can open up a /indow allowing the students to see the instructor from a different angle.

Usually there has to be some kind of assessment of the amount and qualy of work performed and time invested by the student. The method of valuation is important. Although it is difficult, we should try to avoid motiating students with grades. (The effect on a student of receiving a bad rade for their "meaningful object" could potentially be very repressive.)

Instead of grading the students' efforts only with marks, teachers should ncourage them to think about the learning process from beginning to nd. As teachers, we should also be clear about whose opinions or value idgements we are hearing. If we ask for clearly formulated written essays om students, then these aspects can be applied as we assess the work. The

170   *Andrea Pető*

exercises form part of a student's personal development, and they broaden the scope of communication between teacher and student (and among students). They also urge us as instructors to consider what and how we, together with the students, think about the past—and how this may change the futures that we might imagine. It is my opinion that the transformative potential of academia depends on the extent to which we succeed in this task. These exercises might help instructors in Gender Studies classrooms to dismantle disciplinary boundaries and to understand how we are writing our pasts. History is defined as an unfinished project in these exercises, and against this background students become aware of how it is continued and constructed via narratives. History does not end when the narrative about "events" or "objects" is concluded. Narratives transform our understanding of the past, and in the construction of narratives in the exercises, the students are in effect reformulating history. Hayden White's concept of "emplotment" (the encoding and presentation of facts in different narrative genres) can be useful to promote an understanding of why objects are spoken about and to generate insight into who decides which narratives are to become the privileged ones (1978/2001, 223). By the end of the class, students have learned that "history writing" has an alternative: that of examining the historical cultures, communities and agents that produce histories.

NOTES

1. Alluding to the alleged words of French prime minister by the end of World War I, Georges Clemenceau: "War is too serious a matter to entrust to military men."
2. On challenges of how to integrate history in feminist research see Pető and Waaldijk 2011.
3. These exercises were developed as part of the course "Framing Women in History", which was taught at the Department of Gender Studies at the Central European University, Budapest, Hungary; they were developed in cooperation with Berteke Waaldijk (Utrecht University).
4. See more on this in Pető and Waaldijk 2006.
5. The years I suggest to illustrate to my classes what is meant are 1945 as the end of World War II, 1948 as the date of first publication of *The Second Sex* by Simone de Beauvoir or 1956 as a date for the Hungarian Revolution.
6. I taught it, for example, as part of a PhD course in academic and creative writing in Gender Studies at the University of Linköping in Sweden.

REFERENCES

Abu-Lughod, Lila and Catherine A. Lutz. 1990. "Introduction: Emotion, Discourse, and the Politics of Everyday Life." In *Language and Politics of Emotions*, edited by Lila Abu-Lughod and Catherine A. Lutz, 1–23. Paris: Maison des Sciences de l'Homme; Cambridge: Cambridge University Press.

Benhabib, Seyla. 1992. *Situating the Self: Gender, Community and Postmodernism in Contemporary Ethics*. New York: Routledge.

Fleishman, Suzanne. 1998. "Gender, the Personal, and the Voice of Scholarship: A View Point." *Signs* 23 (4): 975–1016.

Fulbrook, Mary. 2002. *Historical Theory*. London: Routledge.

Haraway, Donna. 1991. "Situated Knowledges: The Science Question in Feminism and the Privilege of Partial Perspective." In *Simians, Cyborgs and Women: The Reinvention of Nature*, 183–201. London: Free Association Books.

Heilbrun, Carolyn. 1988. *Writing a Woman's Life*. New York: Ballantine Books.

Koselleck, Reinhart. 1985. *Future Past: On the Semantics of Historical Time*. New York: Columbia University Press.

Mahmood, Saba. 2005. *Politics of Piety*. Princeton: Princeton University Press.

McNay, Lois. 2003. "Agency, Anticipation and Interdeterminancy." *Feminist Theory* 4 (2): 139–48.

Nora, Pierre. 1989. "Between Memory and History." *Representations* 26: 7–24.

Petö, Andrea. 2006. "A Photograph." In *Teaching with Memories: European Women's Histories in International and Interdisciplinary Classrooms*, edited by Andrea Petö and Berteke Waaldijk, 46–50. Galway: Women's Studies Centre, University of Galway Press.

Petö, Andrea and Berteke Waaldijk. 2006. "Memories, Histories and Narratives: Teaching with Memories in Europe." In *Teaching with Memories: European Women's Histories in International and Interdisciplinary Classrooms*, edited by Andrea Petö and Berteke Waaldijk, 21–29. Galway: Women's Studies Centre, University of Galway Press.

Petö, Andrea and Berteke Waaldijk. 2011. "Histories and Memories in Feminist Research." In *Theories and Methodologies in Postgraduate Feminist Research: Researching Differently*, edited by Rosemarie Buikema, Gabriele Griffin and Nina Lykke, 74–91. New York: Routledge.

Smith, Bonnie. 1991. *On Writing Women's Work*. EUI Working Paper HEC no. 91/7. Florence: European University Institute (EUI).

Waaldijk, Berteke. 1995. "Of Stories and Sources, Feminist History." In *Women's Studies and Culture: A Feminist Introduction*, edited by Rosemarie Buikema and Anneke Smelik, 14–25. London: Zed Books.

White, Hayden. 1978/2001. "The Historical Text as Literary Artifact." Reprinted in *The History and Narrative Reader*, edited by Geoffrey Roberts, 375–90. New York: Routledge.

11 Making Theories Work

Kathy Davis

Gender Studies is a theoretical discipline. We all use theory. Doing feminist theory means knowing which theorists are currently *en vogue*, being able to reproduce the right concepts in the right language and displaying an awareness of the correct positions in various debates. Most of us have our own favourite theories—the ones we particularly like or find ourselves inevitably gravitating toward in our research and writing. You probably also have theories that you heartily disagree with; those are the theories you love to criticize.

As important as theory is to most critical feminist scholars, however, it is not an easy thing to write theory. Some of us embark on writing theory by providing long and painstakingly accurate expositions of a theorist's work, replete with impressive lists of references trailing behind each and every sentence and sometimes cropping up mid-way through a sentence as well (see also Davis, Chapter 14, this volume). Others of us may treat theory as a matter of showing one's colours, a judicious dropping of names—a dash of Butler, a bit of Derrida or a fleeting reference to Braidotti—which can help us situate ourselves on the right side of the fence, the fence being whatever is currently considered cutting-edge feminist theory. This allows us to move on without further ado to the business at hand—our research—while leaving the reader to make the necessary connections.

What is missing in both cases is a sense of how we actually engage with a theory. Where are the joyful and painful moments, the eye-openers and the eurekas, but also the doubts and uncertainties which are invariably a part of our engagement with a theory or theoretical debate? What is it that makes you want to draw on a particular theory at a particular point in the research process? And, most important, how is this theory going to actually help you do your own research in a better—that is, more sophisticated, analytically reflexive or creatively critical—way?

WHITHER FEMINIST THEORY?

In 2000 the feminist sociologists Liz Stanley and Sue Wise addressed some of these questions in a path-breaking and controversial article for *Feminist*

Theory.[1] They took issue with what they saw as a troubling tendency within Gender Studies to treat theory as the special preserve of a priestly caste of "theory stars" rather than an activity in which *all* feminist researchers are engaged (Stanley and Wise 2000, 276). This process has led to the canon-ization of a specific kind of theory—meta-theory—at the expense of theory which is grounded in the analysis of material, social and cultural practices. It has established the criteria for what constitutes not only theory but "good" feminist theory.

While Stanley and Wise were critical of the benefits of Feminist Theory (writ large), their primary concern was neither in, as they put it, "identify-ing 'goodies and baddies'" nor in "allocating blame" (2000, 263). Rather, they identified with the rank and file of scholars in the field of Gender Studies: "It is *us*, it is *you and we*, the jobbing academic feminists who are looking and ooh-ing and aah-ing," they wrote (275). We, i.e. the "rank and file", they said, have been relegated (or have relegated ourselves) to the role of "translators", becoming "the recyclers and neophytes who transform the pronouncements of feminist theory into a currency greater than their original value" (274). Feminist theory has become little more than a "translation industry" (262), an endless process of "explaining, simplifying, interpreting, and overview-ing" the theories of a handful of theory stars—a process which, according to Stanley and Wise, "would become largely redundant if 'Theory' was written more accessibly" (266).

The endless replication and translation of the work of theory stars that Stanley and Wise criticize are not simply a matter of redundancy, however. As anyone who has had to read her or his share of "theory chapters" in dissertations and books can attest, this replication is also—quite frankly—boring. Most of us have already read the theories, not only in the original, but in countless recycled versions as well. At a certain point, it becomes difficult to take in another explanation of disciplinary power à la Foucault without suppressing a yawn. The ubiquitous name-dropping which is *bon ton* in contemporary feminist scholarship is even more sleep-producing. It not only disrupts the flow of the text, forcing the reader to stumble through long lists of references before being allowed back into the text, but seriously undermines the author's authority. Too many references gives the reader the impression that the author is unable to say anything without first getting some theoretical backup.[2]

Stanley and Wise locate the problem in how feminist theory is being "done", arguing that it is time for us to stop "performing" the theories of others and instead use theories as resources to help us tell our own story. Anyone who does (feminist) research has a story to tell—this is what doing research is about. This story includes our *intellectual autobiography*[3]—that is, how we become attracted to certain theories, the struggles we invariably have in trying to make sense of them in the context of our research, the things we like and agree with as well as the things we dislike and do not agree with at all, the ways our ideas change as we become more immersed in our research. This is not background noise to the real business of doing theory; it is what doing theory is all about. Thus, Stanley and Wise urge feminist scholars to reclaim theorizing (not Theory) as an integral part of *any* feminist inquiry (2000, 266). Theirs is an impassioned plea for a return to the notion of theory as an active and collective process, which takes as its starting point the shared production of feminist ideas.

In this chapter, I want to take up Stanley and Wise's call to feminist scholars—from the graduate students writing their dissertations to the seasoned academics working on their latest books—to reclaim feminist theory and transform it into something that can help us in our research. How can we engage with theory in such a way that it is not reduced to the tame and obedient performance of the ideas of others? How can doing theory become a personal, passionate and creative enterprise—something that enables us to take risks, embark on unexpected paths and, in so doing, command our audience's full and appreciative attention?

WRITING THEORY

Obviously, there is no simple solution for writing theory. However, I have a modest suggestion—one which will help scholars engage with theories more personally, creatively and adventurously. This engagement will provide a starting point and some of the building blocks for transforming feminist theory into your own theoretical story.[4]

Instead of treating Theory as an authoritative model to be reproduced, theories can be seen as a resource, important, first and foremost, for helping critical feminist scholars formulate their research problems and frame their inquiries in more interesting ways. Theories at their best should allow us to discover the unexpected and to make sense of our research material in ways we could not have anticipated before embarking on our research. Theories should not make us fearful and worried about making mistakes; they should encourage us to be daring, critical and reflexive. Theories are not about telling someone else's story; they are about telling our own.

The method I am proposing owes a debt to much of the work currently being done in qualitative research.[5] For those of us who do qualitative research, one of the first things we learn is to keep a research journal. This is a record of our impressions and experiences in doing the research. It is done alongside the process of thinking about our research problem, collecting material, analyzing and interpreting. Journals allow us to pay attention to values, insights and intuitions as we do research. They contain the preliminary analyses of our material. They are the place where we work through the snags we invariably encounter while doing research. They help us situate ourselves critically in our research, think about the ways our locations shape our research, and attend to power differences at play during the research process. We may use parts of our journal in the book/chapter/article we are writing, but even if we don't, the journal shapes our writing in significant ways.

While research journals are usually considered helpmeets for doing research, they are less frequently applied to the business of theorizing. However, it is my contention that such journals could be a perfect way to appropriate theory, to engage with it in a creative and reflective way, thereby making it work for you and for your research. Just as a person might keep a journal to make sense of her or his research (or, for that matter, life), she might employ a journal to record, explore and work through her or his responses to a particular theory or theories. By reflecting on theory in a personal and creative way, the theory will become less a static display of colours than a friend and a resource for telling an interesting and novel story.

In the following section, I will offer some brief suggestions about how to get started on keeping a theory journal. They are not meant as a recipe to be followed to the letter. You may want to leave out certain steps or add some of your own. It can be applied to the collected works of a particular theorist or to a book, or even just one article. However, I guarantee that it will help you write theory in a different and more imaginative way.

THEORY JOURNALS

The first step is the most prosaic. You need a journal.[6] Some people will want to write their journal on the computer, and in that case, you need a file specifically designated for that purpose. However, others may want to write their journal by hand. I personally prefer keeping my journals in notebooks, usually with an inspiring illustration on the front cover. I like to use a cartridge pen with black ink. The idea that I have to leave my computer in order to write in my journal is appealing to me. Sometimes I head for my living room; other times I sit outside under a tree to write, and occasionally I go to my favourite café. The main thing is to keep the activity of journal writing separate from the actual writing of a book, article or chapter. Writing in a journal is about giving one's thoughts free rein, letting them "flow", and, above all, about *not* being goal-directed. This is not about end products; it is about process.

A good way to begin an entry is to situate yourself. This means describing where you are, what is going on around you, what you are doing and how you feel at the time of the writing. At its most basic level, it means locating yourself in space and time. The feminist sociologist Dorothy Smith has written extensively about the importance of the author locating herself in the text as a prerequisite for doing feminist research. She compares it to the map in the shopping mall with the yellow arrow "YOU ARE HERE" 1999, 5). This marks your location, *where* you are right *now* at the time of writing. This not only places you, the author, squarely in the process of writing about theory ("I am curled up on the couch with my trusty journal, a glass of white wine, and the sounds of Bach cello sonatas wafting through my earphones. The answering machine is on, no one can disturb me . . .").

The experience of writing becomes grounded in the body, in the physical world, and, therefore, provides the starting point for an embodied, personal engagement with theory.[7]

The next step is to collect your first impressions from reading the text. This is *not* the same as a synopsis. Indeed, a basic rule for journal writing is to avoid blow-by-blow descriptions of the theory and its premises. When I ask students to keep journals during classes, for example, I do not accept entries which summarize the content of theory. A journal entry is not about *what* you read but *how* you engage with it. This means being as associative as you possibly can. You might want to put the theoretical text aside at this point and just let your thoughts flow onto the paper. For example, you can write about what struck you especially about the theory, what inspired you and what made you angry or disapproving. You do not have to stick to the main points but can pick out small details, interesting examples or odd observations that catch your fancy. Do not worry if your associations seem trivial or irrelevant. This is all about collecting those aspects of the text that—for whatever reason—appealed to you enough to be remembered. It means taking your reactions seriously!

Once you have collected associations—and be sure to give that plenty of time—the next step is to explore them in more depth. Texts do not stand alone but evoke all kinds of associations with other texts. We all "borrow" meanings from other texts in the course of reading, and these meanings shape how we understand a text. This is what "intertextuality" is about (Kristeva 1980). The other texts may be works by the same theorist which resonate with the text you are now reading. However, you may be reminded of other academic texts that you have read in the same field. Often, reading a text lands you squarely within an academic debate, forcing you to consider what kind of position you would want to take. Intertextuality is not just about the reverberations between academic texts, though. Particularly when you are reading a feminist or critical text, you may be reminded of the current political situation or a specific historical context. A text may make you think of films you have seen or novels you have read. And, last but not least, texts will invariably make you think of personal experiences, encounters or events you have witnessed. Use the journal entry to explore in the broadest possible way the resonances the text has for you and to make connections with a broad tradition of feminist and other texts.

The final section of the entry involves pulling together the experience and interpretations which have emerged thus far. By engaging with the text in such a personal and associative way, you will find that you have become entangled with the theory. You will have a much clearer sense of what it is about the theory which interests you (and why). You will know what you specifically like or dislike about it. You will have glimmerings about how it can be useful for your present research. You will inevitably have many more questions than you had at the outset. This is the moment to pause and consider where you are, to collect any issues that are unclear to you to formulate questions that have emerged, to note areas that you want to explore and issues that you feel need more reflection. This can be written as a series of points to be addressed or as a project or task that you want to take on next. It is a summary of your engagement with the theory, but it also—and more important—signals that your theoretical journey has only just begun.

EXERCISE 35: KEEPING A THEORY JOURNAL

1. *Choose a theorist, theoretical school or concept for your journal entry.*[8]
2. *Decide where and how you want to keep your journal.*
3. *Situate yourself ("here I am").*
4. *Collect associations, first impressions and idiosyncratic details (no synopsis!).*
5. *Think about intertextuality (make connections with other texts, events or debates).*
6. *Take stock (what is useful for your research and why?).*
7. *Reflect on open questions (points that need to be explored).*

CONCLUSION

At this point, many readers will probably already be worrying about how they will find the time to write a theory journal. Most of us are under considerable pressure to publish (or perish), and we have learned to keep our eye fixed firmly on the prize—the end product, the peer-reviewed article in an international journal, the dissertation. Keeping a journal seems, at best, a luxury and, at worst, a waste of our precious time and energy, inefficient for getting our research into a publishable form as quickly as possible. However, I am convinced that journal writing is not going to slow you down and, indeed, may even speed things up. As someone who knows only too well what it feels like to stare at a blank computer screen for hours on end without knowing where to begin, I know that journal writing is one way to manage, utilize and ultimately overcome the inevitable writer's block which is endemic to all academic writing (see also Koobak, Chapter 6, this volume, for a good account of how this works).

Keeping a journal will not necessarily make your task of writing theory quicker. It is not a panacea. One of the most difficult tasks facing researchers is how to integrate a theory into their research in ways that will enable it to work for them. A journal will not eliminate the difficulties that inevitably accompany this process. What it does do, however, is to allow the researcher to engage in a personal and creative way with theories and theoretical texts. It enables a researcher to get to know a theory in an embodied way—not as a fixed body of knowledge to be absorbed or "mastered", but rather as an encounter, as an occasion to explore what is interesting and worthwhile about the theory for the researcher and her specific research project. While I believe that this process makes doing theory more enjoyable and rewarding for the individual researcher, this is not the only—or even the main—reason for keeping a theory journal.

The primary reason is that it will contribute to the production of better critical feminist theory. It will encourage a *reflexive* stance towards the production of knowledge. Theorizing becomes an ongoing process of critically interrogating and revising knowledge in the context of the researcher's embodied interaction with theory.

It will enable a more *creative* approach to theory—one which focuses on the generation of new questions and unexpected perspectives. Theorizing will become less about reproducing already existing knowledge and more about discovering novel connections.

And, finally, it will promote theorizing as a *collaborative* endeavour. It will diminish the problematic distinction between those who *do* theory and those who merely translate or cite it. In this way, feminist theory becomes what it has always been intended to be—the collective process of producing critical knowledge.

NOTES

1. See also some of the critical rejoinders by Petö (2001), Stacey (2001), King (2001) and Lykke (2004).
2. There is, of course, much more to say about the practice of citing the work of others. For example, it is problematic to cite only the big names, thereby neglecting the work of lesser known theorists. At the same time, long lists of references are unwieldy and make the text difficult to read. How to select references judiciously and present them in a balanced way, while situating oneself as an author(ity), would be a topic of another chapter.
3. This term refers to the process by which researchers come to know their subjects, including how they draw conclusions. An intellectual autobiography makes these processes explicit, opening them up to critical reflection and interrogation. See Stanley 1990; Stanley and Wise 1993.
4. The idea that (feminist) theories are stories is nicely set out by Hemmings (2011). I am using a narrative approach to theory as stories we all tell about the world around us, about ourselves and others and about social structures and social change.
5. Here I would refer the reader to the journal *Qualitative Inquiry*, which contains many innovative examples of how to do theory in a grounded but creative and personal way. Handbooks for qualitative research tend towards guidelines and recipes rather than inspiring the would-be researcher to embark on her own journey of discovery.
6. See also Koobak, Chapter 13, this volume, for a lovely rendition of the process of choosing a journal and the important effects this can have on the writing

process itself. I recommend reading this chapter, more generally, in conjunction with the present one as it illustrates many of the points I make here.

7. This method is not unlike how a researcher might begin to engage in a politics of location whereby she explores the ways gender, class, race or ethnicity, national belonging and sexual orientation shape her perceptions, thinking and research practices (see Davis, Chapter 1, this volume; and Brewster, Chapter 4, this volume).

8. Here is another exercise which can be helpful. Choose a theorist. Pick a friend or family member (preferably non-academic) with whom you like to talk. Send this person a letter (or email) in which you explain why this theorist is important to you. You do not need to send this letter. It is just meant as a writing exercise. But it is important to have specific person in mind, and to start your letter with "Dear . . . ." and end it with "All the best" or "Love" and your name. If you are in a group situation, you can read each other's letters aloud and discuss the experience of writing the letter.

REFERENCES

Hemmings, Clare. 2011. *Why Stories Matter: The Political Grammar of Feminist Theory*. Durham: Duke University Press.

King, Katie. 2001. "Productive Agencies of Feminist Theory: The Work It Does." *Feminist Theory* 2 (1): 94–98.

Kristeva, Julia. 1980. *Desire in Language: A Semiotic Approach to Literature and Art*. New York: Columbia University Press.

Lykke, Nina. 2004. "Between Particularism, Universalism and Transversalism: Reflections on the Politics of Location of European Feminist Research and Education." In "Gender and Power 1," special issue, *NORA, Nordic Journal of Women's Studies* 12 (2): 72–83.

Petö, Andrea. 2001. "An Empress in a New-Old Dress." *Feminist Theory* 2 (1): 89–93.

Smith, Dorothy E. 1999. *Writing the Social*. Toronto: University of Toronto Press.

Stacey, Judith. 2001. "The Empress of Feminist Theory Is Overdressed." *Feminist Theory* 2 (1): 99–103.

Stanley, Liz, ed. 1990. *Feminist Praxis: Research, Theory and Epistemology in Feminist Sociology*. London: Routledge.

Stanley, Liz and Sue Wise. 1993. *Breaking Out Again: Feminist Ontology and Epistemology*. London: Routledge.

Stanley, Liz and Sue Wise. 2000. "But the Empress Has No Clothes! Some Awkward Questions about the 'Missing Revolution' in Feminist Theory." *Feminist Theory* 1 (3): 261–88.

12 Making Language Your Own
Brainstorming, Heteroglossia and Poetry

Anne Brewster

I teach both creative writing and Australian Aboriginal literature, and I find it inspiring and sometimes challenging to bring these two interests together. In the courses that I teach on literature, I include creative writing exercises to encourage my students to expand their writing techniques in order to rethink the key theoretical terms in their research. These techniques are drawn from my own writing experiments. In my own writing I find it useful to stop sometimes and think about the terms, concepts, metaphors and phrases that are central to my research and my writing. In the course of my writing I find myself repeating these key terms, and they can become naturalized. I end up taking their meaning for granted, and I become habituated to a certain kind of logic which becomes sedimented into argument. I find that examining the central terms of my argument can be a useful way to think about adjacent issues, ideas and affects which may be obscured by recurrent patterns of thinking.

The work of Mikhail Bakhtin, the Russian philosopher and literary critic, has been useful to me in thinking about the process by which I struggle to articulate my theoretical perspective. Bakhtin has been described as "one of the leading thinkers of the twentieth century" (Lodge 1988, 124). He was interested in the textuality of the novel, in particular. He argues that the novel incorporates many different types and styles of speech which derive from a range of discourses and sub-cultures. He describes the novel (which he saw as more democratic than poetry) as heteroglossic and polyphonic. It is characterized not by a unitary authorial language (or "voice") but by a diversity of social speech types. Although the fiction writer may strive (consciously or unconsciously) to produce what appears to be a monologic or uniform narrative, the diversity of social and cultural voices cannot, Bakhtin argues, be suppressed and assimilated to an overall totalizing discourse. In its polyphony, he suggests, the novel reflects the stratification of the national language, which itself consists of a spectrum of social speech types. These include

social dialects, characteristic group behaviour [and speech], professional jargons, generic languages, languages of generations and age groups, tendentious languages, languages of the authorities, of various circles and of passing fashions, languages that serve the specific socio-political purposes of the day, even of the hour (each day has its own slogan, its own vocabulary, its own emphases).

—(1981, 262–63)

Bakhtin describes the varied speech acts within the novel as "dialogic"; that is, they are engaged in dialogue or conversation with each other. The multiple voices of the novel inflect a range of sometimes conflicting attitudes, beliefs and ideologies, which in turn mirror the stratifications of the social world and its hierarchical power structures. The novel's dialogism reflects the continuous struggle over language in the social world. Language, Bakhtin reminds me, is a material thing, saturated with socio-ideological value. All writers (including the novelist, the scholar and the everyday speaker) inherit a language that is infused with the meanings and associations that others have given it. As Bakhtin puts it:

[T]here are no neutral words and forms—words and forms that can belong to "no-one"; language has been completely taken over, shot through with intentions and accents. For any individual consciousness living in it, language is not an abstract system . . . [It] lies on the borderline between oneself and the other. The word in language is half someone else's. It becomes "one's own" only when the speaker populates it with his own intention, his own accent, when he appropriates the word, adapting it to his own semantic and expressive intention.

—(293)

Bakhtin is especially interested in "tendentious" or authoritative discourses. These discourses, he suggests, "stubbornly resist" challenges to their authority: "expropriating [them], forcing [them] to submit to one's own intentions and accents is a difficult and complicated process" (294). He thus makes me aware of the social nature of language use and the fact that it is laden with value. In using this strong language he focuses on the agonistic aspects of language usage and the struggle involved in negotiations of meaning. But why does he use such strong language? How is language usage a struggle?

KEY TERMS AND FREE ASSOCIATION

I will suggest a writing exercise now to explore some of these issues. I would like you to think about your key terms, those around which your scholarly arguments revolve. I hope this exercise will enable you to recognize the weight of these key terms and the authority they exert on your work. You may like to do this writing exercise alone or in a group. The advantage of doing it in a group is that you can share ideas by reading your work to each other, and this is often productive.

EXERCISE 36: KEY TERMS AND FREE ASSOCIATION

Step One:

The first step is to make a list of key terms that appear in your field of research and your writing. I'd encourage you to think about a range of different discourses. Does your work involve study of the popular media? If so, what are the terms and concepts that circulate there? You probably also draw on theoretical texts; what are some of the key terms and phrases you have been using in your writing? You may be delving into archives and reading other kinds of documents: bureaucratic material, policies, minutes. Or you may be working with a sub-culture or a minority group which has its own style of language, or with other national languages or dialects. What are the terms used in the field in which you are working? Make a list of two to six key terms. Take about 10–15 minutes to do this. You may want to take more time and look over some work you have recently written to identify the words and phrases that have become your key terms.

Step Two:

Once you have made a list, pick one of those words to do some free association writing. With this word in mind simply write down whatever words and phrases come to you. It does not matter how closely or distantly connected they are to the word you have chosen. Allow your imagination to wander. Write continuously for 5 minutes. The basic rule of this exercise is to keep writing. If you run out of things to say at any point simply reiterate the word you have chosen. Or if at any point you feel your writing has completely veered away from the initial meaning of the word, repeat the word in order to bring your thoughts back to it. If you have time and you are waiting for other people in the group to finish, you may like to do the same thing for a second or third key term.

We will return to this list shortly so keep it with you.

I have said that Bahktin describes language as a struggle to appropriate or expropriate "tendentious" or "authoritative" language. And, he suggests,

> [p]rior to this moment of appropriation, the word does not exist in a neutral and impersonal language (it is not, after all, out of a

dictionary that the speaker gets his words!), but rather it exists in other people's mouths, in other people's contexts, serving other people's intentions: it is from there that one must take the word, and make it one's own.

—(1981, 293–94)

Furthermore, he describes this act of appropriation as one of "seizure and transformation" which makes the word into "private property" (294). The concept of private property gives us food for thought. It reminds us about the power asymmetries involved in making language our own. Writers commonly remake and restyle language, turning it into their own "private property". I want to turn to an example of this process of "seizure and transformation" of language, namely, a poem by the Australian Aboriginal poet Lisa Bellear: "Artist Unknown".

Artist Unknown

*(for all indigenous/colonised artists inspired by a visit
to the Art Gallery of New South Wales to look at Destiny Deacon's work)*

Artist unknown
Location Liverpool River
The Rainbow Serpent
Narama and her sons 1948
Acc p1 1956

Artist unknown
Kimberley Area
Hammerhead Shark
And Black Fish 1948
Acc no p15 1956

Artist unknown
Location Oenpelli
Mimi Family 1948
Ochre on cardboard
Original collection presented by
The Commonwealth Government
Acc no p116 1956

Artist unknown
Location
Ochre on cardboard
Mimi man and woman 1948
Acc no14 1956

Artist unknown
Location Milinginbi

184   *Anne Brewster*

Hive of wild honey 1948
Ochre on cardboard
Acc p24 1956

Artist unknown
Location Oenpelli
Crocodile
Ochre on cardboard
Acc no p17 1956

Artist unknown
Location Oenpelli
Two fish 1948
Acc p19 1956

Artist unknown
Divisions of fish
Acc no 22 1956

Artist unknown
Ochre on cardboard
Acquisition number
And purchase date
No name
No tribe
Or clan
Or Language group
No gender
No spirituality
The unknown artist
reads like a memorial

—Lisa Bellear (1993, 141)[1]

This is an example of a "found text" or a "found poem". A found poem comprises text has been transported from a non-literary environment and genre into a literary one. When a "found" text is recast as a poem, we approach the text-as-poem differently, even though the words remain exactly the same. It is now recognized as literature because of the line breaks. The insertion of line breaks in the newly shaped poem works to accentuate particular aspects and effects of the language, for example, to create pauses, rhymes or other kinds of rhythmic patterning which accentuate the poetic effects of what was formerly banal and prosaic text. When we see a text restructured as poetry, the line breaks signal that we should read the text differently; we read more slowly, attending to the poetic qualities of the language rather than its referential significance. Sometimes found poetry produces a comic effect, when language that was intended to be read, say, referentially is transformed into an art object. As Hazel Smith suggests in

The Writing Experiment, found texts "raise vital questions about what constitutes an art object, and why we value some objects as art and not others" (2005, 75). In "Artist Unknown" Bellear produces a found poem by recasting into stanzas the explanatory texts which function as captions explaining the paintings. She informs us in the dedication lines (under the title of the poem) that she came upon the texts from which the poem is fashioned on a visit to the Art Gallery of New South Wales.

A cursory glance at the poem confirms that it is indeed a found poem. The language is clearly referential, conveying information about the titles and content of the paintings, the regions in which they were painted, the dates on which they were painted, the dates when they were acquired by the Art Gallery, the acquisition numbers and the medium of the paintings. A reader familiar with traditional Aboriginal paintings (which have, since the 1960s, become highly prized as art objects in the non-indigenous world, often fetching very high prices) will immediately recognize the paintings' titles as referring to images drawn from Aboriginal cosmology. The Rainbow Serpent is part of an important creation story; the fish and plant images are totemic; the Mimi figures represent spirit beings.

It may seem odd to make a list of the explanatory information accompanying paintings in the absence of the paintings themselves. What does the poem achieve by doing this? What is the point of taking the text out of the gallery environment and recasting it as a poem? For me, the absence of the paintings works to make me aware (as it appears to make the poet aware) of another absence, that of the names of the painters themselves. The absence of the painters' names is noted matter-of-factly by the Gallery ("artist unknown") in its documentation of the paintings. However, the poet emphasizes this absence by grouping these captions together as a string of stanzas and by starting each stanza with the line "Artist Unknown". The repetition of this line brings it forcefully to the viewer's attention (non-indigenous people might otherwise skip over it, for example, if they were in the gallery looking at the paintings).

In the poem the repetition starts to sound mordant to me. I wonder *why* the name of the artist is "unknown". This question leads me directly into the troubled and disavowed colonial history of Australia, into the theft of land, of artefacts, of languages and lives. It reminds me of the colonial history of dispossession. I would like to suggest that the poet reads, in the cataloguing procedure of the state gallery, the perpetuation of colonial processes of appropriation. The aestheticization of Aboriginal paintings and their incorporation within the tradition of Western art seems to erase from public memory much of their spiritual and secret-sacred meanings and functions. The spiritual significance of the paintings relates intimately to a specific Aboriginal clan and to the land in which it lives. Moreover, according to the traditional custom, each of these images and stories probably belonged to a specific member of the clan, and it may have been his or her prerogative alone to reproduce them. All *this* information about the paintings—that is, the information vital to their Aboriginal heritage—has been lost in the process of their "acquisition" by non-indigenous people and institutions. The word "acquisition", a seemingly innocent and neutral term, is defamiliarized in Bellear's text. I read it as a euphemism for expropriation.

Just as the explanatory text, reproduced as a list on a page in a book, points to the absence of the paintings and of the painters' names, so to me it points to loss: the pillage and exploitation of Aboriginal culture. In my reading of the poem the poet makes this explicit in the last stanza of the poem, which no longer contains simply the information about the paintings but her own comment on the many aspects of the painter's identity which have been lost. The list is transformed; it now reads like a sombre and funerary "memorial":

> *Artist unknown*
> *Ochre on cardboard*
> *Acquisition number*
> *And purchase date*
> *No name*
> *No tribe*
> *Or clan*
> *Or Language group*
> *No gender*
> *No spirituality*
> *The unknown artist*
> *reads like a memorial*

In this last stanza the mood of the poem changes. I read the aforementioned text about the paintings not simply as referential information but as evidence of loss and theft. I become aware of the very different function that these paintings could have. In an Aboriginal context, the name, tribe, clan, language group and gender of the painter would have played a crucial role in an understanding of the paintings.

In "Artist Unknown" Bellear, I suggest, has "appropriated" and "seized" (to use Bakhtin's terms) documentary text from an authoritative institution, namely, the Art Gallery of New South Wales, and has infused it with her own authority as an Aboriginal person. This institution, as a signifying organ of the state, defines and legitimizes cultural production, incorporating it into a discourse of nationalism. The text of the labels, which define what is considered important about these paintings within the institutional context, has been "expropriated" by Bellear from the discursive context of the state gallery and repositioned within a literary context. She makes the text compiled by the gallery perform for me a different kind of work—the work of memorialization. In this context the text is significant not only for what it says but also for what it does not say; it foregrounds the impact of colonial violence on Aboriginal culture and the silences it has produced. In her construction of this found poem Bellear is reversing the act of theft visited on Aboriginal people; she expropriates the documentary language to make it work for her.

EXERCISE 37: KEY TERMS AND FREE ASSOCIATION (CONTINUED)

At this point I want to return to a discussion about key terms and to the free association writing exercise we began above. Please turn to the list of free associations that you generated from the writing exercise about key terms. Here are two more steps to this writing exercise:

Step Three:

Examine the words, concepts and images that your free writing has produced.

- *What new ideas do they point to?*
- *How are these ideas related to your topic?*
- *Do the associative words, concepts and images seem odd, uncomfortable or amusing in the ways they relate to the key terms?*

If you have answered "yes" to the last question, ask yourself why that it so. Is this perhaps because they are far removed from the seriousness and gravity of academic work? Have they been excluded from the scholarly domain? If so, why? What might the implications be of including them in your research and writing (even tangentially)? How might you do that?

Take 15 minutes to make some notes in response to these questions.

Step Four:

If these questions have opened up a useful trajectory of ideas for you, you may like to ask yourself a further set of questions:

- *Have the words, concepts and images from the associative writing produced feelings, attitudes or recollections in you?*
- *If so, how do these feelings, attitudes or recollections relate to your research topic?*
- *Can you include them in some way in your writing? (You may have to think about altering the style or structure of your writing to do this.)*

Take 15 minutes (or two years!) to think about these questions and make notes.

If you are in a group it would be very useful for the group members to discuss their ideas at this stage.

OUTCOME OF WRITING EXERCISE—KEY TERMS AND FREE ASSOCIATIONS

This exercise uses free association, which by definition is "free" (to some degree) of logical or rational thinking. It is therefore a way of side-stepping the authority of scholarly discourse, which, I am suggesting, may be useful precisely in order to revitalize the scholarly discourse. In the free associative writing you are in fact expropriating and re-appropriating the key words in your research field, populating them with your own intentions and associations, thereby making them your own. You may also be tracing their various linguistic and discursive histories, genealogies and paradigms. Playful exercises like this can reveal unexpected associations and new understandings of the key terms on which we base our scholarly arguments as we think about the adjacent ideas that they throw up. They introduce heteroglossia into our scholarly thinking and writing by allowing a polyphony of voices, associations, memories, attitudes, ideas and images entry. They show us how "sticky" ideas, affects, memories and values are (that is, how they are always linked to other ideas, affects, memories and values, both intertextually and through lived experience) and how meaning is always contingent and dynamic.

In this exercise the authority of key terms (which may in other contexts seem inviolable, unambiguous and indisputable), especially, for example, the commanding and doctrinal language of theory, can be side-stepped to release tangential meanings, associations and implications, including those which have been silenced, elided, suppressed, marginalized or banished from scholarly work. As in Bellear's poem, the silences and absences in academic writing can be just as telling as the authority with which our key terms are invested. Free associative writing exercises can work to defamiliarize these terms in your research field and make you see them in a different light. This kind of exercise may also encourage you to think about how some of your arguments have become naturalized. You may want to examine the terms which you use repetitively and on which your arguments rely. This may inspire you to modify, qualify or further explain or elaborate them.

KEY TERMS AND THE DICTIONARY—COMPOSING A POETIC COLLAGE

When I did the free associative writing exercise outlined above myself with my own key terms, I chose the word "white", which is central to the critical whiteness methodology I use in my readings of Australian Aboriginal literature. I came up with a string of cognate phrases such as "white man", "whitewash", "white out", "white knight", "white lie", etc. I started to think about the history of these terms and how the term "white" came to be associated with cultural and racial superiority. To see how whiteness

ame to be positioned in discursive hierarchies, I consulted that definitive
:xicon of the English language, the *Oxford English Dictionary* (*OED*), for
he meaning of the word "white" as it is used in these cognate phrases. In
he quote above Bakhtin says that "it is not . . . out of a dictionary that the
peaker gets his [sic] words". He argues that the meaning of words changes
ontinually through usage. What the dictionary *can* give us, however, is a
iachronic cross-section of the history of a word, that is, a compendium of
vhat were considered commanding and reputable sources for and usages
f the word "white". The entries in the *OED* under "white" and its cog-
ate terms ("whiten", "white man", "whitewash", etc.) could be seen as
onstituting a canon of author(itie)s drawn from a wide range of genres,
iscourses and disciplines—including early religious documents, newspa-
ers, legal documents, historical tracts and novels. They provide a very com-
ressed glimpse into the authorizing process by which cultural meanings are
onsolidated (and metamorphose) over time. Of course, it is no surprise that
he vast majority of the sources quoted are by male authors, for example.

Consulting a dictionary is a good way of accessing a very brief and sum-
narized etymology of your key terms. I want now to propose a second writ-
ig exercise which builds on the first one. This exercise allows you to further
rainstorm about the key terms and the concepts, words and ideas that are
entral to your research and writing. It involves doing a poetic collage using
he dictionary. First I will explain how I went about doing my own collage,
nd then I will walk you through the steps of the exercise.

Below is the *OED* entry for the phrase "white man". I have reproduced
he entire entry here as I wanted to show you how vividly polyphonic and
eteroglossic it is. There are many different genres and styles of writing
ssembled here. We can see the "dialogue" between the various genres and
heir various historical periods.

The dictionary entry contains a large variety of what Bakhtin calls "social
peech types". We recognize the various genres and discourses from which
he phrases are excerpted by their linguistic styles. These styles carry traces
f the socio-ideological value of various genres and discourses. Authority
as been conferred on these sources and authors listed under the word
'white" by dint of their inclusion in the *OED*.

OXFORD ENGLISH DICTIONARY ENTRY FOR 'WHITE MAN'

White Man

1. A man clothed in white: cf. WHITE a. 6. In quot. 1691, a surpliced
   chorister. Obs. rare.
   1691 [see WHITE BOY 2]. 1693 *D' Emilianne's Hist. Monast.
   Orders* xix. 216 Of the Order of the White Men. In the year 1399,
   . . . a certain Priest, came down from the Alpes into Italy, . . .

Cloathed all in White, . . . great crouds both of Men and Women
. . . followed him, and took White Cloaths like~wise on their Backs.
2. a. A man belonging to a race having naturally light-coloured skin
or complexion: chiefly applied to those of European extraction:
see WHITE a. *4. the white man's burden*: see BURDEN *n.* 2a; *the
white man's grave*, equatorial West Africa considered particularly
unhealthy for white people.
      1695 MOTTEUX tr. *St.-Olon's Morocco* 12 [The Moors of Tet-
uan] are White-men, pretty well Civiliz'd. 1791 W. BARTRAM
Carolina 96 The centinels . . . perceiving that I was a whiteman,
ventured to hail me. 1835 C.F. HOFFMAN *Winter in West* I.
164 We white men have been spoiled by education; we have been
taught to think many things necessary that you red men can do
well without. 1836 F.H. RANKIN *White Man's Grave* I. p. viii,
[Sierra Leone] bears the terrific and poetic title of the "White Man's
Grave". 1897 M. KINGSLEY *Trav. W. Afr.* 2 My friends . . . said,
"Oh, you can't possibly go there; that's where Sierra Leone is, the
white man's grave, you know." 1904 HAZZLEDINE *(title)* The
White Man in Nigeria. 1924 MAURICE & ARTHUR *Life Ld.
Wolseley* iv. 65 The Gold Coast had well earned the name of "The
White Man's Grave". 1938 X. HERBERT *Capricornia* (1939) iii.
24 The whitemen left the hunting to the [Australian] natives. 1944
F. CLUNE *Red Heart* 19, I dug up his body, souvenired his false
teeth and diaries, and reburied him in whiteman fashion. 1952 P.
ATKEY *Juniper Rock* xiv. 127, I was a bride at eighteen . . . I went
out to the white man's grave. 1956 A. SAMPSON *Drum* xi. 156
As whites regard Africans as natives or boys, not people or men so
Africans never describe whitemen (which they spell, significantly,
in one word), as abantu, or people. 1970 G.F. NEWMAN *Sir,
You Bastard* ii. 67 The street in Hammersmith where Whitmarsh
lodged was so overrun with immigrants that an English-speaking
whiteman was a latterday Livingstone.
      b. orig. *U.S. slang.* A man of honourable character (such as was
conventionally associated with one of European extraction): see
WHITE *a.* 4b.
      1883 *Century Mag.* XXVI. 913/1 You've behaved to me like a
white man from the start. 1887 *Pall Mall Gaz.* 22 June 5 Tricoup
is the President is a white man an extremely white man.

I was inspired by the vividly contrastive styles of the quotes in this d
tionary entry. They seemed to me to constitute a mini discursive archi
of whiteness. I cut and pasted various phrases in order to "record" t
linguistic emergence of whiteness in my own haphazard style. Here is t
collage:

COLLAGE—BASED ON DICTIONARY ENTRY

White Man

A certain Priest (1693)
[C]loathed all in White . . . great crouds
wise on their Backs,
West Africa, equatorial,
unhealthy. Entirely exonerated.

We have been taught, considered
with (1836 F. H. RANKIN), one-eighth
black, MAURICE AND ARTHUR,
earned the name, their long accounts [Australian]
souvenired his teeth (1944). White efflorescence, N.
Brit Rev XXVI.87, overrun his immigrant diaries. I went
out (xi 156) as natives or boys, belonging the
streets, the Moors of Tetuan, you know. Extremely (1970) white

man ventured in vulgar parlance. Horace, conventionally spoiled
trav Thailand, a latterday man of naturally
honourable character (a, 4b) and took
the President (1887 Pall
Mall Gaz. 22) from the start

To me this collage reflects the genealogy of white power. Scattered throughout the *OED* entry for "white man" we see the male figures who have legislated white authority through a range of discourses (religion, history, law, fiction, etc.). The conventions for arranging this material within the genre of the dictionary (inclusion of the authors' names, titles and dates, etc.) bestow status on these sources and usages. A dictionary contains (in the sense of "curtails") meaning and disseminates it. By rearranging the text "found" in the dictionary I wanted to foreground the process of authorization by which certain meanings (those that attach to the word "white man") are naturalized.

EXERCISE 38: KEY TERMS AND THE DICTIONARY—
COMPOSING A POETIC COLLAGE

Step One:

Make a list of six key phrases or words from your research and reading. Pick one word and write free associatively about this word for a few minutes, thinking about cognate phrases (for example, I wrote down *"wash"*, *"white out"* and *"white lie"* as cognate phrases for the term *"white"*). Write down as many as you can think of (at least three or four if possible).

Step Two:

Look these words/phrases up in the OED *(or an equivalent dictionary if you are not writing in English). As you read through the dictionary entries make a long list of phrases (of between one and five words) drawn randomly. Make sure they start with different parts of speech (for example, do not pick phrases that all begin with a verb). Do not forget to include single words. Make sure this is a long list—at least two or three pages, but more if possible (start a new line for every phrase or word).*

Step Three:

Once you have done this, start to join the phrases together (randomly, not consecutively). You may want to preserve the syntax of the sentence, in which case you might have to insert a word here or there, but try to keep this to a minimum. In my collage I did not retain sentence syntax, and I did not introduce any new words. This is a matter of personal preference, so you can decide which style you prefer.

Step Four:

You may like to think about the following questions:

- *What generic sources have been listed as exemplary uses of these words?*
- *What socio-ideological value have these terms held throughout different historical periods?*
- *Has their meaning changed over time?*

Make some notes in response to these questions for 15 minutes. If you are in a group, read your collages and notes to each other.

Bakhtin reminds us that we are social actors in language and that language is active and dynamic rather than static. It is useful to remind ourselves that in our own writing we are appropriating words and repopulating them with our own intentions. We negotiate a language laden with other people's meanings, but we are also continuously engaged in a gendered linguistic and cultural dialogism. As Chris Barker puts it, "we acquire language by internalising the voices of others, and then spend much of our lives re-externalising these incorporated forms in a continuous dialogue with others" (2004, 51).

In composing a collage we are, in effect, creating a found text in a manner that is similar to Bellear's poem "Artist Unknown". When I read "Artist Unknown" it feels rather sombre, and as I discussed above, I experience a sense of loss. It makes me reflect on how one culture's code of museumization strips another culture's code from the artefact that is produced in the process. Like Bellear I am plunging into the archive of the dominant culture, but unlike the artists to whom she refers, the authors I found quoted in the *OED* are known; their names are recorded as authorities in the accretion of the power attaching to the category "white". Hopefully, this exercise will enable you to sketch a map of your own key terms' genealogies, to produce new angles and perspectives on the terms and to deploy them in ways that open up imaginative vistas and enticing entanglements in your writing.

NOTE

1. Lisa Bellear. 1996. "Artist Unknown." In *Dreaming in Urban Areas*. St Lucia: University of Queensland Press, p. 41. Printed with permission from John Stewart (copyright holder).

REFERENCES

Bakhtin, Mikhail M. 1981. "Discourse in the Novel." In *The Dialogic Imagination*, translated by Caryl Emerson and Michael Holquist, 259–423. Austin: University of Texas Press.
Barker, Chris. 2004. *The Sage Dictionary of Cultural Studies*. London: Sage.
Bellear, Lisa. 1996. *Dreaming in Urban Areas*. St Lucia: University of Queensland Press.
Lodge, David, ed. 1988. *Modern Criticism and Theory*. London: Longman.
Smith, Hazel. 2005. *The Writing Experiment: Strategies for Innovative Creative Writing*. Crows Nest, NSW: Allen & Unwin.

13 Writing in Stuck Places

Redi Koobak

> Not to find one's way in a city may well be uninteresting and banal.
> It requires ignorance—nothing more. But to lose oneself in a city—as
> one loses oneself in a forest—that calls for quite a different schooling.
>
> —Walter Benjamin (quoted in Lather 2007, 1)

Like many of my colleagues at the university, I have found myself stuck
at various points in the academic writing process. I have been caught in a
seemingly never-ending maze of stuck places upon stuck places upon stuck
places. In fact, it has happened so many times it would be impossible to
count them. To be sure, most people who do research encounter these stuck
places or moments of being lost, but usually it has not helped much to know
that I am not alone in this. Stuck places in academic writing are frustrating,
and overcoming them requires a lot of hard work. I used to view snags
as momentary setbacks that necessarily had to be and definitely would be
defeated by the end of the writing process. Writer's block occurred because
I was uninformed, ignorant, lazy or simply overloaded with other obliga-
tions and worries; hence, it was something I had to put up with and just try
harder, do better next time. These obstacles were my own fault! In short,
the end result would always have to be a neat and nice progression narrative that moved effortlessly from a problem to a discussion to a possible
solution and after final edits is cleansed of all ambiguities, ambivalences
and stuck places that I might have had to struggle with during the writing
process.

When I found Patti Lather's book *Getting Lost: Feminist Efforts toward
a Double(d) Science* (2007), I was instantly intrigued by her idea of actually focusing on stuckness as a way to keep moving and working oneself
through impossibilities in writing. Although Lather's argument is of course
much more complex, I was happy to pick up something that I thought I
could put to use very directly. What I was indeed inspired by was her simple message: *Learn from your ruptures and failures! Embrace your breaks
and refusals! Love your aporias!* I could not really imagine at first how or

why anyone would look more closely at these stuck moments or, what is more, purposefully *seek them out*, purposefully get off the track and lose oneself in one's research. The kind of enabling stuckness that Lather talks about seemed very different from the static irritant that I had experienced stuckness to be.

At its simplest, Lather's "getting lost", as both a methodology and a mode of representation, means an alternative to "commanding, controlling, mastery" discourses, focusing on places where we are not so sure of ourselves and where this not knowing could be seen as our best chance for a different sort of doing and knowing (2007, 11). This does not mean that there is an innocent, better and all-knowing place to be found when one risks writing differently or otherwise, but using tensions, questions, insecurities, stuckness, ruptures and other stumbling blocks helps to perform the textual double move of doing and troubling knowledge at the same time and thus perhaps locates us more ethically in between knowing and not knowing. Thus, as I have understood Lather, we do not necessarily have to overcome stuck places because focusing on them can be surprisingly productive.

Viewing stuck places as productive moments, rather than temporary setbacks, produces the feeling of research as lived and living experience. Uncertainties, mistakes, contradictions and impossibilities—they all become part of the story. Most important, this methodology of "getting lost" involves realizing that we are not in control and articulating this being lost in our practice of research in order to explore a philosophy of inquiry that is ethically grounded in not knowing. In other words, it is "not so much about losing oneself in knowledge as about knowledge that loses itself in necessary blind spots of understanding" (Lather 2007, vii). In a way, then, getting lost functions as a methodology that is characterized by its inherent reflexivity coupled with the almost stubborn desire to keep moving, doubling and troubling itself along the way.

Using examples from my PhD research, in this chapter I want to examine what false starts, failures, aporias and other stuck places can do for us when situating the experience of impossibility in writing as "an enabling site for working through aporias" (Lather 2007, 16). In between the three stuck stories I present, I suggest some writing exercises and strategies for thinking through and writing in stuck places. The textual examples illustrate different stuck places I have encountered in my research. I have chosen these particular pieces of writing to highlight moments that turned out to be transformative, all shifting the course of my research to quite different effects. I consider these turning points as part of the story of my PhD project—the story that renders research experience not only as the site but also as the data for an engaged critique and articulation of a practice. They all form a story of coming to practice in feminist research.

FALSE STARTS AND DEAD ENDS

I am walking somewhere in Manhattan. Utterly upset. There are long endless streets criss-crossing in front of me, and I feel I am wandering aimlessly. I almost don't see the people around me or notice the buildings in the neighbourhood. It's getting dark. I don't know where I want to go or where I have to be. Rain. As if I wasn't feeling bad enough already. After an hour of discussion—or, rather, being a witness to a passionate monologue by a scholar who writes on the topic I had chosen for my research—I feel devastated and drained of all enthusiasm. For anything. I lack her passion. I lack her knowledge. I lack. How glowing she was! How together! How polished! How proud of her book! And what was I thinking? I never had that kind of passion for this topic. I imagine the rain as part of my frustration. Should I just forget about this topic altogether? But I can't. Can I? How can I possibly let go of it after all this time? I shouldn't be feeling like this. There are plenty of ways to get back on track. For a moment, I suddenly become more aware of my surroundings. Here I am in this city of cities, with only a limited amount of time on my hands. I want to remember this place. I should take pictures. At least. All the photos turn out blurred and out of focus as I keep walking while taking photos and feeling sorry for myself. And it's pouring. After a few shots, I start to like the effect. The amazing blur that I can capture with my cold, wet fingertips, frantically pressing the shutter release, the flashes of car lights all mixed up in a strange collage. Oh my, my feet are killing me. The band-aids don't provide any relief, and the pain is becoming intolerable. I feel like I'm walking on glass. Little pieces of broken glass, piercing the delicate swollen flesh of my toes and heels. I've thoughtlessly enough put on new shoes that my feet are not accustomed to. Not to mention that I've stubbornly decided to keep walking even though I've nowhere to go until my meeting with a friend in the same area an hour later. I keep walking. It would be easy enough to just stop at a café, rest my feet and get shelter from the cold and the wet autumn weather. But I keep walking. Somehow walking seems safer right now. Just keep going. Don't stop. You are safer when you look like you're going somewhere. What just happened? Why am I feeling so upset? And why do I need to keep walking?

* * *

In this short reflection of a memory of a place, I describe a moment when I experienced such a strong sense of being stuck in my research that even talking to a seasoned scholar in the field I was planning to do my research in did not help. In fact, to my surprise, it had quite the opposite effect: I felt I had reached a point when I was no longer sure if this project was really for me. I had to walk the frustration out of me, literally get the stuckness out of my system, dodging the rain and the darkness and the sense of discomfort surrounding my shaky self-confidence. I had to face it: This stuckness was not just a series of false starts for me; it was in fact a dead end. It was time to let go.

In retrospect, it took me a lot longer than that little walk to convince myself that there was no going forward with this topic and I had to start anew. It was not until I was participating in a writing seminar where we tried out an exercise on place writing that I actually made the connection back to how transformative this moment of walking had been for me. The thing with stuckness is that sometimes you feel stuck because you have really reached a dead end—there is no point in holding on to this stuckness if it is not taking you anywhere you want to go. But how do you know if you are really that stuck? How do you know you have made a false start, reached a dead end?

To find out, you really need to take your stuck places seriously. You need to take yourself to your stuck places! Coming to writing is a process, often a long and difficult one. The road to writing can be paved with pain: It can be blistery, slippery, cold, frustrating, uninviting, irrational, insecure, but we keep going because we believe in the promise of arriving at something worthwhile if we just manage to stick to it and keep going despite the discomfort. Writing about that moment of reaching a dead end and needing to walk it through my system made me realize that I needed a different place I could inhabit in order to keep going.

EXERCISE 39: EXPLORE STUCK PLACES

1. *Write a list of false starts or dead ends you have encountered. If you cannot quite place them in your mind, try going to places that are relevant or integral to your research. Go back to moments in time in particular places where something happened that made you feel you were utterly stuck. You can do this either by physically going to that place and observing yourself or by going there through your memories.*

2. *If you are doing this exercise in a group, read out your list to others in the group and discuss.*

3. *Choose one example and write your own story about a difficult moment in your research. Describe the situation: When did it happen, where were you, what were you supposed to do, what did you do? Be concrete: pay attention to perceptions, senses, sounds, smells, colours. Take note of incidental, seemingly insignificant details and things; switch off your cognitive response.*

BREAKS, RUPTURES AND FAILURES

"Hi dear, let's do that interview sometime during the workshop or, for instance, on the bus on the way there."

What?! Puzzlement. My idea of sitting comfortably in some nice, quiet place, looking at her photos together and talking about all the aspects of her art that I wanted to know about, was shattered in a second. How can you even think of doing an interview during a workshop? Or, worse, while travelling on the bus?! That was not an encouraging start.

First day, second day. I was losing hope. Already past lunchtime and it's intolerably hot. Everyone decides to go for a swim.

"Get your gear ready, we'll do it now. That's the best I can offer you."

She has a tendency to disappear. One moment the streak of bright blue hair is here; the next it's as if it had vanished into thin air. The sea is calm, and you have to walk forever until it gets deep enough for swimming. It's full of harmless little jellyfish. You can hardly see them. The icky sticky seaweed is a little more difficult to ignore. She gets a towel, dries herself and puts her colourful dress on.

"Let's walk."

It's the first time I've ever used a voice recorder. I panic for a moment, searching for the right buttons. It looks like I've got the thing to work.

"Ok, now, shoot!"

Eee . . . well. How should I start?

"Why don't we talk in English? That way you don't have to bother translating later."

Again, nothing goes as planned. Shifting language codes suddenly seems unexpected, almost unfathomable, and I am at a loss for words. I mumble She has in a single moment made me forget who I am and what I want I let her speak.

The forest smells of pine trees and late blueberries. We are many, and at some point some people catch up with us. I don't expect anything any more It is all out of my hands. Slowly all that control I supposed I had over the sit uation is slipping away. It is taken from me through interruptions by thos fast walkers who cannot stop themselves from barging in on our conversa tion. Hey, is my recorder invisible? This is my interview. Ssshh. I becom very protective of her words. They are not for sharing. Not now. Not here This is exclusively for my ears only. Her words are mine. Oh, so sorry.

My control over what is happening is further undermined by the wind Should that surprise me? Seaside places are known to be windy. Take it o leave it.

"This is all I can offer you."

The road construction workers are just as ruthless. They tune in with the wind at steady intervals. And the cars! Did I mention the cars? They whirl-wind around us in a constant conspiracy with the unruly sounds of the wind and the construction machines. All I can focus on is the smell of fresh, hot asphalt.

Halfway through a sentence we reach the local store, and she wants to go in for drinks for the evening. I have to stop the recorder. We joke around with the others who have caught up with us again and wander off to other top-ics. I know that this was it, although she leaves me with a vague promise to continue this later, excusing herself for having to go and put on underwear. Oh, the absurdities of the situation. This is not how I planned this. Will I ever manage to decipher these sounds? How do I trust that they are there at all? What if they are all there?

* * *

This piece captures some of the most memorable moments of my very first experience with interviewing. I participated in a three-day summer work-shop in Estonia called [PROLOGUE] EST, which brought together feminist artists, curators, art critics, Gender Studies scholars and government offi-cials, both from Estonia and abroad (see also Koobak and Thapar-Björkert, Chapter 3, this volume). We were all invited to a cottage at the seaside to spend these days together to talk about gender, art, society and politics, articulating and exploring feminist ideas about gender from Eastern and Western European perspectives. The artist I interviewed for my research—Mare Tralla—was one of the main organizers of the event. She is often cred-ited as the first Estonian artist to openly call herself feminist or, as she herself said at the workshop, she was the first artist in Estonia who made a con-scious decision not to be an unconscious feminist. What she was referring to is the way in which many feminists in both Eastern and Western parts of the world have tried to argue that in the former Eastern bloc feminism was "latent" all along and just needs to be uncovered now.

My plan was to interview Mare about her photographic self-portraits for my research about self-representation—she often uses herself, her own body, in her artwork, and I was curious to find out why and what that had brought along for her. As I had met her before, even visited her at her home in London prior to starting my PhD project and she had shared a lot about her art, I imagined the interview situation would be cosy and comfortable, with us sitting down at her place in Tallinn, looking at her self-portraits and just chatting away, like the first time I visited her. This is in fact what she had promised me when she initially agreed to do the interview. And then . . . nothing went as expected. First, there was the frustration that she post-poned the interview, that she proposed to do it during the workshop, that she then wanted to do it while walking back from a swimming break in the sea! I experienced an unsettling sense of loss of control over the situation, and at first I was not even sure what language to speak. I had prepared to speak in Estonian—as we are both Estonian and had previously been speaking in Estonian only (except during the workshops, which were held in English). For her to suggest that we speak in English, because then I would not have to translate later (as I write in English), even further accentuated the fact that I was not in charge here. For the longest time, I did not know what to do with this situation or whether I could use this interview in my work at all. I listened to the recording—it was pretty much useless, with so much background noise that it hurt my ears. So I decided to just write a kind of short story about my stuck moment.

Once I began to focus on this moment of stuckness and converted it into a short text—a form that I could manage and face—I started to think about how this moment could be useful for my research. Did it change anything in my thinking about the topic or the material? What kind of work did it do? What did this stuck moment reveal to me about myself, about the assumptions I had made? How could I take further the reflections that it inspired?

Since this moment was really striking, I began thinking about whether I could use this stuck story as a platform for remembering other difficult and memorable moments, making connections, analyzing. I immediately thought of the sound performance that was presented at the same workshop. Two artists had recorded our seminars during the three days, and they mixed all the sounds together with some pre-recorded noise—whispers, wind, cars, street noises—to create a sound performance. In the performance it felt like well-orchestrated noise, people talking about different things all at the same time, their voices blending in with the background noise, yet it was possible at times to distinguish individual voices. I even recognized my own at one point. The performance really made me think about the state of feminism in Eastern Europe. How do background sounds and voices influence us? Who do we listen to? Who do we hear talking? Do we hear ourselves speaking out loud? When are sounds just noise, and when are they moments that give you ideas? To an outsider who does not really tune in, the multiplicity of voices in the performance could come across as just loud, indecipherable. But if you listened carefully enough, you could feel that there was a purpose to this noise. There is collectivity, and there is individuality.

Sounds can thus function as springboards to jump into other ideas, to tune into all kinds of tones, utterances, resonances, vibrations, melodies, silences, breaks, ruptures. So could my stuck story about the unruly interview material be seen as a metaphor for something else, an allegory? Was I stuck only because of the disturbing noise? Or was I stuck because of my assumptions and expectations, my projections of the interview situation? If I had not written this short extract in this way, what would I have missed? Writing with sounds was a completely novel experience for me, a way of paying attention that required me to tune in to the material differently than my usual approach to analyzing images and visual material allows. Moreover, writing this stuck story enabled me to get away from the idea of a perfect interview. It reminded me of the importance of always having to go with the flow, as I reflected on control, who has it, when it is "lost" for both sides, what is going on in the interaction between the interviewer and the interviewed.

Again, in this moment of stuckness, just the act of beginning to write, even if it was initially only about describing something in detail, was crucial to making my stuckness work *for* me and not against me. Without worrying where I would end up, I was able to let off steam and think through my frustration, opening up for new connections and angles. It was a thought-provoking exercise for realizing yet again that it is of utmost importance to view writing as "a method of inquiry" (Richardson 1997, 2000), as a process, the sole purpose of which is to find something out, something that is not known or cannot be known before writing.

EXERCISE 40: A RECALCITRANT RESEARCH MATERIAL

1. *Write your own version of an impossible interview, approach or material that was difficult to get hold of.*
2. *Focus on what happened. Be concrete: describe feelings, perceptions, senses, sounds, smells and all the "extraneous" stuff.*
3. *After writing this, did you understand something about your research questions or the material you were working with?*
4. *What happened to your project? How did the difficulties become part of your research?*

APORIAS AND INSECURITIES OF MEANING

I first met her on my birthday at the breakfast table. I had wanted to talk to her the day before, but the ever-changing constellations of conversations around us killed the possibility. There was always someone else who grabbed her with words, always someone else who cornered me with endless exchanges of niceties. She appeared so frail, so fragile, so far away. And then suddenly she was there, sitting beside me.

"Happy birthday! Are Leos really good keepers of hearth and home?"

She is Art, I am Academia, both shifting and balancing between small and capital As. Serious representatives of our fields—or at least aspiring to be—and caricatures of ourselves at the same time, blown out of all proportion. We speak in separate tongues, light years apart. Twisting, turning, touching, almost, but not quite. She sends me photos; I send her texts. She is puzzling, obscure, intimate, fragmentary, elusive. I am self-explanatory, overcautious with words, distant, but appear to be complete, together. Two mismatched worlds, each unsure about the other. She has what I have been looking for. She is what I have been looking for. A case study, an object/ subject of analysis, ample material for testing theories and methodologies. I have what she yearns for with her body. Words, concepts, theories, explanations.

"Can we talk outside? It's crowded here."

OMG, what did I do? So sorry, I'm very clumsy today. I spilled influence all over, contaminated my research data, ruined the results! She read my text; she responded. She asked me if she should change her title. She asked me if she should change. Am I allowed to affect my research subject, to mess with her mind? Can I analyze and criticize her art project idea before it makes it to the gallery? Can I teach her, give her advice, point out what I think are her theoretical blind spots and then write it into my thesis? Who am I to guide Art?

But what if she asks for it? What if she wants to be taught, criticized, pushed further? I don't understand her. I don't understand art. She hides it all so well between the lines. She is teaching me, isn't she? We are both each other's teachers. Where do we draw the line? Would we necessarily have to be bounded?

"I left. I wanted to leave you your space."

Look, this is not just any conversation. Let's set the record straight. I mean, I have to. I am being held accountable for my words. My words will be weighed against other words, compared and contrasted, interrogated and cross-examined. My sentences will be tested for quality and compliance with ethics, my chapters searched through thoroughly for suitability and substance. What do I take from her? What do I give her?

"Yes, write about me! Your analysis will maybe make me understand myself better."

Is she giving me anything (besides my dissertation)? What is she taking from me? Everything and nothing, give or take. It's all up for grabs. My struggles, my ignorance, my insensitivity, perhaps also my over-sensitivity, always trying to do the right thing, carefully constructing boundaries between Art and Academia, stubbornly sticking to capital As. She takes it all. My knowledge, my experience, my position as somebody within, while she is not entirely without. I'm just as much of an informant to her as she is to me, an insider, a native, an expert who is in possession of something she doesn't quite have yet. She is preparing for a potentially provocative exhibition; I want to get my PhD. She has her stakes; I have mine.

What if we both just yearn for a dialogue? What if we just need to talk? We make each other vulnerable. I am no more secure in my world than she is in hers. We are both searching. We feed off each other's vulnerabilities but also rely on each other's knowledge and experience. We desire a symbiosis that reaches beyond our immediate selves.

"Let's educate the other photographers; let's publish an article together in *Cheese*; let's take over different media forms and channels."

She's on a roll. We'll be on a roll.

* * *

I wrote this piece on the train while commuting from Linköping to Stockholm, where I was living at the time, shortly after I had met Anna-Stina Treumund, the contemporary Estonian feminist artist whose artwork eventually became my main research subject, after many moments of insecurities and stuckness. I wrote it out of the need to make sense of what my relation was to her and her artwork, and what our sharing of thoughts about feminist art, theory and activism, my guiding of her and hers of me, meant for my research. It was on the spur of the moment that I let my fingers dance on the keyboard. As the landscape rushed past me beyond the window of the train in a continuous flicker, I gave in to words as if wanting to paint a sketchy picture with quick, bold brush strokes, to blow the elements of the story a bit out of proportion, to capture a bird's-eye view in the exaggerations, in excess.

Sense in this case emerged out of that dash of creativity that I associate with the bodily sensation of being transported somewhere, of experiencing the movement of trains, buses and bikes. The body is in motion while the mind can become quiet, still. You can hear your own voice again, coupled with the excitement of going somewhere, the anticipation of arrival, even if it is just a mundane commute between workplace and home. The mind picks up the speed of the body on the moving train; the body relaxes yet retains the feeling of being in movement. The stillness of the mind suddenly sprints. In fact, it gathers its strength from the leftover energy of the body because the body is really just sitting still. Once I dreamed of writing the whole thesis while criss-crossing the country on the train, buzzing with that constant creative rush.

I want to stay with that sense of movement for a moment, with that sense of sitting still yet rushing ahead. Looking back at the first time I met Anna-Stina, the time I attended her first solo exhibition or the countless hours I have spent contemplating her pictures and discussing them with others, I see the reason that pushed me into writing this stuck story—ambivalence—is in fact the feeling that accompanied me throughout the initial stages of the research process. From early on, ambivalence was what I had to make sense of, even when I still could not quite put it into words and was just wishing for clarity once and for all. I was ambivalent about Anna-Stina's photos and what I thought they represented; I worried about how I should approach them as a researcher, a friend, a fellow feminist; I was ambivalent about my relation to feminism, to Estonia, to my feminist education from "the West";

I was intensely ambivalent about writing, as a researcher, about *just* one artist and, moreover, about one who indeed had become my friend.

I remain ambivalent. The difference now is that I know this ambivalence is not nothing; I know it doesn't have to be suppressed or willed away, not yet. I know now that I can claim it: touch it, feel it, hold it up for closer inspection. This ambivalence has meaning. This ambivalence is a reaction to the abyss that separates "me" from "you", "us" from "them", the chasm between one person, one group, and another, differently valued one. It is a response to the void between different differences, hierarchically arranged binaries that time and again present themselves as symptomatic of contemporary ways of organizing knowledge. It was not until I went into that meaning, that ambivalence, and stayed there that I got *some*where. Finding a way in, not in order to explain it away or move quickly beyond it, but rather to get closer, slowly, to that ambivalence, was the key. Making that ambivalence tangible turned out to be a central thinking tool for me. I came to rely on this ambivalence to think, to help this to unfold. Ambivalence became my argument.

For my muse the French author and professor of English literature Hélène Cixous, to think is to think creatively, and to think creatively is to have a courageous relationship to difference. Having a courageous relationship to difference involves a movement towards the other, a crossing over, getting a good grip on the fear of the unknown which feeds destructive thinking. Cixous likens the courageous relationship to difference to "a question of dancing, of the aerial crossing of continents", "a question of acrobatics". She talks of acrobats, who do not focus on separation but "have eyes, have bodies, only for there, for the other" (1991, 79). For acrobats, there is no in-between, no turning back. There is just that "yes" to the jump forward, to that leap of faith. Likewise, I needed to move towards the other, to leap, to jump, to fly straight ahead across the abyss of difference without concentrating on what separates "us" but, rather, on what connects "us". (See also Sissel Lie's discussion of Hélène Cixous' work in Chapter 7, this volume.)

In the context of my thesis, "us" was both the microlevel "us" of Anna-Stina and myself, an artist and a researcher, and our relation to each other, and the macrolevel "us", the more ambiguous relation between feminists in the former Eastern Europe and "transnational" feminists who have tended to exclude perspectives from the so-called Second World, the former Eastern Europe or non-Western Europe, prioritizing the dialogue between the First and the Third World and thus cementing a binary between the Global North and the Global South. Many feminist scholars from the former Eastern Europe have argued for the need to "bring the Second World in" (Grabowska 2012) in order to challenge the binary hierarchical frameworks that are being continuously perpetuated by transnational feminist scholarship; they argue for the importance of the role of the Second World in the ongoing formulations of global understandings of feminism and gender theory (Mignolo and Tlostanova 2006; Blagojević 2009; Pejić 2009; Suchland

2011). Often, I have felt, these attempts have fallen into the chasms that separate "us" rather than keeping the focus on what connects "us".

Before I could leap towards Anna-Stina, though, before I could make that courageous connection, I needed to stay with the ambivalence for a while, to understand how this dizzying array of mixed feelings was produced. I needed to stay in that moment where the body with the racing mind was sitting still on the train. I needed to root myself before shifting, for I could only cross over towards Anna-Stina through deconstructing the homogeneous representation of Second World women as "lagging behind" in relation to the West, while "catching up" is seen not only as imperative but also as just a matter of time. I needed to spell out that ambivalence, created at least partly by the friction between the multiple contradictory allegiances I constantly negotiate, simultaneously. On the one hand, there was my fidelity towards my feminist education from "the West", which evoked certain reductive readings of Anna-Stina's artwork. On the other hand, there was my desire, sometimes, to defend the place I come from, a desire that might not be any less limiting. Rejecting either position in favour of the other was not a viable option because that would entail rejecting a part of myself.

EXERCISE 41: THE WORLD AS SEEN FROM THE PERSPECTIVE OF YOUR INTERVIEWEES OR OTHER "RESEARCH MATERIALS"

1. *Pick your favourite/least favourite research subject and write a first-person account in her or his words about the interview. What if the other is changing and changing you? What if the other becomes the same?*
2. *Give your own account of a dialogue with your "material" where something unexpected arrived, where you felt that the material changed or the material changed for you. Could you use this in your reflection?*

TOWARDS A PRAXIS OF STUCK PLACES

One has to get going. This is what writing is, starting off. It has to do with activity and passivity. This does not mean one will get there. Writing is not arriving; most of the time it's not arriving. One must go on foot, with the body. One has to go away, leave the self. How far must one not arrive in order to write, how far must one wander and wear out and have pleasure? One must walk as far as the night. One's own night. Walking through the self toward the dark.

—Hélène Cixous (1994, 65)

I began to think more about stuckness and the stickiness of stuck places in writing and research, moments when I found myself time and again at a loss, unsure of what to do next or whether to do anything at all. These moments of stuckness tended to be experiences that I could not seem to forget about so that I kept circling back to them until something did come out of them. For that, I needed to trust my writing process, even if that writing was sometimes difficult, impossible, upsetting, unsettling, boring, too easy, too personal, not personal enough.

I adopted Lather's "getting lost" as a methodology that enabled me to embrace moments when I was not so sure of myself and when I could see that this not knowing was my best chance for a different sort of doing and knowing. The exercises I have offered in this chapter open up towards a praxis of stuck places, although they might not always do the trick—sometimes we are indeed just lazy, tired, bored or uninspired or need to read or research more, or perhaps just take a long break. Not every stuck moment is equally productive. But an attentiveness to the potentials of some moments of stuckness, to the unexpected that might arise from stuck places, might be an incredibly efficient way out of a difficult situation in the writing process. Deconstructing moments that feel as if everything has gone wrong helps us to move out of the controlling master discourses. Articulating the feeling of being lost or stuck, exposing stuck places, is likely to mark out the places where we are still lost, up for critique and re-reading, and may thus reveal the necessary blind spots in our knowledge. In effect, "getting lost" or "stuck"—also purposefully—is then a kind of reflexivity that gives the best results when coupled with the stubborn desire to keep moving.

Finally, when none of this works, I have found it comforting to read Chicana feminist author Gloria Anzaldúa's meditation on what to do when you find yourself experiencing writer's block, when you have found yourself in a stuck place. When all else fails, I take out my magic text: "Coming into Play: An Interview with Gloria Anzaldúa". And I just read it. It works every time.

> Yes, you can create your own kind of reading [of the writer's block]. "What is hindering me?" "What is helping me?" "What led to this situation?" Even, "What situation am I in?" Because a lot of times you don't know, you can't figure out what the hell is wrong. And use different symbology systems, different Tarot systems. But mostly I will start pulling out of it, articulating by talking to my friends, working with my dreams, and meditating. And I'll take a walk and I'll go and do an ocean meditation—'cause I live about a block from Monterey Bay, from the Pacific Ocean. So I go down to Light-house Beach here on West Cliff Drive, and I'll sit and I'll just be with the ocean, and watch the breakers come in and watch the birds flying over the crests looking for food, and I'll watch where the sky and the ocean come together, or I'll do a walking meditation, or I'll do a sky meditation—most of the meditations that I do I call creative in that I try to put myself in a state of my

brain waves slowing down to five or six cycles, which is a dream state, a state of semi-hypnosis. And enter into that space, and then record in my journal the thoughts that come to me, the images that come to me. And this is a technique that I use when I teach creative writing, these guided meditations. And that gets me in touch with what is wrong, with what I'm feeling. And a lot of good writing comes out of it, but during the days and weeks and sometimes months when I am in this depressed state, I don't want to articulate it. I don't want to figure it out. I don't want to be helped. I just want to be left alone!

—(2000, 25)

EFERENCES

nzaldúa, Gloria E. 2000. "Coming into Play: An Interview with Gloria Anzaldúa." *MELUS* 25 (2): 3–45.

agojević, Marina. 2009. *Knowledge Production at the Semi-periphery: A Gender Perspective*. Belgrade: Institute of Criminological and Sociological Research.

ixous, Hélène. 1991. "Coming to Writing" and Other Essays. Edited by Deborah Jenson. Translated by Sarah Cornell, Deborah Jenson, Ann Liddle and Susan Sellers. Cambridge, MA: Harvard University Press. Originally published in La venue à l'ècriture by Hélène Cixous, Madeleine Gagnon and Aie Leclerc. 1977. Paris: Union Générale d'Editions, 10/18.

ixous, Hélène. 1993. Three Steps on the Ladder of Writing. Translated by Sarah Cornell and Susan Sellers. New York: Columbia University Press.

rabowska, Magdalena. 2012. "Bringing the Second World In: Conservative Revolution(s), Socialist Legacies, and Transnational Silences in the Trajectories of Polish Feminism." *Signs* 37 (2): 385–411.

ather, Patti. 2007. *Getting Lost: Feminist Efforts toward a Double(d) Science*. Albany: SUNY Press.

1ignolo, Walter and Madina Tlostanova. 2006. "Theorizing from the Borders Shifting to Geo- and Body-Politics of Knowledge." *European Journal of Social Theory* 9 (2): 205–21.

ejić, Bojana, ed. 2009. *Gender Check: Femininity and Masculinity in the Art of Eastern Europe*. Cologne: Verlag der Buchhandlung Walther König.

ichardson, Laurel. 1997. *Fields of Play: Constructing an Academic Life*. New Brunswick: Rutgers University Press.

ichardson, Laurel. 2000. "Writing: A Method of Inquiry." In *The Sage Handbook of Qualitative Research*, edited by Norman K. Denzin and Yvonna S. Lincoln, 923–49. Thousand Oaks: Sage.

uchland, Jennifer. 2011. "Is Postsocialism Transnational?" *Signs* 36 (4): 837–62.

14 Publish or Perish
How to Get Published
in an International Journal

Kathy Davis

Several years ago, I had a conversation with a colleague who had just recei
a rejection letter for an article he had submitted to a well-known journal.
a big name in his field, my colleague was incensed. He announced that
was never going to write another article for a journal. "From now on",
said, "I'm sticking to books." Leaving aside the question of whether it re<
is that much easier to get book manuscripts published, he was certai
right about one thing: publishing articles in scholarly journals can, inde
be daunting.

No matter how long and venerable one's career as an academic has be
publishing an article in a scholarly journal remains an endeavor frau
with uncertainty, difficulties and—in some cases—outright suffering.
an author of more than fifty scholarly articles, I cannot think of a sin
case where the path towards publication was devoid of obstacles: journ
uninterested in publishing my work, unsympathetic reviewers with ruthl
criticisms, not to mention the ordeal of having to cram one's thoughts in
6,000 words of readable text for an "international audience". And yet
do not simply write for ourselves; we want to get our work out in the wo
so that we can share our ideas, the results of our research and our opinic
with others.

In this chapter, I will tackle some of the ins and outs of getting publish
based—somewhat eclectically—on my own experiences as author, jour
editor and reviewer. My experiences have been primarily in the field of G
der Studies. However, I believe that much of what I have to say will
applicable for publishing in the humanities and much of the social scien
as well. I will focus specifically on getting published in what is called t
"peer-reviewed" journal—that is, a journal in which submitted articles a
sent out anonymously for review by experts in the same field as the auth
(see Weller 2001). The idea is that experts will be able to accurately ass
the merits of the article, while the anonymity of the author will guaran
an impartial evaluation.[1] While peer-reviewed articles are not the only kir
of publications which academics produce,[2] they will be my focus here t
several reasons. First, whatever else an academic does in her or his ac
demic career; it is unlikely that she or he can avoid submitting articles

peer-reviewed journals from time to time. Unlike my illustrious colleague, many academics do not see writing books as a viable alternative. If you work in the natural sciences or are a psychologist, books will be regarded as something you write in your free time, i.e. a hobby. "Real" scholarly work always takes the form of articles in peer-reviewed journals. Second, peer-reviewed articles in every discipline tend to be highly valued, particularly according to the bureaucratic standards which are currently used in evaluating academic production. Many universities evaluate departments and individuals based on how many peer-reviewed articles are published in "top journals".[3] This policy puts most academics under pressure to publish articles if they want to find a job, get tenure or receive a promotion. Publishing articles is, therefore, important for anyone interested in pursuing an academic career. And, of course, many academics regard articles as the most effective way of getting their research "out in the world" and communicating the results of their inquiries to an audience of interested colleagues.

While the process of getting published in a peer-reviewed journal is not easy, it is also a process which can be greatly facilitated with some fairly simple and practical advice. To this end, I will address several issues: how to write a journal article, find a journal, and understand the review process, as well as how to revise an article. I will then provide a brief look behind the scenes of a scholarly journal—a journal of which I am co-editor—in order to provide some insight into how things look "on the other side of the fence". And, finally, I will touch briefly on the more general issue of evaluating the work of one's colleagues—that is, the dos and don'ts of giving and receiving criticism—since this is often one of the aspects that makes the process of getting published both painful and rewarding.

HOW TO WRITE A JOURNAL ARTICLE

The first thing to do is to take a look at articles published by others in academic journals. This may seem too obvious to mention, but, strangely enough, many of my students have not considered doing this before embarking on preparing an article for publication. This will immediately tell you that most academic articles are short—between 6,000 and 8,000 words with references and notes is pretty standard for journals. This means that you will have to say what you have to say briefly. You will need to decide at the outset what you can do and, more important, what you cannot do in one article. Since many articles are based on long-term research projects or are parts of books or dissertations, you will invariably have to make some tough decisions. A rule of thumb is that an article has no more than *one* main argument. You will not be able to include everything, no matter how interesting/insightful/essential you think it is. For example, you can provide a theoretical overview and draw conclusions but not present all of your research findings. Or you can describe the research you did and some of your favorite findings, but you will not have space to go into detail about particular cases. Having decided what your argument will be, you will need all the space you have to set the stage, convince the reader that the article is something she or he will want to read, make your argument and close. It helps to remember that this will not be the last article you will be writing on the subject. What is not included in this article can appear in another one.

If the article is based on a dissertation, it is important to remember that you do not have to "prove yourself" in the same way you do for your supervising or evaluating committee. Most journals assume that the author is already competent to write a scholarly article. You do not need to show that you have read everything in the field. Indeed, a journal article with overly long strings of references does not enhance your credibility as scholar ("Can't this author say *anything* on her own authority?"), and it certainly does not increase the readability of the article (see also Davis, Chapter 11, this volume). In a similar vein, while in a dissertation it is important to explain at length how you did your research, in a scholarly article the attention given to methodology should be kept to a minimum.[4]

An exercise which I recommend to beginning (and, perhaps, also to more experienced) writers of scholarly articles is to try to describe your article in a nutshell.

EXERCISE 42: DESCRIBE YOUR ARTICLE IN A NUTSHELL

1. *Describe in one sentence the point of your article. Additional points should be put aside for future reference.*
2. *Explain why your article might be interesting (for example, because of its contribution to a particular scientific or academic debate or because it provides insight into a burning political question or because it offers the perspective of a hitherto neglected group).*
3. *Imagine the potential audience for your article. For whom is your article of interest?*
4. *What can you do to make your article even more interesting?*

This exercise can be done in a group as well. It can be very helpful to get feedback on how to make the point of the article even more interesting, to collect additional reasons why a reader might want to read the article or to come up with other potential audiences. The exercise will also provide a basis for an introduction (see also Lykke, Chapter 9, this volume) and help you focus and organize your arguments.

The next step is to find a suitable journal. Some authors already have a journal in mind to which they want to submit their article. Others prefer to leave this decision until after they have completed their article. In any case, it is not a step which should be taken lightly. For this reason, it can be a good idea to start thinking about possible journals while you are in the process of writing the article.

SELECTING A JOURNAL

In recent years, there has been a veritable explosion of new journals. On the one hand, this makes it easier to find a journal interested in publishing your article. On the other hand, it is more difficult to decide which journal to choose. It is a good idea to approach the selection of a journal as a kind of research project in which you explore the possibilities before making a choice. This can be done by looking at journal websites online or by browsing through back issues in the library.

The first step is to think about the kind of *audience* you want to read your article. Relevant considerations are whether your article is for a disciplinary or an interdisciplinary audience. A journal within a particular discipline (psychology, law) will generally engage in some gatekeeping in order to make sure articles are written in the conventional discourse and have employed the accepted methods and theories of the discipline. An interdisciplinary publication will be less stringent about methods and theories but more attentive to whether the article has a broad appeal and is able to speak across disciplinary borders. There are many journals which cater specifically to younger scholars. You will also need to think about whether you are writing for a more established (mainstream) publication or a more recent journal. The former might carry more weight for department evaluations, but it will also be more difficult to gain entrance as a new author. The latter may be looking for copy and will, therefore, perhaps be quicker to put your article into the review process. Other considerations have to do with the topic, the theoretical or methodological perspective and the degree to which the journal encourages experimental or critical scholarship. You should take some time to peruse the most recent articles in the journal and compare them with your own article. The question to ask is: Can I imagine my article in this particular journal?

Having finished your search, the next step is to make a list of possible journals. My shortlist usually has five journals. You should put your most preferred journal at the top of the list (aim high!). But it is also important to have other options. No matter how perfect you feel that your article is for a particular journal, the editors may not agree, and you want to have some backup in case your article is rejected.

Before submitting your article, you should check the guidelines for authors. They are usually available on the journal's website or on the inside cover of the journal, or they can be requested from the (managing) editor. These guidelines not only will tell you about the general requirements for articles in terms of focus, content and audience but will indicate the desired length and format for references and notes. You are usually asked to provide an abstract and a bibliography. You should submit your article in the format requested and *not* leave this until after the article has been accepted.

"WISHING AND HOPING", OR THE LONG HAUL

Once you have submitted your article to a journal, the most important task ahead of you is to be prepared for what may be a very long and arduous process. Getting published takes a long time, and you should be thinking in terms of years rather than months. You may not get accepted in the first journal to which you submit, which will mean going to another journal (and maybe even another) until you find one prepared to put your article into the review procedure. This having been done, you will need to wait for the reviewers' reports to come in (this takes at least three months but often longer). When the reports come back, you will, in nearly all cases, need to do some revisions—revisions which will, once again, need to be evaluated by the editor and/or reviewers. In some cases, you may need to go through another round of revisions.

Given this situation, you may be asking yourself whether it might not be a good strategy to submit your article to several journals simultaneously. While I admit that the thought has crossed my mind more than once, I advise strongly against it. Journals do not look kindly at submissions which are also under consideration elsewhere, something they may state explicitly in their guidelines. It may seem expedient in view of the long review procedure. However, it is considered to be disrespectful to the work which editors and reviewers put into journal submissions—work which is always done on a voluntary basis. The world of scholarly journals is small, as is the pool of potential reviewers for a particular article. Thus, the chances that you will be "found out" are therefore sizeable, and that would destroy any possibility for further publication in the journal in question. In short, it is not worth it!

Therefore, I recommend the less appealing but more effective strategy of being patient, persevering and, above all, keeping your eye on the main prize: getting your article published. As a case in point, I offer the following account of my first publishing experience: the long and rocky, but ultimately successful, process of getting an article published in a peer-reviewed academic journal. The article was based on my master's thesis. After going through considerable turmoil just to get it on paper (I remember not having the faintest clue about how to actually write an article and going through countless journals to see how older and wiser scholars had tackled the problem), I was fairly sure I had a publishable article. I sent it to a journal which I had always admired. It took six months before I received any news,[5] and when I finally did, it was in the form of three pages, single-spaced, with no less than twenty-four comments! The comments had clearly been drawn

ɔm different reviewers. They were assembled in no particular order and
ɛre contradictory and, for the most part, extremely negative. The worst—
remains etched in my memory forever—was "I wonder if what the author
ιs to say is worth saying at all . . ." At this point, I probably would have
rown in the towel, were it not for an older colleague who jumped into
e fray and gave me a pep talk I will never forget. She assured me that the
ɔmments were not *that* bad. She advised me to read through them several
nes, considering each one separately and asking myself what (if anything)
:ould do. I took her advice, revised the article along those lines and resub-
itted it. This was followed by another wait—this time of nine months.
later heard that the editorial board had folded and that my article had not
ɛen passed on to the new editor but lay moldering in a desk drawer, only
ɔ be discovered quite by chance.) I then received another letter, this time
ith only one page of suggestions for revision. Interestingly, many of these
ιggestions contradicted the first set of criticisms and allowed me to return
ɔ my original text. A sadder but wiser girl, I took a deep breath, went back
ɔ drawing board and revised the article yet another time. Mindful of my
ɔlleague's advice, I changed what made sense and discarded what did not.
resubmitted the article, and, finally, one year later, it was published.[6]

I wish I could tell you that this was just beginner's luck. Unfortunately,
is not. Since then, I have written (and had published) many more articles.
'hile I have become more experienced in writing them and have received
ιany positive reviews, I do still receive rejections and unfavorable or even
ιsty reviews. I almost always have to do some revisions, no matter how
ɔlished my submitted text was. The process *always* takes more time than
would like. However—and this is the brighter side—I have always gotten
ιy articles published eventually. I am firmly convinced that there *is* a jour-
al out there for every article, and you just have to find the right fit (or work
ɔ get it). It might not be in the journal of your first choice, but as I have
iscovered, my second or third choices will sometimes prove to be a better
home" for my article.

I will be returning to the thorny subject of reviews at the end of the
aper. However, for now, having looked at the publishing process from the
ɔint of view of the author, I will "switch hats" and turn to the perspec-
ve of those doing the accepting—or rejecting—of articles for peer-reviewed
ɔurnals—the editors.

'HE EDITOR'S HAT

ɔr more than a decade, I have been involved with a peer-reviewed jour-
al, the *European Journal of Women's Studies* (*EJWS*)—first as an associate
ditor and later as an editor. The journal is fairly typical as peer-reviewed
ɔurnals go. It has two editors who make the initial decision about which
ιbmitted manuscripts can go out for review, choose two reviewers and

make the final decision about whether the edited manuscript will be p
lished. As editors, my colleague and I play an important role in determin
the direction the journal takes in terms of its theoretical and political fo
We have an international (European) board of associate editors who
responsible for reviewing articles in their fields, encouraging contributi
from their geographical areas and participating in discussions about h
the journal should be developing in the future. The *EJWS* also has a m
aging editor who ensures that the review process runs smoothly; mana
the contacts with authors, reviewers, board members and editors; and is
liaison with the publisher.

The journal comes out four times a year, whereby one issue is devote
a specific theme and is edited by one of the associate editors, often toget
with an invited guest editor. Like any journal, the *EJWS* has specific gu
lines. For example, we accept only articles that are *original*, that is, t
have not been published before. The article is expected to be *interdi
plinary*, which is short-hand for "appealing to a broad audience". T
means that we do not accept articles which are aimed at a specific di
pline (psychology, literary criticism) as evidenced by the use of techn
jargon or reference to specific disciplinary theories and debates which wo
not be accessible to readers outside the discipline. Another guideline is t
the journal accepts only *scholarly* articles. This means that policy pap
or research papers which are descriptive and under-theorized tend to
rejected. Since it is a *European* journal, articles are screened for their c
nection to Europe—through the location of the author, the topic or, in so
cases, the relevance to debates within Europe. And, finally, the journa
intended for a *Women's Studies* audience, which means that articles n
to display an awareness of the theories and debates which are part of
field. We not only expect the article to be oriented to a Women's Stud
audience but demand certain recognition of developments in feminist theo
and scholarship. Obviously, these guidelines are specific for the *EJWS*, a
every journal will have its own guidelines. Since guidelines are invaria
abbreviated, they will always require some deconstruction on the part of
author in order to know whether her or his manuscript is suitable for
journal in question.

Journals invariably have set review procedures, and, recently, many of th
procedures have become automated. In the case of the *EJWS*, the author se
her or his manuscript to the managing editor. She checks whether the arti
has an abstract and how many words it contains. If it exceeds the 8,000-wc
limit, she sends it back to the author. If it is complete and not too long, s
sends it to me or my co-editor to decide whether it should go into revi
procedure.

As editor, I read the articles with several considerations in mind. The b
tom line is whether the article fits the aims of the journal and is of suffici
quality to be reviewed. However, I am also keen to find articles that I thi
will appeal to our readers. I do not have to agree with the argument that

author is making as long as the author makes an argument. In fact, I prefer articles which are going to be controversial enough to spark a debate.[7] While it is important that articles are not simply descriptive but also involve some theorizing, I prefer articles that present theory as a discussion or an argument. I am likely to reject policy-oriented pieces (for example, on gender mainstreaming) unless they are framed as part of a theoretical or political debate. In addition to a preference for arguments and debates, I look for articles which are cognizant of developments in feminist theory. For example, I am less likely to accept an article which treats gender as a matter of "sex differences" or "women" than an article which adopts a more intersectional approach (see Davis, Chapter 1, this volume). And, finally, as editor, I am always concerned with moving the journal in a particular direction. For example, in recent years, we have had many discussions about the importance of situating "Europe" in a more transnational context, both in terms of the (colonial) past and in terms of making global connections in the present. Thus, I tend to look less favorably on articles written from a narrowly local perspective (for example, "Rural Women in Southern Spain")[8] and am more inclined to accept articles which are oriented towards making local–global connections as, for example, Gambaudo's (2007) analysis of the relationship between French and Anglo-American feminisms.

The *EJWS* receives from 80 to 110 manuscripts a year, and we reject about 50 per cent of them, mostly at the beginning of the review procedure. After we as editors decide that a manuscript is good enough to go into the review procedure, we select two reviewers. In the interest of getting a good review, we not only look for scholars in a similar field or with the same theoretical orientation as the author but are careful not to ask someone whose work has been specifically criticized in the article. In other words, we want to ensure that the manuscript receives a fair reading.

The reviewers are asked to make a recommendation (accept for publication, accept with minor revision, accept with major revision or reject[9]) as well as to provide comments explaining their recommendation and offer suggestions which will help the author revise the manuscript. While some reviewers recommend rejecting the manuscript, in most cases they ask for minor or major revisions (in only one case in fifteen years have I received an "accept as stands" recommendation!). While it cannot be denied that some reviewers are a bit harsh in the tone of their reviews (a point to which I will return shortly), for the most part I have been impressed by how seriously they take their task and how constructive and comprehensive their comments are.

After the reviews are in (this usually takes about three months), the editor writes a cover letter to the author, including copies of the reviews. In this cover letter, the editor will indicate which parts of the review are particularly important, and she or he will also resolve any contradictory comments in the reviews. This having been done, the author undertakes the revisions and resubmits the article. In most cases, this revision is sufficient, but occasionally there will be additional cycles of revision. At this point, however, the author can be fairly certain that the journal is committed to working with her or him until the article is finally publishable.

SOME NOTES ON REVIEWING THE WORK OF OTHERS[10]

Ideally, a reviewer is a peer—that is, someone who is knowledgeable enough to be able to assess the merits of your work and impartial enough to give you a fair reading. Her or his suggestions are intended not only to ensure that the standards of the journal are met but also to provide constructive criticism which will help you improve and strengthen your article.

Good reviewers will try to keep in mind that, however weak the article may be, the author has gone to considerable time and trouble to write it. They will, therefore, begin the review by giving the author credit for what she or he has tried to do and note the things about the article that are interesting, provocative or well conceived. Good reviewers will not insist that the author share their own theoretical, methodological or normative orientation. They will attempt to take the article on its own terms, rather than expecting it to look like something they themselves would write. But, above all, they will refrain from being unnecessarily harsh or using sarcastic language. They will try to place themselves in the shoes of the person reading the critique.[11]

Unfortunately, not everyone falls in the category of "ideal reviewer". Some reviewers are unpleasant and harsh. They are not always right and, indeed, may have misunderstood the point you were trying to make altogether. While in my experience this is more the exception than the rule, there are still some lessons to be learned, even from the less-than-perfect review. The following suggestions are meant for those who are on the receiving end of such criticisms.

The first rule is to *never*—and I repeat *never*—engage in a debate with the reviewers, no matter how nasty, unfair or just plain wrong they may be. Once reviewers have provided the review, their work is basically finished. It is the editor who will be reading any angry rejoinders, and she or he is more likely to be irritated than convinced. Thus, a better strategy is to treat the comments as the result of the reviewers' willingness to spend their valuable time reading and thinking about your article. Even if the tone of the critique leaves something to be desired, the comments themselves should be treated as a vehicle for improving and strengthening your article.

The second thing to remember is that you do not have to use comments that do not make sense to you or that detract from the point of your paper. Ultimately, you are the one who decides what is helpful and what is not. However, in many cases, when a reviewer has misunderstood your point, this can be a sign that you have not been as clear as you should have been. This can provide a welcome opportunity to clarify or sharpen your argument.

And, last but not least, when you send back the revised article, be polite rather than defensive. Thank the reviewers (and the editor) for the comments, and explain (briefly) what you did with them.

At the outset of this chapter, I mentioned a colleague who decided to avoid the entire ordeal of getting reviewed for a journal because he did not like to have his work criticized. Of course, no one likes to be criticized, and one could argue that he was simply being a bit thin-skinned about his work. However, I believe that there is much more at stake when it comes to accepting criticism. Learning how to take critique on board is not only necessary if you want to get published in peer-reviewed journals. More important, critique is essential for making your work better. It allows you to make your arguments stronger and the focus of your paper clearer. It forces you to compose your ideas in a way which will get them across to your audience. It draws your attention to potentially intriguing aspects of your work that had escaped your attention and alerts you to the—sometimes unforeseen—implications of what you have written. At its best, critique can help you make your article as good as it can possibly be. We all need to find ways to not only criticize one another's work seriously and constructively but also accept critique as the gift that it is or, at least, can and should be.

NOTES

1. Obviously, this procedure is not perfect. Nevertheless, most academics see it as a necessary step towards ensuring that a certain level of quality is maintained in academic work.
2. For example, publications include PhD dissertations, books (academic and popular), book chapters, solicited articles (for special issues of journals) and pieces for popular journals, magazines, newspapers or online blogs. In the course of an academic career, these kinds of publications may even form the bulk of one's scholarly production.
3. The ranking system for determining the top journals varies from university to university. While various "objective measures" like citation indexes and impact factors are employed, politics invariably plays a role as well. For this reason, you should inform yourself about the ranking policies in your own department or university.
4. The same might be said for post-dissertation book projects. I remember talking to an editor of a well-known academic publishing house who laughingly referred to "methodology chapters" as the bane of her existence. "The authors love them, but what reader really cares?"
5. This was the pre-email era when journals did not always send out letters that an article had been received. It would be highly unlikely now not to get an email that your article has been received. In fact, if you don't receive an email, it is a good idea to contact the journal and ask whether they have received your article.
6. For those who are wondering what this infamous article was, see Davis 1986.
7. An example was an article on feminist Darwinism (Vandermassen 2004), which proved so controversial that we ended up publishing a rejoinder (Ah-King 2007), thereby starting a tradition of using articles to provoke debates within the pages of the journal.

8. This is a fictitious title.
9. Many journals also have a "reject and resubmit" recommendation. In the *EJWS*, we have abandoned this category as it often led to endless revisions on articles which had a slim chance of being published in the end. Our policy is to be stricter at the beginning of the process, in that we put in articles which we feel we really want and which have a serious chance of becoming publishable.
10. These comments do not simply apply to reviewing articles for peer-reviewed journals. Throughout one's academic career, one is called on to respond critically to the work of one's colleagues—for example, as discussant at a conference, when writing a book review, as part of a scholarly article. There are good and bad ways of doing this, and it behooves us all to think about the ethics of reviewing (see also Lie, Chapter 7, this volume).
11. I remember getting some very harsh (although helpful) comments from reviewers. I made use of them when revising my text and wrote a cover letter thanking the anonymous reviewer. My editor forwarded her response, which was that she was "pleasantly surprised" that I had responded as I did and that she didn't think she would have been able to do so if she had been in my position! Without wanting to detract from the usefulness of the critique, this suggests that this particular reviewer might have considered a little more carefully how she presented her critique in the first place. See also Davis 2010.

REFERENCES

Ah-King, Malin. 2007. "Sexual Selection Revisited—towards a Gender-Neutral Theory and Practice: A Response to Vandermassen's 'Sexual Selection: A Tale of Male Bias and Feminist Denial'." *European Journal of Women's Studies* 14 (4): 341–48.

Davis, Kathy. 1986. "The Process of Problem (Re)formulation in Psychotherapy." *Sociology of Health & Illness* 8 (1): 44–74.

Davis, Kathy. 2010. "On Generosity and Critique." *European Journal of Women's Studies* 17 (3): 1–5.

Gambaudo, Sylvie A. 2007. "French Feminism vs. Anglo-American Feminism: A Reconstruction." *European Journal of Women's Studies* 14 (2): 93–108.

Vandermassen, Griet. 2004. "Sexual Selection: A Tale of Male Bias and Feminist Denial." *European Journal of Women's Studies* 11 (1): 9–26.

Weller, Ann C. 2001. *Editorial Peer Review: Its Strengths and Weaknesses*. Medford, NJ: American Society for Information Science and Technology.

Postscripts

On (Not) Reading Deleuze in Cairns

Susanne Gannon

Deleuze and Guattari, for instance, argue that a concept should express an event, a happening.[1]

1. Lines of flight[2]

From a jetty in Djibouti and the obscenity of leisure in the west
to a man, a gun, and a dog, in Ecuador.

A forest mandala and a parade of fog
and firewalking for the winter solstice

Coals are a poor conductor, you say
but your voice carries in the thick dark, your fingertips
touch the nape of my spine: burn

2. Haecceity = thisness[3]

Time falls off
Just us now
tangled intaglio
etching bodylines
with our fine
chisels of flesh
and bone
our invisible ink
our breath

3. Univocity[4]

Moon in your mouth
sound of the sea in me
coral driftwood weed
small creatures swim in us
crabs scutter at your wrists:
salt: we are almost all water
At the cellular level, our filaments drift apart
divide, multiply; our surfaces are
littoral zones, subject to moon
tide and the pulsing planet.

NOTES

1. Massey, Doreen. 2005. *For Space*. Thousand Oaks: Sage, 28.
2. "[L]ines of flight, movements of deterritorialisation and destratification"; cf. Deleuze, Gilles and Felix Guattari. 1987. *A Thousand Plateaus: Capitalism and Schizophrenia*. Minneapolis: University of Minnesota Press, 3.
3. "A haecceity has neither beginning nor end, origin nor destination; it is always in the middle." Deleuze and Guattari, *A Thousand Plateaus*, 263.
4. "The essential in univocity is not that Being is said in a single and same sense, but that it is said in a single and same sense, *of* all its individuating differences or intrinsic modalities . . . Being is said in a single word and same sense of everything of which it is said, but that of which it is said differs: it is said of difference itself." Deleuze, Gilles. 1994. *Difference and Repetition*. London: Athlone, 36.

Authors' Aphorisms: A Year of Writing . . .

January:

Don't be afraid to play with fire, but know that it is fire.

In the wilderness inside us there is an unexplored garden.

February:

Your easy reading is my hard writing.

How many times do you have to go to the library ordering books after books after books to realize that what you need to write cannot be found in them?

It's important occasionally (at least once a week!) to take a few moments to gaze out of your window and daydream, thinking of nothing in particular.

March:

The small, insignificant detail can yield a treasure trove.

You have to write a lot of crap to write something worthwhile.

April:

Attend to the body with the body.

Where are you in your text?

Persist!

May:

When you hit a wall (of your own imagined limitations), just kick it in.

Listen to your hunches and take them seriously!

June:

Stay on the brink of the unthinkable.

Writing you must do will lead you towards writing you will enjoy and love to do.

July:

Follow the flow until the flow starts following you.

My best writing is done when I am riding my bike.

August:

One of the hardest things about writing is learning to embrace the moments w' you are most tortuously stuck, to see that they are your friends.

If your text starts looking like a bookcase fell on it, work harder to work your c voice back in.

September:

Try to write something you know that you cannot express.

Write a fragment of your text as if you were somebody else.

October:

Summarize your thesis in two sentences. This is a good focusing exercise.

Is there anything that you haven't done in a long time, such as going to the thea or a concert or taking a walk in the park? This will stimulate your imagination ways that might surprise you.

November:

If you use a lot of theoretical language try this: Take two pages from your thesis a cross out all the theoretical language. Does this make you see your topic or argum differently? (I do not mean to imply that you should not use theory, by the way!

There's no such thing as writing: only rewriting.

December:

Negative criticism can be useful in opening up other vistas and possibilities in y work . . . even though this opening up may not come about immediately.

Should academic prose create tangible images?

Dare what you don't dare.

Contributors

Anne Brewster is an Associate Professor at the University of New South Wales, Australia. Her books include *Literary Formations: Postcoloniality, Nationalism, Globalism* (Melbourne University Press, 1996) and *Aboriginal Women's Autobiography* (Fremantle Arts Press, 1995). She co-edited, with Angeline O'Neill and Rosemary van den Berg, an anthology of Australian indigenous writing, *Those Who Remain Will Always Remember* (2000) and with Fiona Probyn-Rapsey a special issue of *Australian Humanities Review* on whiteness (2007). She has recently published articles on whiteness and Aboriginal literature in *Journal of Postcolonial Writing, Australian Literary Studies, Feminist Theory* and *JASAL*. She has chapters on whiteness in *The Racial Politics of Bodies, Nations and Knowledges*, edited by Barbara Baird and Damien Riggs, and *Practice-Led Research, Research-Led Practice in the Creative Arts (*Edinburgh University Press, 2009), edited by Roger Dean and Hazel Smith.

Kathy Davis is currently senior research fellow at the Free University in Amsterdam, The Netherlands. She has held visiting chairs and research fellowships at Wellesley College, Columbia University and the Radcliffe Institute of Advanced Studies at Harvard University (US) as well as the Maria Jahoda Chair for International Women's Studies at Bochum University in Germany and visiting professorships in Frankfurt and Vienna. Her research interests include sociology of the body, intersectionality, travelling theory and transnational practices, and biography as methodology. She is the author of many books, including *Reshaping the Female Body* (Routledge, 1995), *Dubious Equalities and Embodied Differences* (Rowman & Littlefield, 2003) and *Embodied Practices: Feminist Perspectives on the Body* (Sage 1997), and co-editor of *The Handbook of Gender and Women's Studies* (Sage, 2006) and *Transatlantic Conversations: Feminism as Traveling Theory* (Ashgate, 2011). Her book *The Making of Our Bodies, Ourselves: How Feminism Travels across Borders* (Duke University Press, 2007) was the recipient of several prizes. She is currently working on a book about tango and passion in a transnational perspective: *Passionate Encounters: Dancing Tango in a Globalizing World*, to be published with NYU Press.

Susanne Gannon is an Associate Professor in the School of Education and Centre for Educational Research at the University of Western Sydney in Australia. Her research interests include gender equity in education, creative writing pedagogies and practices, and innovative qualitative research methodologies. She is interested in how theories of materiality, affect and corporeality impact on knowledge production and representation. She has co-edited and co-authored *Doing Collective Biography* (2006, Open University Press, with Bronwyn Davies and others), *Deleuze and Collaborative Writing: An Immanent Plane of Composition* (2011, Peter Lang, with Jonathan Wyatt, Ken Gale and Bronwyn Davies), *Place, Pedagogy, Change* (2011, Sense Publishers, with Margaret Somerville, Kerith Power, Bronwyn Davies and Phoenix de Carteret) and *Pedagogical Encounters* (2009, Peter Lang, with Bronwyn Davies). However, sometimes (often) she would rather write poetry.

Redi Koobak is a postdoctoral researcher at the Unit of Gender Studies, Linköping University, Sweden. She holds a PhD in interdisciplinary Gender Studies from the same university. She has previously held a teaching position at the Department of English, University of Tartu, Estonia, and worked as the Editorial Secretary of *NORA: Nordic Journal of Feminist and Gender Research* (Taylor & Francis). Her current research interests include feminist visual culture studies, feminist theory, queer theory, postcolonial theory, postsocialist feminisms, intersectionality and creative writing methodologies. Her PhD thesis, *Whirling Stories: Postsocialist Feminist Imaginaries and the Visual Arts* (2013), was published by Linköping University Press.

Sissel Lie is a Professor Emerita of French Literature at the Norwegian University of Science and Technology (NTNU), Trondheim, Norway. She has published extensively in Norwegian, English and French on literature from the fifteenth, sixteenth and twentieth centuries as well as two books on academic writing. She is also a fiction writer and author of a number of novels and children's books, as well as a translator from French and English; among other works she has translated W. S. Merwin's *The Vixen* (1996). In English and French, she has published among others the following chapters and articles: "L'image de l'artiste—Hélène Cixous" (2000); "Louise Labé—Dialogue with the Past" (2000); "La Grande Mademoiselle: Writing Memoirs as a Novel" (2002); " 'Without Your Breath on My Words, There Will Not Be Any Mimosa': Reflections on Translation" (2004); "Personal and/or Universal? Hélène Cixous' Challenge to Generic Borders", with Priscilla Ringrose; "Hélène Cixous: 'La Voisine de Beckett?' ", with Petter Aaslestad, in *The European Legacy* (2009); and "Medusa's Laughter and the Hows and Whys of Writing According to Hélène Cixous" (2011).

Nina Lykke is Professor of Gender and Culture at the Unit of Gender Studies, Linköping University. She is co-director of an international Centre of Gender Excellence, GEXcel International Collegium for Advanced Transdisciplinary Gender Studies, as well as scientific leader of a Swedish-International Research School in Interdisciplinary Gender Studies, Inter-Gender. She has been scientific director of the Nordic Research School in Interdisciplinary Gender Studies and managing director of the European Feminist Studies association, AOIFE. She has published extensively within the areas of feminist theory, Intersectionality Studies, Feminist Cultural Studies and Feminist Technoscience Studies, including the following books and edited volumes: *Between Monsters, Goddesses and Cyborgs* (ZED Books 1996, with Rosi Braidotti), *Cosmodolphins* (ZED Books 2000, with Mette Bryld), *Bits of Life* (Washington University Press 2008, with Anneke Smelik), *Feminist Studies* (Routledge 2010) and *Theories and Methodologies in Postgraduate Feminist Research* (Routledge 2011, with Rosemarie Buikema and Gabriele Griffin). She is managing co-editor of the book series *Routledge Advances in Feminist Studies and Intersectionality.*

Andrea Pető is an Associate Professor at the Department of Gender Studies, Central European University, Budapest, Hungary. She has edited thirteen volumes in English, six volumes in Hungarian and two in Russian. Her works have appeared in different languages, including Bulgarian, Croatian, English, French, Georgian, German, Hungarian, Italian, Russian and Serbian. She has also been a guest professor at the universities of Toronto, Buenos Aires, Stockholm and Frankfurt. Her books include *Women in Hungarian Politics 1945–1951* (Columbia University Press/ East European Monographs, New York, 2003) and *Geschlecht, Politik und Stalinismus in Ungarn. Eine Biographie von Júlia Rajk*, Studien zur Geschichte Ungarns, vol. 12 (Gabriele Schäfer Verlag, 2007). Presently she is working on gendered memory of World War II and political extremisms. She was awarded the Officer's Cross Order of Merit of the Republic of Hungary by the president of the Republic of Hungary (2005) and the Bolyai Prize by the Hungarian Academy of Sciences (2006).

Suruchi Thapar-Björkert is an Associate Professor in the Department of Government of the University of Uppsala in Sweden. She has previously held academic positions at the London School of Economics and Political Science, Warwick University and Bristol University in the UK. Her research interests are in four specific areas: gendered discourses of colonialism and nationalism; gendered violence in India and Europe; gender, social capital and social exclusion; and feminist qualitative research methodologies. She has published widely in refereed journals such as *Feminist Review, Ethnic and Racial Studies, The Sociological Review, Women's Studies International Forum, Journal of Gender Studies, Women's History Review* and the *International Journal of Social Research Methodology.*

Index

Page numbers followed by n indicate notes

25–6; Butler, Judith 22; Christian
doctrines/myths/practices 26;
complicating gender 23–4; and
creative methodologies 21;
Crenshaw, Kimberlé 17, 20;
diaspora studies 18; domestic
violence 26; ethnocentricism
17; feminist buzzword 17–19;
feminist theory 18, 19; First
World 25–6; Frankenberg,
Ruth 22; Haraway, Donna 22;
intersectionality defined 18–19;
Lutz, Helma 28n3; Matsuda,
Maria 20; McCall, Leslie 20;
Narayan, Uma 26; narratives
of passing 26; postcolonial
theory 18; qualitative versus
quantitative methodologies
20–1; queer theory 18; situating
yourself 22–3; Smith, Valerie 25;
social geography 22; strategies
for 21–7; summer school
demonstration performance
26–7; Third World 26; "triple
jeopardy" (class/race/gender) 18;
universalistic assumptions 26;
use of the concept 19–21; widow
burning (*sati*) in India 26
intersubjectivity/interaffectivity/
intercorporeality zones 69,
71, 77
intertextuality 176
interviewing 198–201
introductions and conclusions,
resources for writing 116
introductions in academic publications
142–160; body exercise 153;
choreography of six moves 143,
152, 159; Crenshaw, Kimberlé,
"Mapping the Margins"
(1991) 143, 145–150, 160n2;
definitions and background
142–3; denotative language
144, 159n1; experimenting
with your own introductions
151–8; four basic moves
143–4; genealogical analysis
160n3; move 1-establishing
the field 145–6, 155–6; move
2-summarizing previous research
146, 156; move 3-preparing for
present research 147, 156–7;
move 4-introducing the present
research 147–9, 158; move

5-situating the researcher-
subject-narrator 149, 155;
move 6-capturing the audience
149–150, 154–5; Richardson,
Laurel 143; rules in classroom
situations 151–2; Swales, John
143; the tango metaphor 159;
topic association 154; two
added moves for feminist twist
144–5; wrapping up exercise
159–160

Jones, Stacy Holman 107
journals *see* publishing in an
international journal
joy of writing 123–4

Kaplan, Caren 50
Kleinsasser, Audrey M. 109
Koobak, Redi 1, 6, 7–8, 11, 107, 122,
177, 178n6, 199, 224; *see also*
politics of location; research
topics; writer's block
Kostova, Elizabeth 80
Kristeva, Julia, "Toccata and Fugue for
the Foreigner" (1991) 67–8

LaCapra, Dominick 75
language 2–3, 180–193; active and
dynamic 192; appropriation of
words 181–3, 192; Australian
Aboriginal literature 180;
background 180–1; Bakhtin,
Mikhail 180–1, 182–3, 186,
189, 192; Barker, Chris 192–3;
Bellear, Lisa, "Artist Unknown"
(1993) 183–6, 193; creative
writing 180; cultural meanings
189; "found poem" defined
184–5; free association 188;
gendered linguistic and cultural
dialogism 192; heteroglossia
188, 189; key terms and free
association 181–8; key terms
and the dictionary 188–193;
key theoretical terms in research
180; museumization 193; the
novel 180–1; *Oxford English
Dictionary* 189–193; poetic
collage 188–193; Smith, Hazel
184–5; social nature of language
use 181; speech types 180–1,
189; whiteness 188–191; words
as private property 183

Lather, Patti, *Getting Lost: Feminist Efforts toward a Double(d) Science* 194–5, 206
learning and unlearning 109
learning in students 166–7
learning objectives 167–8
learning process 169
Levinas, Emmanuel 69, 71
Lie, Sissel 1, 2, 8–9, 28n5, 151, 159, 204, 224; *see also* resources for writing; writing as a process
literary devices 116–17, 137, 139
literary quotations 138
locatedness *see* politics of location
Lutz, Helma 28n3
Lykke, Nina 1, 5–6, 9, 75, 116, 210, 225; *see also* introductions in academic publications; passionate disidentifications

Mahmood, Saba 168
male-to-female transsexuals 39
Mantel, Hilary 137
"Mapping the Margins" (Crenshaw) 143, 145–150
Massumi, Brian 71, 76
Matsuda, Maria 20
McCall, Leslie 20
McNay, Lois 167–8
meditation 206–7
metaphors 137
meta-theory 173
Middleton, David 87
migrants/nomads/immigrants 48
mobile phones 122
modernist paradigms of Western philosophy and science 18
Mohanty, Chandra T. 48, 51; "Under Western Eyes: Feminist Scholarship and Colonial Discourses" (1984) 31, 35–8, 41–2
monolithic and bounded categories 30, 31; *see also* social identities/categories
Montpensier, Mlle de 111–12, 123
Moreton-Robinson, Aileen, *Talkin' Up to the White Woman* (2000) 65, 78n9
mourning process, in writing as a process 138
multiple and mobile locations versus fixed standpoints 30
multiplicity of locations 51

Muñoz, José Esteban, *Disidentification: Queers of Color and the Performance of Politics* (1999) 31, 32, 34, 35, 39
Murasaki Shikibu 117, 125n2
museumization 193

Nagar, Richa 51, 52
Nancy, Jean-Luc 69
Narayan, Uma, *Dislocating Cultures* 26
Neely, Barbara 88
negative criticism, writing as a process 134
negative reactions, resources for writing 111, 112
nomads 48
non-fiction writing 1
Nora, Pierre 87, 161
"Notes toward a Politics of Location" (Rich) 50
notion of home 48
novels 180–1

object writing 164–6
Olivia Records 39
opening-up and zooming-in writing exercises 99
opinion formation 169
outsider/insider location 47, 48, 49, 59
Oxford English Dictionary 189–193

Paretsky, Sara 88
participatory photography projects 104–5
passionate disidentifications 5–6, 30–46; academic writing and 35; Alarcón, Norma 31, 34, 35, 39; Althusser, Louis 32; Butler, Judith 32, 33, 34, 35, 39; cyborgs ("earth others") 44; definition and theoretical overview 30–2; differential consciousness and 41–2; disidentificatory writing 43–4; Fuss, Diane 32; Gender Dysphoria Syndrome 40; Hirschfeld, Magnus 39; male-to-female transsexuals 39; Mohanty, Chandra T., "Under Western Eyes: Feminist Scholarship and Colonial Discourses" (1984) 31, 35–8, 41–2; monolithic and bounded categories 30, 31; multiple and

Discourses" (Mohanty) 31,
35–8, 41–2
unifying signifier 33–5
universalistic assumptions 26
universalist "we" perspective 50
universalizing identifications of
whiteness 77
unlearning as a way of learning 109
US black feminist theory 18

value system of teaching 169
visual culture theory 97

Waaldijk, Berteke 170n3
Walpole, Horace 111
Weiss, Gail 64, 69, 76
"we" perspective 50
Western philosophy and science 18, 37
white First World feminist scholarship
17, 25, 26
white middle-class woman 64
whiteness 188–191; universalizing
identifications of 77
Whiteness Studies in Australia 6–7,
62–79; Aboriginal Studies 65;
Ahmen, Sarah 71; Australian
Aboriginal literature research
62–5, 71, 76; background
62–4; Behrendt, Larissa 68;
Bellear, Lisa, "Feelings" (1996)
analysis 64, 72–6; bodily
affects 63; border of self and
other 65–7; boundaries and
identities 71; Braidotti, Rosi
77; contact zones 65–9; Critical
Whiteness Studies 22, 64,
65, 68, 77; embodied ethics
of relationality 62, 63–5, 67,
69; embodiment and affective
relations with others 67; face
of the other 69–71; Giroux,
Henry 76; Grosz, Elizabeth
76; indigenous sovereignty 68;
Kristeva, Julia, "Toccata and
Fugue for the Foreigner" (1991)
67–8; LaCapra, Dominick
75; Levinas, Emmanuel 69,
71; Massumi, Brian 71, 76;
Moreton-Robinson, Aileen,
Talkin' Up to the White Woman
(2000) 65, 78n9; Nancy, Jean-
Luc 69; power relations 64,
65; relationality and affect
71–5; "settler" nations 71;

universalizing identifications of
whiteness 77; Wiegman, Robyn
75; Weiss, Gail 64, 69, 76; white
middle-class woman 64; writing
about place 62–3; zone of
intersubjectivity/interaffectivity/
intercorporeality 69, 71, 77
white women's position within Western
feminism 50
widow burning (*sati*) in India 26
Wiegman, Robyn, 75
Wikipedia 122
Wise, Sue 172–4
Wolf, Diane 103
Women in the Third World book series,
Zed Press 36–8, 42
women of colour 17
women's historical narratives in India
57
women's historiography 167
Woodman, Francesca 106
words as private property 183
Worsham, Lynn 109
writer's block 1, 7, 194–207; Anzaldúa,
Gloria 206–7; aporias and
insecurities of meaning 195,
201–5; background 194–5;
Benjamin, Walter 194; blind
spots of understanding 195,
206; breaks/ruptures/failures
198–201; dream state 207;
exploring stuck places 197;
false starts and dead ends 195,
196–7; First World 204; focusing
on stuckness 194–5; Global
North and Global South 204;
interviewing 198–201; Lather,
Patti, *Getting Lost: Feminist
Efforts toward a Double(d)
Science* 194–5, 206; meditation
206–7; recalcitrant research
material 201; resources for
writing 113, 115, 124; Second
World 204, 205; semi-hypnosis
207; Third World 204; towards
a praxis of stuck places 205–7;
Tralla, Mare 199; transnational
feminist scholarship 204;
Treumund, Anna-Stina 203, 204,
205; in writing as a process 128,
129, 130
writing: academic careers and 1;
academic style of 88; alternative
practices of 4; combining

Lightning Source UK Ltd.
Milton Keynes UK
UKHW020950180819
348129UK00016B/210/P